International Political Economy Series

General Editor: **Timothy M. Shaw**, Professor of Commonwealth Governance and Development, and Director of the Institute of Commonwealth Studies, School of Advanced Study, University of London

Titles include:

Francis Adams, Satya Dev Gupta and Kidane Mengisteab (*editors*)
GLOBALIZATION AND THE DILEMMAS OF THE STATE IN THE SOUTH

Preet S. Aulakh and Michael G. Schechter (*editors*)
RETHINKING GLOBALIZATION(S)
From Corporate Transnationalism to Local Interventions

Elizabeth De Boer-Ashworth
THE GLOBAL POLITICAL ECONOMY AND POST-1989 CHANGE
The Place of the Central European Transition

Edward A. Comor (*editor*)
THE GLOBAL POLITICAL ECONOMY OF COMMUNICATION

Helen A. Garten
US FINANCIAL REGULATION AND THE LEVEL PLAYING FIELD

Randall D. Germain (*editor*)
GLOBALIZATION AND ITS CRITICS
Perspectives from Political Economy

Barry K. Gills (*editor*)
GLOBALIZATION AND THE POLITICS OF RESISTANCE

Richard Grant and John Rennie Short (*editors*)
GLOBALIZATION AND THE MARGINS

Takashi Inoguchi
GLOBAL CHANGE
A Japanese Perspective

Jomo K.S. and Shyamala Nagaraj (*editors*)
GLOBALIZATION VERSUS DEVELOPMENT

Stephen D. McDowell
GLOBALIZATION, LIBERALIZATION AND POLICY CHANGE
A Political Economy of India's Communications Sector

Ronaldo Munck and Peter Waterman (*editors*)
LABOUR WORLDWIDE IN THE ERA OF GLOBALIZATION
Alternative Union Models in the New World Order

Craig N. Murphy (*editor*)
EGALITARIAN POLITICS IN THE AGE OF GLOBALIZATION

D0958284

Michael Niemann
A SPATIAL APPROACH TO REGIONALISM IN THE GLOBAL ECONOMY

Markus Perkmann and Ngai-Ling Sum
GLOBALIZATION, REGIONALIZATION AND CROSS–BORDER REGIONS

Ted Schrecker (*editor*)
SURVIVING GLOBALISM
The Social and Environmental Challenges

Leonard Seabrooke
US POWER IN INTERNATIONAL FINANCE
The Victory of Dividends

Timothy J. Sinclair and Kenneth P. Thomas (*editors*)
STRUCTURE AND AGENCY IN INTERNATIONAL CAPITAL MOBILITY

Kendall Stiles (*editor*)
GLOBAL INSTITUTIONS AND LOCAL EMPOWERMENT
Competing Theoretical Perspectives

Caroline Thomas and Peter Wilkin (*editors*)
GLOBALIZATION AND THE SOUTH

Kenneth P. Thomas
CAPITAL BEYOND BORDERS
States and Firms in the Auto Industry, 1960–94

Geoffrey R. D. Underhill (*editor*)
THE NEW WORLD ORDER IN INTERNATIONAL FINANCE

Amy Verdun
EUROPEAN RESPONSES TO GLOBALIZATION AND FINANCIAL MARKET
INTEGRATION
Perceptions of Economic and Monetary Union in Britain, France and Germany

Robert Wolfe
FARM WARS
The Political Economy of Agriculture and the International Trade Regime

International Political Economy Series
Series Standing Order ISBN 0–333–71708–2 hardcover
Series Standing Order ISBN 0–333–71110–6 paperback
(*outside North America only*)

You can receive future titles in this series as they are published by placing a standing order. Please contact your bookseller or, in case of difficulty, write to us at the address below with your name and address, the title of the series and one of the ISBNs quoted above.

Customer Services Department, Macmillan Distribution Ltd, Houndmills, Basingstoke, Hampshire RG21 6XS, England

European Responses to Globalization and Financial Market Integration

Perceptions of Economic and Monetary Union in Britain, France and Germany

Amy Verdun
Jean Monnet Chair
European Integration Studies Director
European Studies Program
University of Victoria
Canada

First published in hardcover 2000

First published in paperback 2002 by
PALGRAVE MACMILLAN
Houndmills, Basingstoke, Hampshire RG21 6XS and
175 Fifth Avenue, New York, N.Y. 10010
Companies and representatives throughout the world

PALGRAVE MACMILLAN is the global academic imprint of the Palgrave
Macmillan division of St. Martin's Press, LLC and of Palgrave Macmillan Ltd.
Macmillan® is a registered trademark in the United States, United Kingdom
and other countries. Palgrave is a registered trademark in the European
Union and other countries.

ISBN 0–333–71200–5 hardback (*outside North America*)
ISBN 0–312–22913–5 hardback (*in North America*)
ISBN 1–4039–0059–0 paperback (*worldwide*)

This book is printed on paper suitable for recycling and made from fully
managed and sustained forest sources.

A catalogue record for this book is available from the British Library.

The Library of Congress has cataloged the hardcover edition as follows:
Verdun, Amy, 1968–
European responses to globalization and financial market
integration / Amy Verdun.
     p. cm. — (International political economy series)
   Includes bibliographical references and index.
   ISBN 0–312–22913–5 (cloth)
    1. European Monetary Union—Public opinion. 2. Monetary unions–
–Europe—Public opinion. 3. Europe—Economic integration—Public
opinion. 4. Competition, International—Public opinion.
5. Statesmen—Europe—Attitudes. I. Title. II. Series.

HG925.V47 1999
332.4'566'094—dc21   99–39485
                                                     CIP

10	9	8	7	6	5	4	3	2	1
11	10	09	08	07	06	05	04	03	02

Printed and bound in Great Britain by
Antony Rowe Ltd, Chippenham and Eastbourne

To my parents

Contents

List of Tables

Preface

In April 1989 the Delors Report on Economic and Monetary Union (EMU) in the European Community (EC) was published. The report described a possible road to EMU to which all twelve EC central bank governors agreed. Its aim was that, in time, the Member States of the EC would have one central monetary policy, and to realize this would 'require further steps in all areas of economic policy-making' (Delors Report, 1989: 16). Although it seemed to be an important report, with far-reaching consequences, I did not find it widely debated or discussed publicly, either amongst the general public, or amongst political parties, interest groups, business, or monetary institutions. It seemed obvious that creating an Economic and Monetary Union would put policy-making issues at a higher level of decision-making (i.e. away from the national governments and institutions to the EC level). It would at least substantially restrict the policy-making capacity at the national level. I wondered *why* it was not discussed more, and *why* nobody voiced any fear over loss of influence in the policy-making process.

This led me to look at views held on EMU by trade unions, employers' organizations, the Finance Ministry and the central bank in the Netherlands. The main conclusion of this earlier research was that in a small open economy, such as the Netherlands, policy-makers perceived that there was already virtually no leeway for monetary authorities to pursue independent monetary policies. Over the past thirty years the Dutch central bank has, in fact, very much followed the policy of the German Bundesbank. Interestingly, the actors were well aware of this themselves, and appear to be not at all concerned with the loss of sovereignty in this area of policy-making (Verdun, 1990).

Trade unions and business associations in the Netherlands have been more positive than the monetary authorities towards EMU plans. The trade unions saw it as a way of regaining a say in policy-making, which they *de facto* had already lost a long time ago. Businesses welcomed the idea of a larger market and fewer national rules and regulations. Eventually officials in the central bank and Ministry of Finance held a similar positive view on EMU. They considered EMU to be a vehicle with which to institutionalize a 'German-type' monetary policy regime. For the Netherlands this would mean that EMU would not change the earlier Dutch monetary policy. The monetary authorities had, however, only during the 1980s become very positive towards EMU. This enthusiasm was mainly due to the boost it was hoped it would give the Internal Market. It seemed that these institutions were less concerned about the loss of sovereignty, lack of sufficient economic convergence and possible monetary arrangements, or a premature completion of EMU than they had been previously. Puzzled about the lack of concern about losing sovereignty, and some popular control over policy, I decided to pose the same question to actors in three major Member States.

Acknowledgements

This book has taken a long time to materialize. Initial research was started way back in 1989 after the publication of the Delors Report which provided the blueprint for Economic and Monetary Union (EMU) for the European Community (EC).

In 1989–90 I conducted a small study on the perceptions of EMU in the Netherlands. While interviewing monetary authorities, political parties and social partners I found that there was little or no concern about this next important move towards economic and monetary integration. Puzzled by this result, I decided to embark on a larger research project focusing on three larger EC countries. Content with the kinds of responses received in the Dutch case study, I decided again to hold interviews based on semi-structured questionnaires and simply *ask* the European monetary experts about their organizations' perceptions of EMU.

Having conducted such a study in 1989–90 I was well aware of the little theorizing about European economic and monetary union that had been done at that point in time. In the late 1980s few political scientists were studying and conceptualizing the economic and monetary, or the general European integration process. Thus the idea was born to set this research up as an explorative research, not a rigorous testing of any particular theoretical approach. Eventually I decided to reflect on the traditional integration theory as the logical theoretical body of literature.

Writing a book of this nature presents its author with a long list of institutions and persons to thank, as one has to learn a lot from other people. I feel this has been particularly true for me, as this research project involved studying contemporary attitudes, covering an interdisciplinary field and focusing on three countries unknown to me at the start. I cannot possibly express my thanks adequately to all those who have inspired, taught, corrected and supported me during these past years. My apologies to those whom I have forgotten to acknowledge.

I would like to start by thanking the people who helped me collect the data necessary for my research. Many have been very generous, allowing me an hour or more of their precious time. Because some of them wish to remain anonymous, I shall mention only the organization of their employment. These are: in Brussels, the Economic and

Social Committee of the European Union, the European Commission, UNICE, the ETUC, the ETUI, the European Savings Bank Group. In London, the Bank of England, Her Majesty's Treasury, the CBI, the TUC, the TWGU, the IoD, BIEC, NEDO, Barclays Bank, Lloyds Bank, the *Financial Times*, and the *Observer*. In Germany, the Bundesbank, the Bundesministerium der Finanzen, the BDI, the DGB, and IG Metall. In Paris, the Banque de France, the Ministère de l'Économie et des Finances, the CNPF, the CFDT, the CGT, FO, the AMUE and the AFEC. In the Netherlands, the Ministerie van Financiën.

I would like to thank several officials of DG II of the European Commission in Brussels who spent much time with me during my five-month internship at DG II in 1991–2. They put in considerable effort, listening and explaining in great depth to me, a political scientist, the issues involved in creating EMU and its possible implications. They are: Declan Costello, Stephan Lehner, Horst Reichenbach, Ludwig Schubert, Thierry Vissol, and Helmut Wittelsberger. A special word of thanks goes to Alexander Italianer, Alain Morisset and Marc Vanheukelen.

The European University Institute (EUI) and the Dutch Ministry of Education and Sciences generously provided a grant which funded most of the research expenses. A European Union Human Capital and Mobility Research Grant which I held at the University of Essex and an Internal SSHRC Grant provided by the University of Victoria enabled me to finalize the book manuscript. Furthermore, the European University Institute provided the ambience to work steadily on the research project. Its excellent facilities and wonderful surroundings made it a splendid place to study. My thanks go to the EUI for supplying these facilities. Special thanks go to the staff of the language centre, Elenore Eckmann, Nicki Hargreaves, Nicki Owtram and Colette Kleemann. Gratitude is also expressed to the wider EUI academic community for engaging in lively academic debates.

I have received a lot of useful feedback from the academic community when I presented (parts of) this book. I would like to thank the participants of conferences and panels at the EUI, the Canadian Political Science Association meetings, the European Community Studies Association conference, as well as the participants of the staff/student colloquium at the University of Bradford and the participants at the European integration/public policy seminar at Harvard University.

Since I started, various persons at different stages of the research project have generously given me their advice. I would like to thank Alan Cafruny, Thomas Christiansen, David Coen, Charles Goodhart, Erik Jones, Gerd Junne, Kathleen McNamara, Andrew Moravcsik,

Louis Pauly, Claudio Radaelli, Jeremy Richardson, Philippe Schmitter, Adri Smaling and Niels Thygesen. A special word of thanks goes to Martin Marcussen for reading and correcting the whole manuscript (twice!) and for encouraging me to express myself more clearly. Timothy Shaw, the International Political Economy series editor, is thanked for his continuous support and useful suggestions.

But above all, my deepest appreciation and gratitude go to my supervisor and co-supervisor, Roger Morgan and Susan Strange, whose enthusiasm, constructive criticism, support and commitment I shall never forget. Without doubt, their importance as an example for me will remain unequalled.

Finally, I would like to thank my daughter Zoey, who was born in 1992, and my partner, Paul Schure, for having shared with me the joys of life. This project could not have been realized, however, without the dedicated support I received from my parents. For all these years of supportive love I would like to express my deepest gratitude: *heel, heel hartelijk bedankt.* It is to them that this book is dedicated.

AMY VERDUN

University of Victoria, BC
Canada

List of Abbreviations

AFEC	Association Financière Européenne de Credit
AMUE	Association for the Monetary Union of Europe
BB	Bundesbank
BdF	Banque de France
BDI	Bundesverband der Deutschen Industrie
BENELUX	Belgium, the Netherlands, Luxemburg
BIEC	British Invisibles Export Council
BIS	Bank for International Settlements
BoE	Bank of England
BOP	Balance of Payments
CAP	Common Agricultural Policy
CBI	Confederation of British Industry
CDEP	Centre of Decision for Economic Policy
CFDT	Confédération Française Démocratique du Travail
CFSP	Common Foreign and Security Policy
CGT	Confédération Générale du Travail
CNPF	Conseil National du Patronat Français
DG II	Directorate General II (Economic and Financial Affairs)
DGB	Deutscher Gewerkschaftsbund
DM	Deutschmark
EC	European Communities/European Community
ECB	European Central Bank
ECOFIN	Council of Economic and Finance Ministers
ECOSOC	Economic and Social Committee of the EC/EU
ECSC	European Coal and Steel Community
ECU	European Currency Unit
EDC	European Defence Community
EEA	European Economic Area
EEC	European Economic Community
EFTA	European Free Trade Association
EMCF	European Monetary Cooperation Fund
EMF	European Monetary Fund
EMI	European Monetary Institute
EMS	European Monetary System
EMU	Economic and Monetary Union
EP	European Parliament

EPC	European Political Community
ERM	Exchange Rate Mechanism
ESCB	European System of Central Banks
ETUC	European Trade Union Confederation
ETUI	European Trade Union Institute
EUA	European Unit of Account
Euratom	European Atomic Energy Community
FFM	French Finance Ministry
FO	Force Ouvrière
FRG	Federal Republic of Germany
GDP	gross domestic product
GFM	German Finance Ministry
GNP	gross national product
HMT	Her Majesty's Treasury
IGC	Intergovernmental Conference
IG Metall	German Metal Workers' Union
IoD	Institute of Directors
IMF	International Monetary Fund
IPE	International Political Economy
MCA	Monetary Compensatory Amount
NEDC	National Economic Development Council
NEDO	National Economic Development Office
NIC	newly industrializing country
OCA	Optimum Currency Area
OECD	Organization for Economic Cooperation and Development
OMOM	'One Money, One Market'
OPEC	oil producing exporting countries
PU	Political Union
RPR	Rassemblement pour la République
SEA	Single European Act
TEU	Treaty on European Union
TUC	Trades Union Congress
TWGU	Transport and General Workers' Union
UK	United Kingdom
UNICE	Union of Industrial and Employers' Confederations of Europe
VAT	value added tax

1
Introduction

The present study is concerned with one of the most topical issues in contemporary European integration: Economic and Monetary Union (EMU). EMU implies the transfer of national sovereignty over monetary policy-making to a European Central Bank, while macroeconomic policy remains at the level of the Member State. Budgetary deficits and public debt ratios are subject to rules. This transfer of national sovereignty can arguably be considered to be one of the most far-reaching formal transfers of sovereignty to the European level that the European Community (EC) Member States have witnessed to date.

Paradoxically, this study was triggered by the observation, in the late 1980s following the publication of the Delors Report in 1989, that there was little general debate about EMU. As mentioned in the preface, a pilot study was conducted in 1989 examining the perceptions of domestic actors in the Netherlands towards EMU (Verdun, 1990). That study found that there was little or no debate about EMU. Political parties, trade union representatives, employers' organization officials and monetary authorities in the Netherlands did not perceive EMU to make that much of a difference. This was a remarkable result for such a far-reaching proposal for European economic and monetary integration. Obviously the Dutch actors had grown accustomed to gearing national policies closely towards those pursued in neighbouring countries, in particular those in West Germany. Still, this result was puzzling and counterintuitive. Surely actors in other countries, in particular larger Member States, would not hold this view?

But clues for understanding this apparent general attitude to EMU should not only be searched for in the present. A brief look into the past reminds us that in the 1970s the plan to create EMU in the EC was adopted, but then failed. Hence, a core question emerged: were actors silent because they all agreed on its need or did they think it was unimportant, or unlikely to happen?

At present the EMU concept can be described as: a union with a single currency, a single monetary policy, and on the economic side merely provisions to ensure the necessary convergence and discipline to strengthen the monetary objective. This particular concept of EMU results from various European proposals, and ultimately from the outcome of the 1991 intergovernmental negotiations. Neither economic literature nor political science 'integration' literature 'predicted' that this particular type of EMU would necessarily come about as a logical result of the integrated European market. So why did this particular design of EMU come about?

This book will address these issues in considerable detail. In order to give a proper assessment one needs to consider the context in which the EMU plan gained momentum. In the late 1980s and early 1990s the European integration objective had regained success, after a period of great difficulty which characterized the early 1980s. With the prospect of the completion of the '1992'-Internal Market programme, support for European integration was found at various levels of society and in each of the twelve EC Member States. EMU came to be seen as a logical next step in the integration process. Moreover, as 'globalization' of the international and the domestic economy became an ever-occurring phenomenon, it was feared that national policy-making autonomy was being reduced (cf. Coleman, 1996; Pirages and Sylvester, 1990; Porter, 1993; Rosamond, 1995; Strange, 1996). This study adopts a loose definition of the term 'globalization'. It can roughly be described as the phenomenon of increasing interdependence of economic and political actions and transactions which transcend national borders.[1] Financial market integration, which had already been part of the broader globalization phenomenon, increased in the EC after the decision in the 1980s to liberalize capital movements. Furthermore, the success of the European Monetary System (EMS) in the second half of the 1980s also clearly indicated that policy coordination implied reduced policy autonomy. For most of the Member States monetary policy was 'made in Germany'; policy effectiveness was achieved by shadowing German monetary policies. Hence, one currency, a single monetary policy and economic convergence came to be considered by politicians, economists and commentators as the solution to the problems of loss of autonomous policy-making effectiveness at the national level (cf. Padoa-Schioppa, 1987). It became clear that having free trade, free movement of capital, fixed exchange rates and monetary policy autonomy was untenable. Tommaso Padoa-Schioppa labelled this the 'inconsistent quartet' (cf. Padoa-Schioppa, 1994: 4).

Smaller member states had already for some time accepted that the policy-making antonomy of individual organizations and governments had decreased in recent years (see Jones, Frieden and Torres, 1998). However, until recently, policy-makers of larger European countries had tried to formulate policies mainly on the basis of perceived national interests. The widespread positive acceptance of EMU during the late 1980s in France and Germany, and even the less negative sounds in Britain, were therefore interesting developments. The apparent support for EMU presents an interesting case study for understanding questions often posed by scholars of International Political Economy (IPE): how much national policy-making autonomy remains against the background of an increasingly global economy? How do various political actors deal with this reduced policy autonomy (see *inter alia* Dyson, Featherstone and Michalopoulos, 1995)? Finally, the case of EMU points to the importance of changes in beliefs about the conduct of economic and monetary policy-making (see also Marcussen, 1997; McNamara, 1998).

1.1 Theoretical framework

The progress of European integration has had a chequered history of progress and stagnation. In fact, it is the very 'ebb and flow' of the integration process which has puzzled many observers (see for example Corbey, 1993, 1995; Haas, 1976; Hoffmann, 1966; Milward, 1992; Moravcsik, 1991, 1998a; Taylor, 1983). Intergovernmentalists have focused on the role of national governments in protecting 'national interests' through the process of European integration. Their claim is that national governments do not lose power through this process. National governments only participate in the European integration process to safeguard national interests. According to some, they even go a step further, and use the integration process to try to gain power *vis-à-vis* their domestic political actors – a process referred to as two-level games (Dyson, 1994; Moravcsik, 1993a; Putnam, 1988; Wolf and Zangl, 1996). The neo-functionalists have emphasized how the European integration process has an inevitable drive forwards, and that eventually, for purely 'functionalist' and 'technocratic' reasons, policies will have to be conducted at the European level (Burley and Mattli, 1993; Haas, 1958; Lindberg and Scheingold, 1970; Sandholtz and Zysman, 1989). Though a clear definition of 'the' intergovernmentalist approach and likewise 'the' neo-functionalist approach is increasingly difficult, and the sharp divisions between the two camps have become somewhat blurred over the years, the question of why integration happens, and what are the roles of the various actors, is still at the core of the grand theorizing about European integration. Recently there have been a great number of contributions to the literature which do not attempt to explain the *whole process* of integration. Rather they emphasize *parts of the process* and look at various policy processes, actors and modes of governance in the integration process (see for example, Bulmer, 1983, 1994, 1998; Caporaso, 1996, 1998; Caporaso and Keeler, 1995; Cornett and Caporaso, 1992; Huelshoff, 1994; Kohler-Koch, 1996; Marks, Hooghe and Blank, 1996; Peterson, 1995; Pierson, 1996; Risse-Kappen, 1996; Stone Sweet and Sandholtz, 1997; Wallace, 1996a, 1996b; Wessels, 1997). This book will, however, try to contribute to the scholarly tradition of grand theorizing and to clarify which factors give rise to increased/decreased support for European integration.

The present study will offer a so-called 'eclectic approach' to European integration which tries to explain why integration happens. It is eclectic in that it adopts elements of both the intergovernmental and neo-functional traditions. From the intergovernmentalist approach it adopts the claim that national governments aim at European integration to try to promote 'national interests' through the European integration process. The eclectic approach also applies this claim to societal actors, and suggests that their attitude to European integration has also to do with the fact that they perceive European integration as a useful instrument for influencing policy-making in order to protect their interests. From neo-functionalist thinking the eclectic approach takes on the idea that policy-making can indeed *spill over* into other policy areas, and that there inevitably is an important role for experts and technocrats in the policy-making process. The eclectic approach incorporates from the larger International Political Economy literature the assertion that increasing globalization, and its result – the reduction in national policy autonomy – strongly determines the policy-making process and hence international cooperation, and in our case European integration (among others, see Pauly, 1992; Strange, 1994, 1998). Hence, this 'eclectic approach' is an attempt to explain the progress towards further European integration by taking domestic, European and global factors into consideration. It examines how the European (monetary) integration process became considered as (part of) the solution to existing problems.

1.2   A short historical background to EMU

The lessons of the 1970s – the negative effects of double-digit inflation and economic stagnation ('stagflation') as well as mounting public debts – made governments recognize the limits of demand-led government expenditure. From the early 1980s it became increasingly acknowledged that low inflation was a necessary condition for economic growth – the ultimate goal of governments, organizations and institutions. The often-quoted example of an unsustainable divergent monetary policy is that of France in 1981–3 (Hall, 1986; Petit, 1989).[2] Hence Member States started to aim for monetary stability and integration. However, terms such as monetary 'stability' and 'union' cover a wide range of possibilities. An example of the former is the Exchange Rate Mechanism (ERM) of the European Monetary System (EMS), which is a system of fixed *but adjustable* exchange rates. The creation of a monetary 'union' implies a common monetary policy, with irrevocably fixed exchange rates, or a single currency. To avoid conflict among participating monetary authorities, the EC central bankers advocated the creation of a European monetary institution, which would be solely responsible for the conduct of a single European monetary policy. Thus it would be left to one institution, the European Central Bank, to decide on the level of interest rates, the money supply, and the acceptable rate of inflation. Obviously this implies that the Member States transfer formal monetary sovereignty to the Community, but leave adjacent matters of macroeconomic policy-making to be decided by national governments.

The far-reaching implications of the monetary union become even clearer when its underlying economic preconditions are studied in depth. To achieve a single monetary policy successfully, national budgetary and fiscal policies need to be coordinated. This stems from the natural relationship between monetary and fiscal policies, that is, the 'fiscal/monetary policy mix' (cf. Johnson, 1994; Mundell, 1962; see also Cairncross, 1981). The Community budget compared to the federal budgets of existing federal states has been quite small.[3] Hence, national fiscal policies may have to be coordinated to enable a proper policy mix.

In the 1970s some scholars, the so-called 'economists', believed that economic convergence should precede the fixing of the exchange rates. Others, the 'monetarists',[4] were convinced that monetary harmonization would induce economic coordination. The EMS contains elements of both schools of thought, although the system was believed in the success years of the EMS to be more 'monetaristic'. After the pound sterling and the Italian lira plummeted from the ERM in September 1992 and several other currencies devalued, eventually leading to the widening of the bands to ±15 per cent in August 1993, it became clear that the 'economist' argument could not be underestimated. If the underlying economic indicators are not sound, the exchange rate will come under pressure, and eventually will have to be adjusted, which was the case with the Italian lira. Yet it also made clear that global financial markets can upset economically 'sound' national currencies with speculative attack, which was the case of the French franc.

Considerable differences of opinion exist concerning the role of budgetary and fiscal policies in EMU. In 1977 a Commission report, the MacDougall Report, advocated a more substantive role for the Community budget, of around 2–2.5 per cent in the intermediary period, and eventually 5–7 per cent of Community GDP, instead of the 1 per cent at the time, and indeed at present. This concern with a greater redistributive role for the Community budget was not shared by the Delors Committee. Its authoritative blueprint on how to create EMU, the Delors Report, came out in April 1989. It mentioned 'binding rules' on the 'size and the financing of national budgetary deficits', but disapproved of setting up, as advocated for monetary policy, a central-ized European institution for the pursuit of economic policy, or any other type of supranational cooperation in economic policy-making (Delors Report, 1989: 23). These recommendations were formally accepted by the Heads of State and Governments at the 1991 Maastricht Summit. It was decided that the subsidiarity principle would be applica-ble to economic policy-making. Nevertheless, to ensure the success of a single European monetary policy, 'economic convergence' between the participating countries of the monetary union is required. It remains unclear exactly how this convergence is supposed to be achieved by relying merely on the subsidiarity principle and limits on budgetary deficits.

In the years following the ratification of the Maastricht Treaty there was a lively debate on the interpretation of the Maastricht convergence criteria, and also on how to ensure full compliance to the rules once countries had adopted the single currency. The Germans initiated a 'Stability Pact' which outlined how fines would be imposed on Member States who did not comply to the rules on debts and deficits which was eventually adopted by the EU.[5] The French proposed the creation of an informal body that would discuss economic matters. Eventually the so-called Euro-X Council was called into life. It is com-posed of two members from each of the Member States participating in EMU, and two members from the European Commission. Yet it was to do no more than informally discuss economic matters, serving the Ecofin Council and the European Council.[6]

From the above it follows that EMU incorporates an innate diffi-culty, a contradiction, or a paradox. National governments retain their freedom in the economic sphere, on the condition that they use their economic policies in a 'healthy' way, that is, so as not to endanger economic convergence. What, however, does this economic convergence mean? The Commission advocates cooperation in 'all aspects of economic policy and performance that significantly affect Community objectives', meaning 'supply and demand trends, price and cost developments, public finance, financial markets and the underlying economic policy orientations' (Commission of the European Communities, 1990a: 20). Three macroeconomic aggregate indicators are seen as potentially threatening to monetary stability when they do not converge: government debt, budgetary deficits and their financing.

In a broader sense, economic convergence is often used when referring to equal levels of performance among Member States, in terms of productivity and welfare. The coordination of credit, budgetary and wage policies is also a necessary prerequisite to monetary integration (Balassa, 1975: xii). This interpretation is not the one used in the Delors Report. It made very clear that economic convergence means discipline:

> Without such coordination [of national budgetary policies] it would be impossible for the Community as a whole to establish a fiscal/monetary policy mix appropriate for the preservation of the internal balance.... Monetary policy alone cannot be expected to perform these functions. Moreover, strong divergences in wage levels and developments, not justified by different trends in productivity, would produce economic tensions and pressures for monetary expansion. ... As regards wage formation and industrial relations, the autonomous negotiating process would need to be preserved, but *efforts would have to be made to convince European management and labour of the advantages of gearing wage policies largely to improvements in productivity.*[7] Governments, for their part, would refrain from direct intervention in the wage and price formation process.
>
> (Delors Report, 1989: 24)

However defined, economic convergence seems to set the *boundaries* within which the national government and its actors can still move as they see fit, as long as their policies do not pose a threat to monetary stability. The presence of convergence is the key to the success of EMU.

Evidently, monetary policy cannot be pursued without *de facto* affecting macroeconomic policy instruments and policy objectives. In this book it is argued that its implications go beyond merely accepting upper limits on budgetary deficits and public debts. It is argued that the implications of monetary integration *spill over* to other policy areas. This effect was considered, however, not so much an intended effect, but rather as following from the *dynamics* of the process of monetary integration. Negotiations, policies and perceived interests are based on partial comprehension of EMU. This study examines whether actors in considering the costs and benefits of EMU went beyond the formal implications on monetary and budgetary policies when making their judgement. This study examines whether, and if so, how actors anticipated EMU to affect other policy-making areas and the wider economic implications more generally. The book will study to what extent actors perceived EMU as giving rise to an increasing neo-liberal market orientation, and restructuring of the welfare state, and the way in which national macroeconomic and welfare/labour market policies were conducted more generally.

1.3   Selection of actors

This book focuses on four actors: central banks and Ministries of Finance, the employers' organizations and the trade unions. The first two represent the monetary authorities, that is, the institutions or bodies that have been the major national actors responsible for monetary policies. Representatives of monetary authorities participated in the negotiations for the drafting of EMU. The latter two, the social partners, may be regarded as representing the two main actors in modern societies; namely, enterprises and workers. They are often referred to when tighter monetary and fiscal policies request discipline, and flexibility in the labour market (cf. Dornbusch, 1991). When EMU is fully operational, domestic adjustments will take place in the labour market. Moreover, in the view of the monetary authorities the social partners are *supposed* to direct their policies so as to ensure competitiveness of the various industries in their country. In an earlier three-stage blueprint for creating an EMU, the Werner Interim Report (1970), this fact had already been acknowledged. The report emphasized the importance of the consultation between the Community institutions on the one hand, and the social partners on the other (Werner Interim Report, 1970: 4). However, by 1989, when EMU was once again on the agenda, this dialogue had become a monologue. As a result of changing views on the role of social partners in economic policy-making, the 1989 Delors Report stated that European management and labour *would have to be convinced* of the advantages of gearing wage policies largely to improvements in productivity. In addition, as was mentioned above, governments were advised not to intervene in the wage and price formation process (Delors Report, 1989: 24).

The reason for studying Britain, France and Germany was to study three 'large' Member States. As mentioned above, a similar study on the Netherlands conducted in 1989 showed that in a small open economy the role of the policy-makers is reduced (Verdun, 1990). Therefore, the countries chosen here are three bigger EC countries, with a strong historical background on state sovereignty.

This book examines the perceptions of EMU in Britain, France and Germany by making a distinction between the 'national interests' and the 'interests of the different actors'. Several authors have directly or indirectly examined the role of these or similar actors in the European monetary integration process. Some authors have questioned the role of national governments in representing the interests of their electorate (Vaciagio, 1991: v) or of the domestic vested interests such as industry and finance (Frieden, 1991). Others have stressed the fact that EC membership has strengthened the role of the state *vis-à-vis* domestic actors (Milward, 1992; Moravcsik, 1994, 1998b). Moreover, various authors have explained that when actors in the policy process formulate their perceived 'national interests', the fact that their country is an EC/EU member already shapes the way this national interest is conceptualized (Moravcsik, 1994; Pauly, 1992; Sandholtz, 1993a). Kenneth Dyson's authoritative study on EMU stresses how the EMU process should be seen as a 'two-level game' (Dyson, 1994; see also Dyson and Featherstone, 1996). Finally, authors have stressed the need to understand the notion of *issue linkage* when examining the interests of various actors in achieving monetary integration (Garrett, 1993; Lange, 1993; Martin, 1993). Nevertheless, even if the insights of the above authors have helped clarify the EMU process, insufficient systematic research has been conducted as to examining exactly *why* domestic actors thought EMU was or was not in their best interest.

The question posed here is formulated in an explorative manner, and seeks to collect the information from the actors themselves: what are the perceptions of the interests of different actors towards EMU, and how, in their view, does EMU serve or frustrate their policy objectives? Embracing more than just the monetary aspects of EMU, the book will try to make clear what the presumed relationship is between 'monetary' and 'economic' union. The spill-over effect of EMU via the market mechanism to other policy areas, such as fiscal and social policies, will be investigated. The period under study runs roughly from the launching of the Delors Report to the ratification of the Maastricht Treaty, although a detailed account is also given of the history of EMU in the 1960s, 1970s and 1980s, with special focus on the attitudes towards the Werner Report.

1.4   Aim of the study

The puzzling observation that has triggered this research was the apparent consensus in favour of EMU in 1989–90. This study set out to examine the perceptions of EMU in three 'major' Member States, that is, Britain, France and Germany. Its findings will shed light on the way individual actors perceive policies to defend the interests of their organization, and how national interests can be seen. It will also show how various actors within each of these three countries respond to the changes in the global economy and increasing interdependence.

The book aims, first, to present a study of the literature on Economic and Monetary Union. It examines what the economic theories and political science/international relations theories tell us about economic and monetary integration.

A second aim of the book is to evaluate the history of EMU in order to understand why economic and monetary integration plans occurred – that is, what triggered a plan? What were its aims? What were the motives of various actors? Why did it go wrong or succeed? The answers to these questions regarding the earlier plans serve as a framework to anticipate the answers to these questions concerning the current EMU process.

The third aim is to understand the perceptions of EMU as held by the four different actors in three countries in particular during the period 1989–92. The findings will also be compared across, and within, the three countries. The study will characterize what the typical 'national', and what the typical 'actors' perception' of EMU is. Because the interviews were held twice, that is, in two successive periods, the data will also be compared over time focusing on whether the perceptions of EMU were the same during the 1991 intergovernmental conferences and in 1992 – a year which was characterized by treaty ratification difficulties and exchange rate crises.

The fourth aim is to offer an alternative theoretical approach, introducing an eclectic 'theory' which will help in understanding the economic and monetary integration process, and related phenomena studied here.

1.5 Assumptions and levels of analysis

A number of assumptions were made concerning the aspects or elements that were thought to have been influential in determining the actors' perceptions of EMU. The implications of creating an Economic and Monetary Union may not have been fully examined before actors had made up their minds on whether or not they agreed to EMU. There are many reasons for this: it is not known what EMU will look like until it has been agreed to; the effects of EMU may be so extensive that it is next to impossible to comprehend its intended or unintended effects; the actors may have merely wanted to institutionalize the ERM because it was operating very successfully; actors may have thought it was desirable to participate in a process of monetary integration; there may have been domestic political or geopolitical reasons for wanting to move forward, etc.

To evaluate which of these factors were decisive one needs to examine the motives for favouring or opposing EMU at different levels. Was the perception of EMU determined by global change, by political or economic factors in the domestic economy, or were the actors involved in monetary issues so much part of a financial elite that they all had similar ideas about EMU? Hence, to examine the perceptions of EMU, three levels of analysis are proposed here: the level of the global or political economy, the domestic level, and the level of the actor as an agent. To understand exactly which motives led them to perceive EMU to serve or frustrate their interests it is useful to differentiate actors' use of 'economic' and 'political' motives.

At the level of the *political economy or at the global level*, a number of factors have changed over the past thirty years. It may be these factors which have weakened the actors' opposition to surrendering sovereignty in the area of monetary policy-making. Countries have become more interdependent and national policy-making effectiveness has gradually decreased. These developments are related to changes such as the growth of global production, the liberalization of the (capital) markets, the tremendous growth of the financial markets, technical innovation in general, and financial innovations in particular, the challenge posed by Japan and the NICs to the American and European producers. These changes have resulted in increasing competition between the United States, Japan and Western Europe. Capital and production mobility has confronted national governments with more elusive market-actors. Mobility has developed asymmetrically in Europe. Where capital and most factors of production are mobile, people do not tend to respond to small changes in the same way as capital does. Products can be produced anywhere, and can be imported from or exported to anywhere. Money can be borrowed by and lent to anyone. Nations have become part of a larger whole, whether they like it or not. It has become clear to many that autonomous European countries cannot keep up with competition, or sustain more than low rates of economic growth, and hence they cannot afford an ever-expanding welfare state. More importantly, the rigid structure of the European industrial society makes it difficult to adjust to these global changes, in particular compared to the United States. These important structural changes in the global production structure of modern society – which shall be referred to in this study as 'change in the global economy' – have challenged the traditional powers of a nation state. Today a nation's success is calculated in terms of productivity, efficiency and competitiveness. In Europe the only way of combating this loss of power at the national level is to cooperate with one's natural partners (trade partners or countries in close geographic proximity). Consequently, it is generally believed that the European Internal Market – the 1992 programme – will solve some of these problems. Creating a monetary union, however ill-defined, may have been perceived as offering a step towards regaining some of the power that had been lost at the national level. It may be a step in the dark, but it is at least a step.

At the *domestic level* actors need to respond to the changes in the global economy. This means that policy-makers have to explain the policy choices to their constituency. However, it is clear by now that the governments and societal groups notice that they have limited leeway for making policy decisions. In addition, policy-makers have come to realize that the 'old' structure of the welfare state needs to be revised if a country wants to be able to compete in the global economy. Legitimation is needed to 'roll back the state' on the one hand, and 'accept the facts of life' on the other. Examples of the former are the need to privatize, cut budget deficits, and increase labour flexibility. Examples of the latter are the fact that policy-making cannot be pursued effectively in isolation from the policies of neighbouring countries, such as monetary policy when capital can move freely, and when the Single Market has led to some policy harmonization and has increased economic interdependence.

The third level of analysis is the *level of the actor.* 'Actors' are defined in this study as the representatives of the four organizations – central banks, Ministries of Finance, employers' organizations and trade unions. The representatives that have been selected are those who are responsible for the drafting, formulation or conduct of monetary policy. Actors can thus be considered part of a policy-making 'elite' on EMU. They are monetary specialists and they judge how policies should be directed based on their knowledge of *monetary policy-making*. Decision-making as a whole has been divided into various compartments, and requires narrow, highly specialized expertise. An individual official will of course not be able to comprehend the full effects its organization's decisions will have on the society as a whole. Such an official will, however, be able to indicate which are the likely consequences of the monetary policy decisions. Policy-makers with specialization in other fields have difficulty in understanding the monetary specialists' decisions, and what consequences these decisions have for their field of expertise. Thus, due to the segmentation of policy-making, the dynamic and spill-over effects are seldom scrutinized by the decision-makers.

In order to understand why these monetary specialists in the various organizations and institutions may have been in favour of EMU as was set out in the Delors Report it is necessary to consider whether this positive attitude could be related to the fact that EMU would give monetary policy-making a more dominant role in society. After all, the European Central Bank would operate largely independent from politics as does a Constitutional Court in a Member State.

In any event, when examining the actors' perceptions of EMU it is useful to identify when the respondents refer to each of these three levels. In addition, the book will also study when they use 'pure' economic or monetary arguments, and when political ones in support of their position. The concluding chapter discusses the evaluation of this analysis.

Summarizing, this book evaluates the perceptions of EMU as well as the perceived policy implications that the representatives of central banks, Ministries of Finance, employers' organizations and trade unions bear in mind when discussing EMU. What do these actors think is going to be affected by EMU? In its aim to understand EMU this study will go beyond the mere *formal* loss of national sovereignty over monetary policy and restrictions on macroeconomic policy areas. To understand the deeper implications of EMU it is necessary to examine the effect of EMU on social policies, competitiveness, growth and unemployment. In addition, one needs to evaluate which policy instruments can still be used to combat successfully a country-specific shock – the most recent example of such a shock being German reunification.

How will the loss of monetary instruments, and the limits on the level of budgetary deficits and government debt, influence policy-making at the national level? And what kind of implications do these losses have on the interests and policy-making of trade unions, industry and monetary authorities? In other words, what spill-over effects of EMU do the various monetary experts in central banks, Finance Ministries, employers' organizations and trade unions anticipate?

1.6   The research question

The central assumption of the present study is that monetary integration *spills over* to other areas of policy-making (budgetary, fiscal and social policies), and it is going to affect economic growth, employment and the distribution of wealth. This is also why it is generally thought that monetary integration would have to be paralleled by some economic integration; hence the Werner and Delors Reports called for an *Economic and* Monetary Union. However, the Delors Report, and subsequently the Maastricht Treaty, focus mainly on the monetary aspects of EMU, and understand Economic Union to entail merely restrictions on budgetary deficits and public debts. Here this type of EMU is christened 'asymmetrical EMU'.[8]

The notion of 'asymmetrical EMU' implies the asymmetry between the contents of the 'Monetary' and the 'Economic' Union. The former relates to the positive integration of monetary policy at the Community level, implying a complete transfer of sovereignty to a new supranational institution, the European Central Bank (ECB). The 'Economic Union' refers mainly to negative integration (completing the Single Market) and acceptance of binding rules on budgetary and fiscal policies in order to support the price stability objective of the new ECB. Contrary to what is decided with regard to monetary policies, no new institution will be set up in the economic field of policy-making, as no single economic policy has been envisaged. Even though the Treaty on European Union envisaged the establishment of a cohesion fund to support the economies of the four weakest countries, this cannot at all be considered to be equivalent to a single economic policy.

The four main questions of this study can be briefly restated: (i) what are the reasons for choosing an 'asymmetrical' EMU? (ii) what are the perceptions of monetary authorities and social partners of EMU? In particular: (iii) how, according to them, will EMU affect their policy objectives? And (iv) how do actors perceive EMU as serving or frustrating their interests?

Of course it is almost impossible to judge the effects of EMU prior to its conception and indeed creation. Thus, the actors had to make their own judgement as to the implications of EMU for monetary and other policy areas. This study started out aiming at inspecting the actors' perceptions of EMU and how they claim it will serve or frustrate their aims. In addition EMU itself is analysed in order to give an indication of what effect it could be expected to have on policy objectives, and how these effects might be expected to spill over to other policy areas.

The theoretical framework is presented in Chapter 2 in response to the traditional theories of integration. In Chapter 8 the various theoretical approaches are evaluated and there is an analysis of why the actors came to hold their perceptions, and what can be learnt about perceptions of different socioeconomic groups and institutions in the policy-making process.

1.7   The research method

The data were collected by conducting 75 interviews with representatives of the organizations involved, whose job it was to follow European monetary integration, and to draft policy statements of their organization towards the monetary developments. Most of the interviews were conducted with officials in central banks, Ministries of Finance, employers' organizations and trade unions, which form the core of this study. Some interviews were conducted with other monetary experts, such as European Commission officials in DG II, members of the Economic and Social Committee, officials of various major banks, the president of the Association for the Monetary Union of Europe and many others. The interviews were held on the basis of a semi-structured questionnaire, in two periods, early 1991 and autumn 1992. The interviewees were asked during the interview how EMU was perceived by their organization, how it served the interests of their organization, and so on. Most interviews were conducted in the mother tongue of the interviewee. However, to improve accessibility of the replies, all quotations have been translated. The original quotes as well as the transcripts of the most important interviews are reported in Verdun (1995).

The economic and political science literature on European integration is reviewed in Chapter 2. Chapter 3 provides a historical background to European (monetary) integration until the launch of the EMS. Chapter 4 discusses the relaunch of the EMU project in the late 1980s and early 1990s. Chapter 5 describes the research method chosen for this study. Chapter 6 provides the perceptions of EMU as derived from the interview material. Chapter 7 draws a comparison between the national and the 'actoral' attitude of EMU. Finally, Chapter 8 sums up the perceptions of EMU and concludes with a reflection on integration theory.

2
Economic and Political Theories of Integration

Why did the EMU project emerge? What do the economic and the political science bodies of literature tell us about economic and monetary integration? This chapter reviews the literature of both economics and political science on the subject of European integration in general, and European economic and monetary integration in particular. It asks two questions. First, what are the driving forces behind the integration process according to the various schools of thought? Second, what are the 'costs' and 'benefits' from integration according to these theories? The first two sections discuss the economic rationale behind integration, and the economic theories on integration. The third section gives an account of the theories of regional integration, which focuses on neo-functionalist, intergovernmentalist and more recent approaches. The fourth section discusses the different explanations of EMU itself that have been offered by various scholars in recent years. The chapter closes by suggesting a revised theoretical framework which clarifies the drive to EMU.

2.1 Economic rationale behind integration

The concept of 'integration' is relatively new. It was not until the 1950s that it reached widespread usage in economic and political science literature and public policy-making (Machlup, 1977). The first time the term 'integration' was used to mean *combining separate economies into larger economic regions* is thought to have been in the 1930s. In the 1960s Balassa emphasized that integration referred to both the process as well as the state of affairs, and that the absence of discrimination was crucial (Balassa, 1961: 1). Tinbergen referred to integration as being an 'optimum' of international economic cooperation (Tinbergen, 1965: 3), as well as the creation of an 'optimum policy' for participating countries (Tinbergen, 1965: 57). Apart from rather general objectives these early writers did not elaborate on why, how and, especially, *at what cost*, the larger economic region is beneficial to the participating economies.

Economists have generally distinguished four forms or stages of economic integration: (i) free trade areas, in which the associated countries agree to remove the barriers to trade between them but all may have different barriers to third countries; (ii) customs unions, in which a common external tariff is decided upon *vis-à-vis* non-associated countries; (iii) common markets, which embody a customs union and allow capital and people (labour) to move freely in the area; (iv) economic unions with centralized or harmonized decision-making concerning monetary, fiscal and other policy areas (cf. Robson, 1987: 2; Swann, 1988).

Definitions of economic union

The least well defined of the four forms of integration, and the one which is at the heart of the present study, is the economic union. In this stage, according to the different theories on international economic integration, the member countries have agreed to create a lasting integrated area, which 'limits the unilateral use of certain instruments of economic policy' (Robson, 1987: 2), or as Swann has defined it: 'a common market in which there is also a complete unification of monetary and fiscal policy. The latter would be controlled by a central authority and in effect the member countries would become regions within the union' (Swann, 1988: 12). In recent years a differentiation has been made between 'economic union' on the one hand, and 'complete economic union':

> *Complete economic unions*: which are common markets that ask for complete unification of monetary and fiscal policies, i.e., a central authority is introduced to exercise control over these matters so that existing member nations effectively become regions of one nation.
>
> (El-Agraa, 1990: 2)

Willem Molle uses 'full economic union' to describe that state of affairs. Economic union refers to a less far-reaching stage in the integration process. He adopts the following definitions, which are worth quoting in full:

> *Economic union* implies not only a common market but also a high degree of co-ordination or even unification of the most important

areas of economic policy, market regulation as well as macro-economic and monetary policies and income redistribution policies. Not only is a common trade policy pursued towards third countries, but external policies concerning production factors and economic sectors are also developed. The *monetary union* is a form of co-operation which, on top of a common market (notably free move-ment of capital), creates either irrevocably fixed exchange rates and full convertibility of the currencies of the member states, or one common currency circulating in all member states. Such a union implies quite a high degree of integration of macro-economic and budget policies. The *economic and monetary* union combines the characteristics of the monetary union and the economic union. In view of the close interweaving of monetary and macroeconomic policies, integration evolves mostly simultaneously for both policy fields. *Full economic union* implies the complete unification of the economies involved, and a common policy for many important matters. The situation is then virtually the same as that within one country. Given the many areas integrated, political integration (for example, in the form of a confederacy) is often implied.

(Molle, 1990: 13)

Hence, depending on which policy areas are harmonized, and on what basis it is created, the original notion of 'economic' union is now referred to as 'full economic union'. It may include various policies; it may consist of a 'common' or 'single' market, a monetary union, a payments union, a fiscal union, a social union, a political union, a full union, a federation or, in fact, even a completely new state.

European economic and monetary integration

When the EC embarked on further economic integration in the 1960s it separated currency matters from other matters (such as market integration, budgetary and fiscal policies). Various EC Commission reports labelled the former 'monetary' union and the latter 'economic' union, which subsequently taken together were called Economic and Monetary Union (EMU) (cf. the Barre Report, 1969; the Werner Report, 1970; and the Delors Report, 1989; see also Chapter 3 below). For analytical purposes academic authors have generally accepted this dichotomy (see, among others, Christie and Fratianni, 1978; Molle, 1990; and Tsoukalis, 1977: 32; for a discussion of 'economic union' see also Emerson, Giovannini and Thygesen, 1991; and Pelkmans, 1991).

The Delors Report[9] adopted the economic–monetary dichotomy and applied a narrow definition. The economic union consisted of not much more than the Single Market, that is: (i) a common market, (ii) policies strengthening competition and the market mechanism, (iii) common policies aimed at structural change and regional development, and (iv) macroeconomic policy coordination including binding rules for budgetary policies (Delors Report, 1989: 20). The monetary union, on the other hand, was defined as (i) 'a currency area in which policies are managed jointly with a view of attaining common macroeconomic objectives', (ii) capital liberalization and integration of banking and financial markets, and (iii) the elimination of margins of currency fluctuation and the irrevocable locking of exchange-rate parities (Delors Report, 1989: 18–19).

Reflecting on the previous section regarding the definition of economic union, it can be concluded that the term 'Economic and Monetary Union' as it is used in the Delors Report, in Community jargon, and as subsequently was incorporated in the 1992 Maastricht Treaty, is a subset of the original theoretical concept of 'economic union'. As is discussed in Chapter 3, part of the reason for the choice of the name 'Economic' and 'Monetary' Union, rather than for example 'European' Monetary Union, lies in its historical origin. In addition, the usage of the term 'EMU' was a result of the dispute between the *monetarists* and the *economists* over which element of economic integration should come first: currency matters or other macroeconomic policies.

The 1980s and 1990s revealed yet another reason for maintaining this economic–monetary dichotomy, namely that consensus appeared to exist on how to reach the monetary union, and what monetary union would consist of (that is, transferring sovereignty to a supranational monetary institution, having fixed exchange rates and gearing monetary policy towards low inflation). However, concerning other macroeconomic policy areas it proved difficult to agree on transferring competence to the supranational level. Thus, it has been decided that no *de jure* institutional transfer of sovereignty should take place. The term EMU may have facilitated separating these issues. The irony, of course, is that enforcing a single monetary policy limits the freedom to conduct macroeconomic policy-making – in particular, budgetary and fiscal policies – but it will also affect level and distribution of government spending. Or, in other words, Tinbergen's *optimum economic policy* concerning monetary policy will affect the conduct of other macroeconomic policies. As was mentioned in Chapter 1, the present study examines whether indeed the actors in the policy-making process agreed to an asymmetrical EMU *precisely because* they could agree on transferring competence in the monetary field to the Community level, and they *explicitly did not* see the need for a parallel transfer in the economic field. The reasons for this reluctance are also examined.

2.2 Theories of economic integration

The previous sections illustrated that in the literature the term economic union is rather ill-defined and covers various areas of policy-making. In the late 1980s the emphasis was on monetary integration, and coordination of the related policy areas, such as budgetary and fiscal policies, to safeguard success. This section examines the motivations for forming an 'Economic and Monetary Union'.

The main literature associated with the creation of Economic and Monetary Union focuses on Optimum Currency Areas (OCA) (McKinnon, 1963; Mundell, 1961), and on 'credibility' (Artis, 1994; Artis and Winkler, 1997; Talani, 1998; Winkler, 1996; Woolley, 1992).

The theory of Optimum Currency Areas

The question central to the theory of Optimum Currency Areas (OCAs) is: which area could ideally benefit most from the use of a single currency? Deriving from the idea that exchange between countries can take place more efficiently with a single monetary unit, the task is to discover the costs for a country without its own currency.

Suppose that a small country is deliberating whether to adopt the currency of its (much larger) neighbouring country. To join this neighbour to form an area with a single currency the applicant would need to have substantial economic interaction (trade) with this neighbouring country. Moreover, joining in a monetary union (which is what having a single currency means) might distort the economic environment. It has been found that the rate of distortion is lower when the members of the future monetary union have domestic economies similar in structure implying that they have comparable economic levels and modes of production, types of industry and productivity (Commission of the EC, 1990b; Taylor, 1995).

When the members of the future monetary union adhere to these criteria, and an area with a single currency is created, adjustments can no longer be made by varying the exchange rate between the participants of the union. Here the substantial difference between 'fixed but adjustable' and 'fully fixed' rates comes in. Thus, the most important cost for the applicant country is the abolition of the exchange rate instrument. The theory of OCAs states that in these areas instruments other than the exchange rate instrument would have to be used for adjustments; for example, prices and wages may have to fluctuate corresponding to the business cycle, and to changes in productivity and/or competitiveness. With regard to the EEC the conclusion was that it was *not* an OCA (Commission of the EC, 1990b, 1991a; Eichengreen, 1990, 1993; Gros and Thygesen, 1998; Sachs and Sala-i-Martín, 1989; Taylor, 1995).

Even though the EC was not considered an OCA several authors in the early 1990s argued that it would still make sense to have a single currency in the EC (for example, Commission of the EC, 1990b; de Grauwe, 1997; Gros and Thygesen, 1998; Thygesen, 1990). The main reasons put forward were: (i) differences between the participating countries in the 1990s were small; (ii) already the usage of exchange rate adjustment was limited due to the commitment to stable rates and the interdependent nature of the domestic economies of the Member States; (iii) when the exchange rate instrument is used by national politicians, it often only provides a short-term benefit, yet a medium and longer-term cost; (iv) or, as Burda and Wyplosz (1993: 420) have bluntly stated 'If North and South Germany – or East and West Germany – can form a successful currency area, why not the EMS countries?'

The OCA theory also camse under attack as a result of conclusions reached by recent studies, which elaborated that 'currency confidence' and 'risk expectations' contribute significantly to sustaining or frustrating economic activity and growth (cf. Artis, 1994; Winkler, 1996). If the launching of a single currency successfully reduces the premium paid for the usage of money, this will be beneficial to the participating countries, but only if these benefits outweigh the costs of abandoning the exchange rate instrument. However, increasingly it was thought that devaluations were not beneficial, as they depended on the balance between imports and exports. Moreover, it was argued – though not always convincingly – that devaluations tended to be inflationary, thereby reducing their positive effect (see also Fitoussi *et al.*, 1993; Gros, 1996). In fact, in the second half of the 1980s an important consensus in economic thinking had emerged. The idea that a trade-off exists between inflation and employment had been abandoned. Aiming for low inflation had become considered the best policy option. With respect to the benefits of trade, it was assumed that fixed exchange rates provided more security, hence, again a lower risk premium, and thus producing more economic growth.

Benefits of EMU

What are considered to be the benefits of EMU? Many benefits refer to the full exploitation of the benefits derived from a larger European Single Market – more internal competition and increasing economies of scale. If the specific benefits of monetary integration are considered – that is, the advantages of having fixed exchange rates or a single currency – the gains would also include: elimination of transaction costs of converting currencies of the participating countries, the end of exchange rate insecurity in the area, and thus, a lower risk premium, less need for large foreign exchange reserves, a stronger role of the common currency in the world economy (see *inter alia* Thygesen, 1990). In fact, more subsequent benefits might occur as a result of complete integration of markets (Gros and Thygesen, 1998). Moreover, in the specific EC case an important argument considered in favour of EMU is the fact that when one monetary policy is conducted, it will replace the EMS and the actual 'copying' of German monetary policies. In many countries interest rates were higher than in Germany as a 'risk premium' because inflation had occured in the past. EMU would eventually get rid of that. Finally, EMU would enable monetary authorities to regain some power over economic and monetary policies lost as the contemporary international economy has witnessed great mobility of capital across national borders, but also as a result of copying German policies. The latter argument, of course, does not hold for German monetary authorities. In addition to political motivations, one of the reasons why German monetary authorities might consider EMU to be attractive could be because it would end competitive devaluations of other currencies and the gradual appreciation of the Deutschmark (van der Ploeg, 1991: 158).

Costs of EMU

Turning to the costs of economic integration, in particular EMU, the main cost which is generally accepted is the loss of the devaluation option. Two other instruments, seignorage and monetary financing, are also lost, but are considered to be of lesser importance. The former refers to money creation which generates revenue due to the fact that central bank liabilities are mostly non-interest bearing. The abandonment of the latter, financing by printing money, is consistent with aiming for price stability. As monetary financing of the national budget creates inflation, it is considered an undesirable policy option, under the EMS arrangement. According to the 'One Market, One Money' Report (Commission of the EC, 1990b), eight of the twelve EC Member States in the late

1980s had a low level of seignorage revenue, that is, around 0.5 per cent of a country's GDP (see also Gros and Vandille, 1994).[10]

Much has been written about the value of devaluation as a policy instrument (Buiter, Corsetti and Roubini, 1993; de Grauwe, 1997; Eichengreen, 1990, 1993; Gros, 1996; Gros and Thygesen, 1998). From the late 1980s until the 1992–3 crisis in the EMS, it was considered a policy instrument of the last resort. As stated above, the argument was that devaluations generated gains only for the very short term but in the longer term they generated losses; inflation would thus soon rise considerably.[11] It is also argued that the adjustment of exchange rates on one occasion would create the expectation that future adjustments might follow. These adjustments, in turn, would lead to more exchange rate insecurity which could only be countered by higher interest rates and greater risk premiums. Another premise was that one devaluation would lead to others. Competitive devaluations would set in motion a train of protectionism. This domino effect is again open to doubt. The 1992–5 ERM experience illustrates this point.

It is interesting in itself that the loss of the exchange rate instrument was the core argument on which the debate about the 'costs' of EMU has focused during the preparations and the meetings of the Inter-governmental Conference on EMU.[12] This reflected the official line set out by the EC Commission. The major work in the field, 'One Market, One Money',[13] and the so-called 'background studies' were written by officials of the Directorate General for Economic and Financial Affairs (DG II) of the EC Commission and external experts selected by DG II to calculate the costs and benefits of EMU. Public debate at the time had not focused on EMU.

In subsequent years the EMU plans *did* attract more criticism (see *inter alia* Feldstein, 1992). In the early 1990s criticism focused on implications of EMU on the use of fiscal policy. The argument was that the centralization of monetary policies would require the need for diversion in fiscal policies as all countries would have different policy objectives, and different social and economic conditions (see *inter alia* van den Bempt, 1993; Buiter and Kletzer, 1991; Van Rompuy, Abraham and Heremans, 1991; Wyplosz, 1991). Thus, according to some, limits on fiscal policy would endanger the ability of national governments to achieve stabilization (Johnson, 1994), which in turn could require transfers funds, which some found undesirable (Goodhart, 1990; see also Masson and Melitz, 1990). By contrast, however, it was also argued that a federal system of transfer systems would need to be put in place to ensure stabilization (see *inter alia* Goodhart and Smith, 1993;

Majocchi and Rey, 1993; more generally see European Commission, 1993a, 1993b). Other points of concern were the rigidity of the convergence criteria, in particular the requirements concerning public debt and budgetary deficits (Buiter, 1992; Buiter, Corsetti and Roubini, 1993). At the beginning of the 1990s it was thought that meeting these criteria for some countries implied that it would be virtually impossible for governments to conduct counter-cyclical policies (see *inter alia* Giovannini and Spaventa, 1991).

The convergence criteria laid down in a protocol of the Maastricht Treaty are: (1) price stability, that is, inflation may not be higher than 1.5 per cent of that of the three best-performing Member States; (2) no excessive deficits may exist, that is, government debt may not exceed 60 per cent of GDP, and government deficit may not exceed 3 per cent of GDP; (3) the national currency must be participating and respecting 'normal fluctuation margins' in the exchange rate mechanism of the EMS; (4) long-term interest rates may not be higher than 2 per cent of that of the three best-performing Member States in terms of price stability. In addition, to enter the third stage of EMU, the Member States' central bank should be independent of the national government.[14]

Other costs which are not dealt with by OCA theory are uneven allocation and distribution of the wealth generated by the creation of a currency zone. Even if economic and monetary integration leads to greater wealth on aggregate, individuals, sectors, or regions might not gain if the wealth is not redistributed (Molle, Sleijpen and Vanheukelen, 1993). The fact that the differences between European regions are large (in terms of economic structure, per-capita income, unemployment, productivity, etc.), implies that the costs and benefits may well be unevenly distributed over the various Member States. This is perhaps the largest potential cost for individuals and regions. The cohesion fund was partially set up to deal with possible negative distributive effects of EMU.[15] However, if the costs of EMU affect certain individuals and regions more than anticipated, they will have to address their *national* authorities, as the European Commission and national governments consider larger Community transfer payments undesirable (see also Van Rompuy, Abraham and Heremans, 1991; Wyplosz, 1991). Indeed, in the early 1990s a report stated that the Community budget should not grow to more than 2 per cent of Community GDP. The federal budget of mature federation is around 40 per cent (European Commission, 1993b, see also 1993a. For further discussion see Biehl, 1990; 1994; Biehl and Winter, 1990; Panic, 1992; Radaelli, 1996, 1997; Verdun, 1998c, 1999c).

Besides these concerns over either the restrictive role of national fiscal policy in EMU or the lack of fiscal federalism, EMU has been criticized for being inadequately designed from a political perspective (see for further discussion Verdun, 1998a, 1998c and Verdun and Christiansen, 2000). Some argued that EMU was too much of an institutionalization of German politics and institutions without the same German domestic checks and balances (Hall, 1994; McNamara and Jones, 1996). Thus, the EMU design was criticized for not being embedded into a political framework, thus rendering accountability and responsiveness problematic. Others argued that the lack of political linkages and the absence of a clear hegemon would make EMU in the long run unsustainable (Cohen, 1993).

Now that the economic costs of full EMU have been mentioned, it should be clear that the costs of reaching EMU lay first of all in the transition to EMU, in which monetary and budgetary criteria will need to be reached in order to start the third phase (see also Kenen, 1995). Furthermore, the dynamics of EMU might affect various individuals, industries and geographical locations differently, thereby unequally distributing the costs and benefits of EMU across the European Union (see Table 2.1 which summarizes these benefits and costs of EMU).

Table 2.1   Economic benefits and costs of EMU

Benefits
- International trade increases efficiency by allowing countries to specialize in activities in which they are relatively productive.
- Benefits from economics of scale.
- Greater efficiency in the use of money (decrease of transaction costs, leading to lower risk premiums).
- The European currency as world currency/reserve currency.
- Safeguard policy effectiveness, 'optimum policy-making' (avoiding the leaking away of policy measures to neighbouring countries by harmonization).
- Lower inflation in Europe.

Costs
- Adjustment costs. Even when the nation as a whole might benefit from trade, the adjustment process might involve unemployment of labour or capital of either a temporary or structural nature, thus leaving income distribution distorted. The problem is aggravated when economic integration takes place on an inter-sectoral rather than intra-sectoral level.
- Loss of the exchange rate instrument. Useful instrument for adjustment. The recent cases are Britain, Italy, Spain, Ireland, Portugal. The cases of Britain and Italy are interesting as they devalued, but managed successfully to keep inflation rates from rising accordingly.
- Costs related to restrictive use of budgetary and fiscal policies by individual governments.

2.3 Political theories of integration

Why and how does integration of countries into a larger whole take place? This section tackles this question. It will briefly survey the various integration theories. It discusses why and how, according to these theories, integration takes place. What are the mechanisms that give rise to successful integration? When does integration come to a halt? Who are the key actors according to the various theories? Which sectors or policy areas are likely to integrate first? More broadly, what are the costs and benefits of integration? The first part deals with the functionalists, followed by the neo-functionalist theory. This is followed by a brief discussion of the supranationalist and the federalist perspective on integration. Next, the intergovernmentalist approach is discussed. The core focus here is on the neo-functionalism–intergovernmentalism dichotomy, even though more recent approaches are also discussed. The review closes with an amendment to the integration theories which provides this study with a theoretical framework; an eclectic 'theory' of integration.[16]

This chapter aims at anticipating what conventional wisdom and prevailing theories would have supplied as a provisional answer to the core question posed in this study. By the same token the eclectic 'theory' presented is a first attempt at reconceptualizing the economic and monetary integration process. Its evaluation is presented in the last chapter.

Functionalism and neo-functionalism

The founding father of 20th-century functionalism was David Mitrany. In the interwar period he constructed a concept of regional integration whereby the nation states would try to co-operate to solve the problems they had in common, sector by sector. Its theme was the development of a 'working peace system' (Mitrany, 1943/66). The idea was that successful international co-operation could attract loyalty, which would be shifted away from the nation state. This approach did not envisage replacing the nation state with a supranational state. Its goal is seen as 'a complex, interwoven network of cross-national organizations performing all the traditional welfare-functions of the nation-state while at the same time rendering war impossible' (Pentland, 1973: 70). It reminds one contemporary writer of the present-day EC subsidiarity principle (Holland, 1993: 15). Mitrany recognized that integration would probably not take place automatically. Functional units would cooperate at an international level (Mitrany, 1975: 124–32). Thus, international committees were to be set up to replace the state bureau-cracies. Once the units form a political community surrender of sover-eignty will be gradually surrendered to the international (supranational) level of government (Mitrany, 1943/66, 1975; see also Claude, 1966: Chapter 17; Groom and Taylor, 1975; Haas, 1964: Chapters 1–4; Pentland, 1973; Sewell, 1966; Taylor, 1990).

Neo-functionalism provided a first systematic theory of regional inte-gration. In explaining European integration the most influential work was carried out by the American political scientist Ernst B. Haas, *The Uniting of Europe*, and *Beyond the Nation State* (Haas, 1958, 1964). His neo-functionalist theory differed from functionalism in that his approach to integration was more politicized (see for a discussion of neo-functionalism see Harrison, 1974, 1990; Pentland, 1973; de Vree, 1972).

First, in the neo-functionalist view, integration does not take place automatically, but evolves as a result of 'learning'; it is a political process (Haas, 1964: 48, 456). However, once the integration process has taken place in certain sectors the process will *spill over* to other sectors. In 1964 the spill-over effect of international decisions was defined as: 'policies made in carrying out an initial task and grant of power can be made real only if the task itself is expanded' (Haas, 1964: 111).

Second, the integration process goes beyond the level of the states, bureaucracies and governments, and also takes place in trade unions, political parties, interest groups, etc. When conflicts and clashing inter-ests exist among these groups, the groups will eventually try to strike package deals at the supranational level in order to resolve these con-flicts. Third, as a result of the first two mechanisms, the integration process itself will result in increased political institutionalization. Building a larger political community requires the creation of new institutions, to which sovereignty will be transferred. The political actors, in turn, will eventually shift their loyalties and expectations towards supranational institutions (Haas, 1958: 7–8, 16, 299–301). As mediators these institutions play an important role in taking forward the integration process (Haas, 1964: 111, 492–6; 1958: 32–59).

Resembling the approach of the earlier functionalists, Haas's road to integration was a sectoral approach (Haas, 1958: 104–5). Integration was seen as a process. However, in his preface to the second edition of *The Uniting of Europe*, Haas responded to his critics that there were areas and conditions in which spill-over was less likely to occur (Haas, 1968: xxii–xxiii). A distinction was made between the effect of the process on so-called *high politics* and *low politics* (George, 1991: 32; Hoffmann, 1966: 884–901; Taylor, 1983: 9). The former consisted of defence policy and external affairs, while the latter included what was named 'welfare politics', that is, economic policies, social policies, agriculture and so forth. This separation was made to explain why certain areas of policy-making might integrate faster than others. Policy-making areas in the domain of 'high politics' were considered an essential part of state sovereignty, and of great interest to politicians. Integration would thus first take place in 'technical' sectors, in which politicians and interest groups showed no 'ideological' interest. The neo-functionalists believed that if a supranational authority could function as a mediator and make package deals at the supranational level, integration would first happen in those sectors. The integration process would also depend on the aims of statesmen and non-governmental elites (Haas, 1968: xxii–xxv). Integration would only happen smoothly and nearly automatically if both the statesmen and the elites were aiming at incremental–economic objectives.

Having reached integration in some areas of policy-making the mechanism of *spill-over* would facilitate further integration. The concept embodies the idea that if integration takes place in one policy area it will influence other policy areas. As loyalties were shifted to the supranational level in the area of 'low politics' it would eventually spill over into 'high politics'. A recent example of this mechanism would be the fact that the Member States in 1990 decided that in parallel to the Intergovernmental Conference on EMU an IGC on Political Union had to be convened. Economic and monetary affairs fall into the category of 'low politics', whereas the foreign and security policy fall into the category of 'high politics'. Another example of spill-over is that Member States' governments realize they need to harmonize the levels of indirect taxation as a result of the successful completion of the removal of trade barriers and qualitative restrictions on trade. Maintaining different levels would distort competition. Hence, integration has spilled over to the fiscal sphere.[17] This step-by-step approach would shift the focus of policy-making to the new centre, to which the political loyalties would then be transferred.

To specify how integration proceeds, a distinction was later made between 'functional' and 'political' spill-over (George, 1985). The former incorporated the idea that integration of one sector would necessitate the integration of another. The latter suggested that political integration would eventually result from the gradual integration of the various sectors.

In the 1950s and 1960s neo-functionalism flourished as an 'explanatory theory' of European integration (Haas, 1958, 1964; Lindberg, 1968; Lindberg and Scheingold, 1970, 1971). Though neo-functionalism provided a systemic theory, others had meanwhile also made significant contributions to the literature on regional integration, such as the transactionalist theory of Karl Deutsch (Deutsch, 1954; Deutsch *et al.*, 1957; Deutsch *et al.*, 1967).

When neo-functionalism failed to explain the developments of the late 1960s, the 1970s and the 1980s it was then put aside by many scholars. Even Ernst Haas himself was disappointed about the failure of the Werner EMU plan, as he stressed that it was generally thought that it was needed for a proper functioning of the common market. 'EMU is puzzling because superficially it looks like a natural candidate for successful spillover' (Haas, 1976: 195). However, he also concluded that EMU failed 'because France and Germany disagreed fundamentally on the respective merits and priorities of monetary and economic policy as methods of management. Furthermore, Britain wanted neither' (Haas, 1976: 195).

More recently, however, some writers have again recognized the merit of neo-functionalism (Burley and Mattli, 1993; Feld and Mahant, 1986; George, 1991; Pijpers, 1994). Several authors have proposed supplementing or amending the neo-functionalist theory (cf. Corbey, 1993, 1995; Schmitter, 1992; Tranholm-Mikkelsen, 1991). Another author concluded that, though it might prove useful for understanding the political effects of market integration, neo-functionalism could not help in understanding the progress of political integration (Mutimer, 1989: 100–1).

After the totally unexpected and unpredicted boost to European integration in the second half of the 1980s, it was widely thought that evidence for the neo-functionalist *spill-over* mechanism was once again to be found. Examples are the revival of the EMU plan in order to consolidate the Internal Market, but also the introduction of the qualified majority voting procedure in some areas of European policy-making (cf. H. Wallace, 1990).

During the recent revival of neo-functionalism the theory had been adopted with some adaptations and/or supplements. Attention is once again drawn to the concept of spill-over. Borrowing from George (1985) Tranholm-Mikkelsen adopts three categories of spill-over (although the third category was renamed): functional, political and cultivated spill-over. *Functional spill-over* is used to describe the process of successful integration in one policy area causing integration in other policy areas.

The mechanism of *political spill-over* is at work when the 'elites' (governmental and non-governmental actors) start directing their policies to the supranational rather than the national level.

> The idea is that such elites will undergo a learning process, developing the perception that their interests are better served by seeking supranational rather than national solutions. They will therefore refocus their activities, expectations, and perhaps their loyalties to the new centre. Such reorientation will lead to calls for further integration, hence providing the process with political impetus.
>
> (Tranholm-Mikkelsen, 1991: 5)

The third mechanism, *cultivated spill-over*, captures the role of institutions, especially the European Commission, in ensuring that the integration process moves beyond the lowest common denominator. Tranholm-Mikkelsen states that the Commission has always pursued a neo-functionalist agenda, but has done even more so since 1985.

Dorette Corbey (1993), also refers to the two aforementioned categories of functional and political spill-over, but uses a different label for the third category, namely *geographical spill-over*. In her work she re-evaluates the integration theories and concludes that the neo-functionalist theory is most adequate in explaining the European integration process due to the fact that it explicitly anticipates the response to integration. Her *dialectical functionalism* incorporates the stagnation period into the process of European integration (Corbey, 1993). Her research leads her to conclude that when integration has successfully taken place in one policy sector it will result in Member States safeguarding adjacent policy areas against EU impact and in protecting formal national autonomy in those policy areas. In a later stage it is conceivable that policy competition will increase in those adjacent policy areas. If state intervention or policy rivalry in these policy areas become counter-productive, Member States will demand further integration, either by initiating it themselves, or by having the European Commission play the role of initiator (Corbey, 1995: 265). It is however not clear when 'counter-productivity' takes place.

Philippe C. Schmitter, who had already contributed to the discussions of neo-functionalist integration theory in the 1960s and 1970s, recently also contributed to re-examining the usefulness of the neo-functionalist heritage (Schmitter, 1971). In his recent contribution he applies the neo-functionalist perspective to the Single European Act and the Maastricht Treaty, and it seeks to examine how much spill-over has actually taken place since 1950 (Schmitter, 1992). The second aim is to assess which type of Euro-polity is emerging. He attributes the reason why the neo-functionalist strategy has again become relevant to two changes in the European policy environment, of which only the second bears a relationship to neo-functionalism. The first is the subjective feeling that Europe as a whole was destined to decline in its competitiveness, *vis-à-vis* the rest of the world, and in particular the Pacific Basin and North America. The second is the realization that European governments cannot pursue policies in isolation which are completely different from other Member States, as was convincingly demonstrated by the French President François Mitterrand's socialist experiment of the 1980s. Moreover, it became clear that such policy experimentation could have negative effects on growth and monetary stability. His conclusion is that the neo-functionalist perspective can be of help in anticipating and interpreting the interdependencies between the actors and interests of Member States but it does not clarify how interactions with external actors are likely to influence the eventual outcome (Schmitter, 1992: 60).

Stephen George, in his evaluation of neo-functionalism, concludes that the 'idea of functional spillover pressures does have some validity' (George, 1991: 33). However, he has problems with the concept of political spill-over. In particular it fails to identify the relevant political actors and it is inadequate in conceptualizing the political processes in the Member States. Furthermore he stresses the need to re-examine the economic assumptions underlying the neo-functionalist thought. In particular George questions the assumption that the economic benefits of integration would be equally spread amongst the Member States. Finally, he suggests focusing on the EC as participating in a wider international context (George, 1991).

Supranationalism or federalism

If neo-functionalism is taken in its broadest sense supranationalism and federalism are incorporated into it. Lindberg and Scheingold (1970) refer to supranationalism to explain the compromise strategy decided upon by Jean Monnet in the 1950s. Ernst Haas uses the notion of 'supranationality' as a style of decision-making: 'a cumulative pattern of accommodation in which the participants refrain from unconditionally vetoing proposals and instead seek to attain agreement by means of compromises upgrading common interests' (Haas, 1964: 64–6, quoted in Keohane and Hoffmann, 1991: 15).

Uwe Kitzinger (1963), when discussing supranationalism and sover-eignty, stresses the need to focus on supranational decision-making. He observes that a feature of the Rome Treaties is that 'a state pledges itself to take *measures as yet unknown* provided they are decided by a certain procedure...' (Kitzinger, 1963: 60, emphasis in the original). He then states: 'Supranationality only starts to come into play when a state agrees that it is willing to carry out decisions to which it is itself opposed. Most obviously, such a situation arises when it has agreed to be outvoted if necessary by other states – either by a simple or by some weighted or qualified majority. Let us call this governmental suprana-tionality' (Kitzinger, 1963: 61). The actors focused on, however, are not so much societal groups such as trade unions and political parties, but the national governments and the supranational actors. National governments will with regard to some areas of policy-making hand over sovereignty to an authority at the supranational level. The institu-tionalized supranational authority, for example the European Commis-sion, will then ensure that the international bargaining will exceed the lowest common denominator.[18]

Resembling supranationalism, federalism is closely associated with it but has as major objective the creation of a new federal or confederal state. Jean Monnet's approach to the construction of Europe is most famous for having had federalist aspirations (see Monnet's *Mémoires*, 1976; see also Burgess, 1989; Duchêne, 1994; Holland, 1993; Mayne, 1966; Pryce and Wessels, 1987). Federalism stresses the need for politi-cal and juridical institutions in order to achieve European integration. The core actors in this view are the supranational authorities and bureaucrats. This view has not regained much popularity recently because of various factors such as the British dread for the famous 'f' word, but also the Community's lack of advance towards a political community, the limited powers of the European Parliament.

A critique of neo-functionalism

In the late 1960s and 1970s European integration stagnated. The European Communities witnessed economic down-turn, and protec-tionism prevailed in most EEC countries. It was widely felt that neo-functionalism had been unsuccessful in predicting the developments in the EEC (cf. Pentland, 1973; W. Wallace, 1990; Webb, 1983). As mentioned above, even Ernst Haas himself drew this conclusion (Haas, 1975). The scholars of interdependence argued that the scope of neo-functionalism had been too narrow (Keohane and Nye, 1975). It had not sufficiently taken either domestic or international political and economic processes into consideration (Webb, 1983: 4). In addition 'integration' did not seem the most appropriate label for the process of policy co-operation in Europe of the 1970s and early 1980s.

Robert Keohane's work of the 1980s culminated in what he called 'neoliberal institutionalism'. His assumption was that 'state action depends to a considerable degree on prevailing institutional arrangements' (Keohane, 1989: 2). In 1990 and 1991 Keohane and Hoffmann contributed again to the debate on European integration by insisting that the institutional change in the EC can be understood only by accepting 'competing hypotheses'. They accepted the spill-over mechanism, but claimed it leads to successful integration only under certain conditions. These are to be found in the international political economy and the mere chance of having national preferences converge (particularly those of Britain and France). They concluded that their findings were consistent with regime theory (see below). It is however puzzling what they meant by 'spill-over'. With regard to monetary integration they stated: 'Nothing in the functional logic of spillover requires a European central bank or a single currency.' (Keohane and Hoffmann, 1991: 26) Their reason is that they assumed that the intergovernmental bargain would prevent spill-over:

> Ultimately, unless there is a radical change of policy in London, its partners will have to choose between a compromise or a break with Britain. Compromise would probably mean a European currency... and no European central bank. To create a system with a central bank would require not only overruling British objections but stifling the reservations of other influential parties, including the Bundesbank itself.
>
> (Keohane and Hoffmann, 1991: 26)

A critique of neo-functionalism tends to focus on three elements. First, in the late 1960s, the 1970s and the early 1980s its predictions concerning integration seemed not to have been supported by reality (cf. Taylor, 1983). Second, it did not take the external conditions into account. Third, it underestimated national sentiments related to sovereignty and national identity. Intergovernmentalists such as Stanley Hoffmann responded to the last two elements.

Intergovernmentalism

Hoffmann (1966) stressed that the nation state would remain the most logical unit in the international system for three reasons, which he labelled 'national consciousness', 'national situation' and 'national-ism', the latter term referring mainly to a national doctrine or ideology (Hoffmann, 1966: 867–8). He criticized neo-functionalism and stressed that integration was unlikely to take place in what he referred to as 'high politics'. In the 1980s this view was further supported by the Eurosclerosis and Europessimism. Intergovernmentalists held that it was an illusion to think that the European nation states would dissolve in the larger European Community (Hoffmann, 1982; Taylor, 1983).

In response to the renewed interest in European integration illus-trated by the signing of the Single European Act and the Maastricht Treaty, Andrew Moravcsik has launched 'a liberal intergovernmentalist approach' which builds on these earlier ideas (Moravcsik, 1993b; see also 1991, 1994 and 1998b). In this view national governments are the most powerful actors and are the most appropriate negotiators to secure national interests. European integration is thus mainly seen as inter-state bargaining. The state is assumed to be a rational actor.[19] The national preferences of the state are determined by their evaluation of the costs and benefits of economic interdependence (Moravcsik, 1993b: 480–1). Consequently, the outcome of this bargaining process is determined by the relative strength of the nation states involved. Although the outcome of European integration is seen to have been determined by the role of national governments, the possibility of domestic forces, including societal actors, playing a role in shaping national preferences is not discarded (Moravcsik, 1993b: 487–95).

The intergovernmentalist approach supplies a good insight into how the bargaining mechanism takes place at the level of the European Council meetings. For example, it is very well applicable to explaining the power-play between the larger Member States. An illustration of this mechanism is how the choice of a president or the location of a new EC institution has tended to involve 'deals' between Britain, France and Germany. The Benelux countries as well as the Southern countries have been very frustrated about these dealings. Examples are the British–French deal on the European Regional Development Bank which became located in London, with the Frenchman Attali as its president; the European Monetary Institute and thus the European Central Bank being placed in Frankfurt; and finally, the choice of Jacques Santer as the EU Commission president, which was the result of a 'compromise'. The French and Germans supported the Belgian candidate Dehaene, and opposed the Dutch candidate Lubbers. The British vetoed the Belgian candidate, and finally the choice was made for the 'compromise candidate': a Luxemburger.

An intergovernmentalist approach is however disinclined to credit European integration to structures, institutions or cooperation between actors other than those voicing the state preferences. On the contrary, it claims that the EC or EU institutions strengthen the power of governments in two ways (cf. Milward, 1992; Moravcsik, 1994). First, by borrowing insights from a functional theory of regimes (Keohane, 1983, 1984) and regime theory (see Rittberger, 1993), it argues that inter-state bargaining is facilitated by the increase in efficiency which results from the existence of a common negotiating forum. Second, the intergovernmentalist approach stresses that national political leaders have strengthened their position *vis-à-vis* domestic social groups: 'By augmenting the legitimacy and credibility of common policies, and by strengthening domestic agenda-setting power, the EC structures a "two-level game" place that enhances the autonomy and initiative of national political leaders – often ... a prerequisite for successful market liberalization' (Moravcsik, 1993b: 507; on two-level games see also Putnam, 1988).

Though the efficiency argument is not very convincing (that is, power struggles, clash of interests and so on can easily disrupt possible 'efficiency'), the second mechanism, whereby national political leaders have strengthened their domestic position, provides a useful insight into how the national constituencies are persuaded to accept further economic integration. The great strength of the liberal-intergovernmentalist approach lies in combining intergovernmental power struggles and domestic pressures for understanding the bargaining process at the level of the European Council (see in particular Moravcsik, 1998a).

Evaluating the usefulness of approaches and introducing a new approach

The history of the EEC has witnessed several doctrines, theories or approaches discussed above, explaining European or regional integration. They differ in their emphasis on what determines integration: what factors activate the integration process, which policies will be affected first, which actors play the largest role in achieving integration, and why various actors are likely to favour or oppose integration. By evaluating the theories of integration presented above, some remarks can be made in the light of the present research.

The intergovernmentalist critique on neo-functionalism has emphasized that 'integration' will more easily happen in areas of 'low politics' than in those of 'high politics'. In order to examine the usefulness of the neo-functionalist 'predictions' it would be necessary to clarify whether economic and monetary integration should indeed both be placed in the original category of 'low' politics, or whether 'economic' and 'monetary' policies need to be subdivided into separate categories, that is, into 'low' or 'high' politics. It will indicate why actors might agree to surrender monetary sovereignty to an authority at a supranational level (because it is low politics), but have great fear in doing so with regard to other 'economic' policies. The ones examined here are budgetary, fiscal, social policies (including the national social security system), labour policies, etc.[20] The conclusion of the data collection will clarify the underlying motives for treating monetary and economic policies differently.

A second aspect of neo-functionalist thought that seems decisive for the present study is the concept of *'spill-over'*. As was illustrated above, an argument often heard in favour of an EMU for Europe is that it is needed in order for Europe to benefit fully from the Internal Market. This leads to another question: what, in turn, will be the spill-over effects of EMU? As was mentioned in the introduction, shortly after an Intergovernmental Conference on EMU was envisaged it was decided to convene in parallel an IGC on Political Union. This study will show how much the actors have taken spill-over into consideration, and which areas of policy-making are perceived to be affected by it.

A third feature of neo-functionalism that seems applicable to the present research concerns the role of the various actors, Ministries of Finance, central banks, and employers' organizations and trade unions. Neo-functionalist literature claims that organized interests, that is, trade unions and employers' organizations, will be the first to try to safeguard their objectives at the supranational level, because they see the issues as non-ideological (depoliticized), and that they will be the first to shift loyalties to the higher level. The present study evaluates where the actors feel their strongest loyalty is, and at which level they can best safeguard their interests.

As has been pointed out by critics, the original neo-functionalist thought unfortunately did not take into consideration the external circumstances, which can be influential factors to trigger or oppose integration. This aspect was rightly pointed out by Haas himself, the interdependence theorists and intergovernmentalists. The present study will clarify how much actors have been influenced by external factors in their policy formation and preferences.

The intergovernmentalist view anticipates only a small role for European supranational institutions in the integration process. Any role they play would be a mere administrative one; for example, governments could delegate the task to administer a bargaining result previously agreed upon. Intergovernmentalist writers see European integration as a result of national governments trying to safeguard their national domestic interests. In addition, they claim that the more powerful countries determine the outcome of the bargaining. Their core focus in understanding European integration is to look at the power-play between national governments. Their claim is that the outcome of European integration is the logical consequence of inter-state bargaining. In this view, merely by looking at what the interests of the most powerful Member States are one can understand the process of integration. However, the liberal intergovernmentalist approach stresses that domestic actors help shape the perception that governments hold of the national interest. In the present study of the perceptions of EMU, this domestic factor is also examined.

2.4   Explanations of EMU – a literature survey

Throughout the 1980s the development of European integration theory virtually came to a halt. Few authors were examining why European integration happened, and how it could be explained. The economic and monetary integration process happened in a moment of theoretical limbo. Theorizing about it happened only after the EMU project had been incorporated in the Treaty. Puzzled by the acceptance of creating an EMU in the EC/EU, many authors have since 1992 investigated what caused this progress in European monetary policy-making (for a recent review of the literature see also Verdun, 1998e). Let us look at a number of these explanations.

In his authoritative article Wayne Sandholtz suggests that a combination of five factors made the EMU agreement possible in the late 1980s (Sandholtz, 1993a; cf. Pauly, 1992 and Campanella, 1995). First, there existed domestic support for monetary and price stability. Second, the Internal Market programme and increasing internationalization of financial markets generated the need for a regime of monetary stability and gave rise to a widespread sense of Euro-optimism surrounding the 1992 project.[21] Third, some governments (for example, the French, the Italians and the Benelux countries) who had been participating in the EMS and had shadowed German monetary policies, desired a greater voice in EC monetary policy.[22] Fourth, German reunification implied that Germany needed to show the rest of Europe that it would remain committed to the European integration objective.[23]

Finally, EMU was considered desirable by the EC Member States to institutionalize their commitment to low inflation (Sandholtz, 1993a: 37–8). Though Sandholtz' account is very persuasive, his analysis centres mainly around issues of domestic politics and international (institutional) solutions to these domestic problems.

David Andrews' analysis into the origins of the EMU agreement emphasizes in particular the role of global factors. He stresses that the EMU process cannot be understood merely by looking at spill-over mechanisms or domestic politics. His argument is that external developments provided the major impetus for the Maastricht Treaty (Andrews, 1993: 118). In particular, structural changes in economics and politics led to national governments' redefining of interests. The global integration of financial markets and the interdependence of the European economies have made national monetary authorities governments less capable of pursuing independent monetary policies (Andrews, 1993, 1994).

Andrew Moravcsik (1993b, 1994, 1998b) emphasizes the fact that the EMS and the EMU negotiations were part of a strategy of national executives to gain more domestic control given that international interdependence was reducing the room for manoeuvre of national politicians (Moravcsik, 1994: 38–51; see also Milward, 1992). Moravcsik's earlier analyses do not discuss the recent EMU process. On the basis of other parts of the integration process he argues that national executives have increased their importance *vis-à-vis* domestic actors by using progress in the European integration as legitimation for difficult domestic policy decisions. Moravcsik's analysis rejects the idea that the integration process may have an internal dynamic which may push forward the integration process. The analysis also plays down the role that the EC/EU institutions or transnational actors would have in the integration process.

In his provocative new book, *The Choice for Europe*, Moravcsik (1998a) however *does* discuss at great length the negotiations that led to the EMU arrangement in the Maastricht Treaty. His main proposition is that national governments acted rationally and aimed at safeguarding their own national interests. He treats the national governments as 'unitary actors', not because they *are* but because they *act as if* they are unitary. His conclusion is that the EMU package in the Treaty is in no way a result of unintended consequences, or path dependence. Rather, it is the result of careful negotiation and bargaining of national governments, reflecting in particular the interests of the most powerful Member States. In his view the process can be best analysed by assuming that national governments formulate preferences, then engage in inter-state bargaining and finally decide whether or not to delegate or pool sovereignty (Moravcsik, 1998a: 473).

Aware of the challenges that the EMU arrangement poses for neoreal-ism, Joseph Grieco (1995) offers a revised neorealist analysis of the process. In his analysis the 'voice opportunities thesis' may help explain why countries such as France, Italy and many smaller Member States favoured EMU; by creating the ESCB monetary authorities of these countries could regain power that was lost to the Bundesbank. Moreover, assuming that there are external challenges to be met, it could be considered consistent with neorealist assumptions that countries cooperate multilaterally in order to be strong enough to face a hegemonic power (Grieco, 1995: 40). Grieco criticizes the neo-functionalist concept of 'spill-over' as not functioning properly in the case of EMU. He argues that 'simultaneity of financial liberalization *and* the decision to seek EMU would not appear to be in acord with the spillover hypothesis' (Grieco, 1995: 33). However, Grieco does not address the fact that the decision to liberalize capital by 1 July 1990 had been decided *before* the Delors Committee came out with its report. In fact, the Delors Committee decided to let the first stage of EMU *coincide* with the first date of full capital liberalization in the EC. So, one could well argue that spill-over was at work at this particular point in time.

In the July 1993 issue of *Economics and Politics*, various authors exam-ine the reasons behind the success of the EMU project.[24] Barry Eichengreen and Jeffrey Frieden state the obvious by stressing that the process was determined by *political* rather than *economic* factors because according to them: 'neither economic theory nor economic evidence provides a clear case for or against monetary unification ... The absence of a clear economic justification for EMU leads us to conclude that events in Europe are being driven mainly by political factors' (Eichengreen and Frieden, 1993: 89). In order to explain political consensus in favour of EMU they discuss three sets of political considerations, that is, interstate bargaining, issue linkage and domestic distributional factors. They conclude that no single factor can explain the EMU process, and that the outcomes are a result of all the political considerations taken together (Eichengreen and Frieden, 1993: 98).

Two other authors in the same issue, Geoffrey Garrett and Lisa Martin, each focus on specific aspects of the EMU negotiations. Garrett examines why Germany accepted the type of EMU agreed to in Maastricht. He rejects the usual interpretation of the Maastricht Treaty which views the EMU arrangement as re-creating the German model at the European level. Writing in 1993, he claims that EMU could well lead to higher inflation because 'Membership was not limited to countries that mimic the German commitment to price stability' (Garrett, 1993: 105). He concludes that the reason for Germany's acceptance of this 'suboptimal outcome' is to be found in the international circumstances at the time of the Maastricht negotiations; that is, German reunification and the demise of the Soviet empire, which gave Germany broader political interests to deepen European integration. With the benefit of hindsight it can be noted that German policies have tended to demand a 'strict' interpretation of the Maastricht convergence criteria for entering EMU, a policy choice which Garrett does not seem to have anticipated. An analysis by C. Randall Henning (1994) clarifies the process with which the German government moved towards accepting EMU. The Bundesbank was more sceptical than the German government and was concerned about 'weaker Member States' participating prematurely in EMU. The Kohl government was willing to accept EMU if it was firmly based on German principles of stability and central bank independence (Henning, 1994: 228–37).[25]

Lisa Martin's article in *Economics and Politics* examines the ways in which formal institutions and decision-making procedures have constrained the EMU process (Martin, 1993). Her thesis is that the final EMU arrangement was a result of issue linkages (that is, not only achieving EMU, but also incorporating in the Treaty a cohesion fund, the Social Chapter, and extending the powers of the European Parliament). She stresses that these linkages were possible as EMU was negotiated in a particular institutional set-up, namely an Intergovernmental Conference aimed at amending the Treaty of Rome. As a consequence, all Member States ultimately could veto the final outcome. The final package had to please (or at least not enrage) every Member State. As the Treaty had to be ratified this implied that the package had to be acceptable to the negotiators as well as their national parliaments. Thus, she discards a purely intergovernmental analysis of the EMU negotiations. From her analysis we may start to understand why some countries, for example 'poorer' Member States who may not be able to join EMU right away, still accepted EMU.

In an article comparing the Nafta agreement with the Maastricht Treaty Helen Milner, much like Lisa Martin, concludes that domestic politics and the institutional set-up are the most important variables in explaining the EMU agreement. In her view the role of the Commission and of its President should not be diminished, but 'National political leaders' interest in monetary union was what brought the issue back to life' (Milner, 1995: 351). Her analysis takes the increasing international economic interdependence and dominance of German policies as a given, and hence political leaders responded to domestic pressure in addition to the changed international environment.

Kathleen McNamara, another author who examines the role of domestic politics, also comes to the conclusion that 'domestic politics do matter' but only if one moves beyond the level of sectoral interest group pressures on government action. Instead, McNamara points to the fact that policy-makers need to respond to 'continued uncertainty over what constitutes the correct prescriptions for monetary policy' (McNamara, 1994: 21). She points to the role of ideas in bringing about – or 'helping to construct' – perceptions of national interests. In her view the relatively under-examined role of changing ideas is in need of study in order to understand diverging and converging interests in the move towards EMU. She argues that the constraints of international capital mobility and the neo-liberal consensus on monetary policy led to 'the consensus of competitive liberalism' (McNamara, 1998: 166). Her excellent book on the idea formation underlying the EMS clarifies the importance of converging policy objective prior to the EMU initiative having been relaunched (a comparable ideational study of economic and monetary policy change is provided by Marcussen, 1998a, 1998b, on the role of ideas and knowledge see also Radaelli, 1995, 1997).

So far Kenneth Dyson has written the most comprehensive study of economic and monetary integration in the Community in a monograph entitled *Elusive Union: The Process of Economic and Monetary Union in Europe.*[26] His central argument is 'that the EMS and EMU policy process is best understood as composed of a distinct set of interdependent bargaining relations and rules of the game, embedded in a framework of structures that they have a limited, and fluctuating, capacity to influence' (Dyson, 1994: x). His book looks at the policy actors, the bargaining relations and what he calls 'structural power in the international political economy'. Regarding the actors, his thesis is that the EMU process is shaped by the 'will and capacity of the central actors involved'. Four factors influence this will and capacity. First, the actors have to operate in a 'scene', a 'two-level game' (see also Putnam, 1988). Moreover, these central actors have also held certain economic beliefs. Thirdly, these actors are confronted with changing structural conditions in the international political economy, and lastly, their will and capacity to create EMU is heavily influenced by their experience with the European economic and monetary integration process, notably the EMS and EMU (Dyson, 1994: 10–17). Finally, with respect to 'structural power', Dyson refers to control over a wide range of factors in the external environment (see also Strange, 1994). These include, among others, control over the anchor currency, control over supply and demand of capital, control over 'economic fundamentals' and, notably, the 'control over the key ideas and beliefs informing the policy process, in particular the "capture" of the EMS policy process by economic ideas of "sound money" and the prevalence of political beliefs about European union' (Dyson, 1994: 16).

This latter emphasis on the importance of monetary experts is also found in a recent paper by David Cameron in which he examines the process leading to EMU. In his analysis he questions whether the process should be seen as primarily supranational or intergovernmental. His conclusion is that both types of politics were important, but that:

> the EMU initiative also witnessed a *third* type of politics that involved *neither* the national governments of the member states *nor* actors embedded in the supranational institutions of the Community but, rather, *transnational* actors.
>
> (Cameron, 1995: 73–4)

The transnational actors he refers to are monetary officials who were members of the Monetary Committee or the Committee of Central Bank Governors. Cameron points to the fact that these actors not only represented their national governments, but also met one another regularly as their meetings were highly institutionalized. Cameron's line of thinking reminds us of the work done by Rosenthal (1975) on the Werner Report, in which she draws similar conclusions. The role of experts is discussed further in Verdun (1998b, 1999a).

Erik Jones, Jeffrey Frieden and Francisco Torres (1998) offer an analysis of EMU by examining various smaller Member States. The interesting phenomenon observed here is that they find that there is no 'small country explanation' of why EMU happened. EMU seemed to occur because it served all participants at the same time in different ways. However, the analyses of several smaller Member States point to international factors, globalization and financial market integration as having been important for the realization by national monetary authorities of the limited room for manoeuvre in macroeconomic and monetary policy-making. Yet at the same time, it is clear that congruence of national interests was crucial in pushing forward the EMU process. Still they do not at all claim that monetary integration is in any way inevitable.

2.5   An eclectic theory of integration

Below an eclectic 'theory'[27] of economic integration is presented. It is 'eclectic' as it does not exclusively build on any single existing theory. The main phenomenon it tries to understand is why actors within a given country at times seem to favour integration without a large debate about its desirability or the distribution of the costs and benefits, whereas at other times the issue of redistributing the gains from integration is at the forefront of the debate.

Phases of integration – a 'model'

In the proposed 'model' of integration of the eclectic theory, three phases can be identified. The event that triggers the start of the integration process is that a country feels threatened by external effects. It perceives its economic performance to be deteriorating, and it sees very little opportunity to address these problems by finding domestic solutions, that is, pursuing domestic policies in isolation will not solve the problem. It perceives cooperation with other countries, that is, with those that experience the same problem, as the most logical solution to the problem.

In the case of Western Europe, for example, governments of several European states share an awareness that the newcomers in industrial production of manufactured goods have a comparative advantage. In addition the strengths of Japan and the United States have brought about the realization that European countries have very limited influence on global developments if they do not act in concert. Moreover, the mobility of production and capital makes it obvious that a response to the challenge should be found in cooperation with countries that face the same problems. As a result, according to the model of integration of the eclectic theory, the member nations seek cooperation among themselves to protect a part of the world market for free trade by collective bargaining.

The model envisages that, to support the strategy of cooperation, the domestic actors temporarily settle their differences. Hence, in this phase the country appears to act as if it were a so-called 'unitary actor'. By doing so it avoids letting the domestic struggle frustrate the larger strategy of addressing the challenge posed by the global political economy. All domestic actors agree that the nation as a whole must unite first, in order that the *whole country* gains (that is, pull in more production, be more competitive).

Summarizing, in the model, Phase One of integration shows a country in which citizens are aware of the need to stand together as a nation and are willing to cooperate in order to achieve the aim of strengthening the position of the country *vis-à-vis* the rest of the world. The internal distributional struggles are temporarily set aside. In addition the country very willingly cooperates with other countries to increase the total economic activity of the cooperating countries, thereby generating aggregated wealth for the cooperating or integrating group of countries, increasing its bargaining power on the global level, and protecting itself from the rest of the world.[28]

When the first phase identified by the eclectic theory of integration has been successfully achieved, the second phase will manifest itself. The indicator that shows that Phase One has been completed is that the integration or cooperation strategy has been established and is operating successfully. This implies that it is delivering the greater wealth to the cooperating or integrated group of countries. It is important for the successful completion of this phase that the participating countries and the domestic actors accept that it is still necessary to incur some adjustment costs at the domestic level, but that eventually the aggregated wealth generated by the cooperation strategy will flow back into the country. If the countries and the actors within these countries do not hold this view, Phase Two of the model is bound to fail, and the country will fall back to Phase One, or even retreat back to its position before it started participating in the process.[29]

In Phase Two the nation state will try to obtain at least its proportional share of the accumulated trade and production of the integrated whole. At the domestic level the various social and political actors within the country will try to identify the 'redistributive issues', but will refrain from embarking on internal struggle. They will try to coordinate their views, and say similar things, and try to speak 'with one voice' to their governments, to the other nations and to supranational institutions of the area. When a dispute is difficult to resolve, employees and labour, being relatively abundant, will have to 'give in'. They are aware of the need to enlarge the cake first. Later they may strive to have it equally divided.

In the third phase, when the integration objective is completely fulfilled, the country's domestic redistributive struggle is bound to return. This struggle is to be expected if labour has pre-empted the process by agreeing, and has not seen an 'equal' share of the cake. An indication that the country has successfully achieved Phase Three occurs when the group of countries have managed to reach the final integration aim that was started in Phase One. It now has more economic wealth within its geographical boundaries, that is, the economic competitiveness of its production is safeguarded. To the extent that the integrated area was trying to respond to the challenge of the global economy, it now has found a way to exert more influence over global processes, or it is at least capable of having a more influential response to the challenge.

In this phase the domestic redistributive debate will arise again with great intensity. The domestic actors have been postponing demands so as not to endanger the strategy of the country as a whole in finding a way to combat the challenge. However, in this third phase domestic actors want to make up for the 'loss'. They feel they have a right to an equal share of the larger cake. Employees, consumers and trade unions will remind industry and enterprises, even governments, that the area has consolidated its position in the world economy, and that now is the time for giving them bigger pieces of the cake. This can be done by raising wages, employing more people, improving working conditions, increasing social benefits, etc. Enterprises, for their part, will be hesitant to redistribute the increased national income. They will, for example, argue that it is impossible to render more of the profits to the employees, because that would raise the price of their products in the world market, thereby causing a deterioration in their newly gained competitive position. If the pressure on an enterprise is considered by its management to be too strong, it might announce its intention of leaving the country.

With respect to the various member countries it can be expected that the less prosperous will demand more equitable redistribution of the enlarged cake which was acquired through regional integration.

This process of integration in three phases, set out above, is a very simplified model of the various national actors' motivations for proceeding with integration. It tries to explain why various actors sometimes seem to agree to integration, and at other times oppose it. The unequal position of employees in the largest economies has resulted from changing circumstances in the global economy, as was mentioned in Chapter 1. This includes increased productivity, a capital-intensive mode of production, technological innovation, the relatively high level of wages in the developed countries, low labour mobility though high capital mobility resulting in the transfer of production to low-wage countries, and the world-wide abundance of labour as opposed to capital. Each of the actors calculates the perceived costs and benefits of starting with Phase One, and will then patiently await Phase Three. Thus, the real question of redistribution is initially postponed but will have to be addressed in the third phase.

Consequently, looking at countries in Phase One of the integration process, one would expect to find consensus about integration in the country, and less debate on the distributional effects of economic integration. Once the integration process has been substantial and successful, one would expect the domestic debate to reappear and, in the last phase, be completely present. These phases are an attempt to try to explain why actors in Member States can passively accept a plan for economic integration, which will only *on aggregate* benefit everyone. However, the further the integration process progresses, the more the actors in the Member States are worried about its implications for sovereignty and redistribution. Chapter 8 draws some conclusions about how this 'model' may help in understanding the fluctuating support for integration.

3
A History of European Monetary Integration

At the outset of the European integration process, in the second half of the 20th century, it had not been decided whether the Member States should or should not eventually have a single currency. Though it was not written into the Treaty of Rome, it may have been in the back of the minds of the founding fathers of 'the European Community'.[30] An often-quoted phrase of Jacques Rueff rightly stresses the symbolic importance attributed to money for the success of the integration process: *'L'Europe se fera par la monnaie ou elle ne se fera pas'*.

This chapter provides a historical survey of the development towards economic and monetary integration. It describes the conditions that triggered the launching of the plans, and it examines why economic and monetary integration plans failed to mature, by focusing on the differences of opinion between the Member States on how to approach EMU, and the changes in the international context. The leading questions in this chapter are: how and why did the EMU plans rise and fall, what were the objectives of economic and monetary integration, and how was it to be achieved? More specifically, what were the motives of the governments of the Member States for embarking on economic and monetary integration, and why and when did they dismiss the plans or abandon them? The focus with regard to the earlier EMU plans is mainly on France and the Federal Republic of Germany (FRG) and less on the UK as that country was not a member of the Community until 1973. Special attention is given to the first EMU plan, the Werner Report. This chapter will examine why the common EMU goal lost general support only a few years after the project was launched. The next chapter will deal with the establishment and success and failure of the European Monetary System (EMS), the relaunch of the EMU project in the 1980s (the

Delors Report) and the subsequent negotiations leading up to the Maastricht Treaty.

This chapter discusses chronologically the developments in the EEC that led to the European monetary integration plans. It is divided into four main sections. The first section sets out the origins of the EC and the role of economic and monetary policy coordination in the Rome Treaty. The next section discusses the period 1958–69 and focuses on the attempts in the 1960s to institutionalize monetary cooperation. The third section covers the period 1970–4 which focuses on the first EMU plan, the Werner Report and its aftermath, on the Snake and on the changes in the international (monetary) situation. The attempts in 1975–7 to boost the EMU are described and the failure of the EMU plan is analysed in the fourth section.

3.1 Three communities

When the European Community for Coal and Steel was set up, it was mainly a reaction to the West German *Wirtschaftswunder* which followed the Second World War. To minimize the risk of war, Robert Schuman and Jean Monnet in May 1950 put forward a plan for a common market for coal and steel, in which equal access to these products would be guaranteed, and discrimination on the basis of nationality would be abolished. The future of Europe would be secured by creating a 'European federation which is indispensable to peace'. The 'Schuman Plan' was the basis for the Treaty of Paris, which was signed in April 1951 by six Member States ('the original Six'), namely Belgium, France, Italy, Luxembourg, the Netherlands and West Germany. The most powerful country in Western Europe at that time, Britain, stayed out of the new organization (Lipgens, 1982; Milward, 1984).[31] The drafting of the European Atomic Energy Community (Euratom) and the European Economic Community (EEC), took place from 1955 to 1957. They were signed in Rome on 25 March 1957, and came into force on 1 January 1958.[32]

The EEC was by far the most ambitious of the three European Communities (EC). It advocated a transition to a European common market, with free movement of goods, services, persons and capital. The main emphasis was on the progressive elimination of tariffs and quantitative restrictions and on the suppression of national discrimination. The first step was the transition to a customs union within twelve years. In this union tariffs and quotas on trade between the members were removed and a common level of duty was raised on goods entering the union from third countries. Its creation, thus, the 'transition period', was completed ahead of time in July 1968.

Though very ambitious, there was no explicit mentioning of either economic or monetary *union* in the Treaty of Rome. Economic and monetary policy *coordination*, however, was mentioned in articles 103 to 109. Article 103 reads that Member States shall regard their conjunctural policies as a matter of common concern and shall consult each other and the Commission on measures to be taken. In article 104 it is stated that Member States ought to pursue the economic policies needed to ensure equilibrium in their balance of payments, but it clearly allows for parity changes if needed 'to ensure the equilibrium of its overall balance of payments and to maintain confidence in its currency, while taking care to ensure a high level of employment and a stable level of prices'. Article 105 declares that economic policies should be coordinated. Article 106 calls for the removal of exchange controls in connection with those transactions in goods, services and factors liberalized under the common market arrangement. Article 107 specifies that 'each Member State [shall] treat its policy with regard to rates of exchange as a matter of common concern'. Furthermore, the management of economic affairs would remain at the level of national policy-making (EEC Treaty, 1957: art. 145). Article 108 declares that the Commission will recommend appropriate remedial measures, when a Member State is in balance of payments difficulties. If these measures prove to be insufficient the Council of Ministers may grant mutual assistance. If not, or if this does not eliminate the difficulties, the Commission can authorize the Member State to institute protection. The Council can, however, overturn such a measure. Finally, article 109 leaves Member States the possibility of applying for protection in the case of a sudden crisis although the Council can call for the suspension of such an action.

Thus, looking to the Rome Treaty for a first step on the path to Economic and Monetary Union, no proposal is found about either centralized control of macroeconomic policy-making or monetary policies. However, it was clearly recognized that creating a customs union meant increasing economic interdependence among the members. As there was no consensus for further institutionalized joint macroeconomic or monetary policy-making, nor binding rules on any of these policies, the Treaty voices the necessity for consultation and coordination in general terms. Douglas Kruse notes that the Treaty provides all elements of monetary union, with the exception of fixed exchange rates or a common currency:

> That the Treaty should go so far in this direction [of monetary union] reflects the recognition that unrestricted convertibility and economic policy co-ordination are essential to the free movement of goods, services and the factors of production.
>
> (Kruse, 1980: 14)

But the Treaty had, in fact, also not envisaged two other important elements of a monetary union, that is, free convertibility of currencies and liberalization of capital flows.

Clearly, the Rome Treaty aimed at further longer-term integration, the ultimate objective being a united Europe (Monnet, 1976). At the time of its drafting it was simply not acceptable to put forward plans limiting national autonomy on exchange rates and other elements of monetary policy. Under Bretton Woods it was in fact not really necessary, as it *de facto* installed a system of fixed but adjustable exchange rates (Brown, 1987). This international monetary system was based on a gold-dollar standard, providing the system with a vehicle currency (see also Strange, 1976; Ungerer, 1997). The major currencies were pegged to the US dollar, and the US Treasury had agreed to sell gold to foreign central banks at the official price of $35 per ounce. The EEC countries accepted the obligations of the Bretton Woods Agreement which implied that they would seek approval of the International Monetary Fund with respect to certain exchange restrictions, multiple currency or discriminatory currency arrangements as well as taking the responsibility for converting certain foreign-held balances (Tsoukalis, 1977). Another reason why a separate European system of fixed exchange rates at this time seemed premature, was that until 1961 the countries of the EEC were still bound by the transitional arrangements provided by article XIV of the International Monetary Fund (IMF). The external convertibility of the Six EEC national currencies and Britain formally became possible in 1961. Despite all these existing arrangements, the drafters of the Rome Treaty were convinced that a European system of fixed exchange rates would prove necessary after the realization of the common market. Though given the international circumstances, they did not anticipate its specific features.

To strengthen the general objectives for macroeconomic coordination the Treaty called for a Monetary Committee as an advisory organ.

The Monetary Committee was composed of senior officials from each of the Member States Finance Ministries, the deputy governors of the central banks, and two representatives of the Commission. It was established in 1958 and had two main tasks.[33] On the one hand it had to review the national and Community monetary and financial situation. On the other hand it was to give advice, on its own initiative, or when its opinion was requested. Consultation was obligatory when exchange rates were altered or in need of mutual assistance (EEC Treaty, 1957: art. 105; see also Verdun, 2000a).

3.2   Between the Rome Treaty and The Hague Summit (1958–69)

Between the drafting of the Rome Treaty and the first concrete plan for Economic and Monetary Union (EMU) in 1970, it became clear that further attempts needed to be made to fill the gap in the Treaty in the field of monetary policies.[34] However, none of the initiatives launched in the 1960s would materialize. In January 1959 the European Parliament proposed a development towards an organization similar to the Federal Reserve System in the United States. Furthermore, a plan to create in stages a European Reserve Union and a common currency was also put forward by an American monetary expert, Robert Triffin (1961, 1968). As early as 1960 he pointed out, in his book *Gold and the Dollar Crisis*, that a fundamental contradiction existed between the mechanism of creating dollars for the world market and international confidence in the system – the 'Triffin dilemma'. Helped by the French president Charles de Gaulle's action to convert dollars into gold, Triffin would prove right to fear that eventually the chronic American deficit would undermine confidence in the dollar. He proposed the creation of a European Fund to help preserve international liquidity and reduce dangers of instability, which resulted from the use of national currencies as international monetary reserves. Triffin's plan was later adopted by Jean Monnet's 1962 Action Committee for the United States of Europe (Commission of the EC, 1962). The EC Commissioner for economic and financial affairs, Robert Marjolin, was strongly in favour of Monnet's plan (Marjolin, 1986; Marjolin *et al.*, 1975). In 1959 the Belgian Foreign Minister, Mr Pierre Wigny, called for an EEC unit of account which would replace the dollar as a reserve currency, and provide the EEC with financial independence. A European unit of account would not so much solve European problems, but rather enhance Europe's financial role in the international monetary system (Commission of the EC, 1960; Tsoukalis, 1977: 53; see also Verdun, 1998d).

The Commission of the European Communities played an important role in the further development of economic and monetary coordination in Europe by drafting several proposals for coordination in the macroeconomic policy field. In 1960 a Short-Term Policy Committee was set up to monitor the demand management policies of the Member States. With the ongoing process of economic integration, national economic policies were increasingly affecting other members. In 1962 Monnet's Action Programme was launched, emphasizing again more economic coordination. In 1963 the Commission made specific proposals calling for coordination in four national economic policy areas: domestic monetary policy, international monetary policy, exchange rate policy and budgetary policy (Commission of the EC, 1963a, 1963b, 1963c). After initial hesitance the Council of Ministers of the EC in 1964 agreed to accept the Commission's proposal. Hence, by 1964 a Committee of Central Bank Governors, a Budgetary Policy Committee and a Medium-Term Policy Committee had been created (Ludlow, 1982: 16). Together with the already-existing Monetary Committee and the Short-Term Policy Committee the Community now had five of these committees.[35]

Failing monetary integration in the 1960s

As the 1960s drew to a close, Europe became increasingly aware that the type of voluntary coordination set up a decade before had failed. During the 1960s the Member States could not reach further monetary coordination, even though, by 1965, the Commission had adopted the introduction of a common EEC currency as one of the major strategic objectives (Tsoukalis, 1977: 60). Several explanations can be given for this failure of monetary coordination.

First, according to Swann (1988: 177–8), the Six were still very preoccupied with the consolidation of the type of Community that the Rome Treaty had originated. The debate at this time was dominated by questions concerning majority voting, and the French resistance to the British application. Secondly, the continuing payments surpluses and mounting reserves of the Member States left very little incentive to proceed with monetary integration, a reason given by Bloomfield (1973: 7). However, it has become generally understood that this is only part of the explanation. It is necessary to include the EEC Common Agricultural Policy (CAP) for a complete comprehension of a mechanism which Tsoukalis has called 'the Agricultural Mythology'

(Tsoukalis, 1977: 59–63). He argued that it was an illusion to assume that the currencies could be pegged when prices of agriculture were quoted in European units of account. As the farmers received a fixed nominal price expressed in national currency for their products, the widespread belief was that devaluations would prove to be less attractive for monetary authorities as the national prices of agricultural products would have to rise with the amount of the devaluation. Revaluations would, by the same token, lead to lower domestic prices, which would be unacceptable for the national farmers. This mechanism, indeed, showed its limits when in 1969 the French franc and the West German Deutschmark devalued and revalued respectively (Franck, 1987).[36] Balassa (1975: 178) emphasizes that there was widespread belief throughout the Community that the existing exchange rate parities would not encounter difficulties. Deficit countries found other ways to cope with their balance of payments problems. In 1964, for example, Italy sought and received help from the US, rather than from the Member States, to resolve its deteriorating balance of payments problems. The latter solved its own problems by *de facto* printing money (increasing its liabilities denominated in US dollars), while Britain applied a stop–go policy to safeguard the exchange rate. Moreover, as mentioned earlier, most countries ran comfortable surpluses so that the illusion was maintained that parities could hold without policy coordination.

The Barre Report

By 1967 and 1968 there appeared to be a need for increasing coordination (Rosenthal, 1975). The exchange rate crisis of the late 1960s provided an important incentive. In November 1967 the pound sterling devalued – an event which ended a period of seven years of no parity changes. Its political implications were significant as it emphasized that the Bretton Woods system was under attack. In January 1968, two years before he was approached to chair a group whose task it was to lay out the path to economic and monetary union, Pierre Werner, the Prime Minister of Luxembourg, submitted a plan for action. It called for a European Fund, an EEC mutual aid system and the progressive irrevocable fixing of exchange rates of the Member States.

A month later the Commission published its response to the international events with a memorandum analysing the implications for the Community. Resembling the 'plan for action', it pointed out that trade patterns were already affected by the events and that therefore exchange rates should be viewed as a matter of common interest. It proposed to study:

> the adoption of identical ranges of fluctuations in respect of non-member countries, not only to facilitate commercial and financial relations within the Community, but also to make possible a common position for the Member States should non-member countries adopt floating exchange rates.
>
> (Commission of the EC, 1969: 3)

Next, it urged for the study of 'the definition of a European unit of account which would be used in all fields of Community action requiring a common denominator' (Commission of the EC, 1969: 4). Day-to-day fluctuations of the parities of the Member States currencies needed to be eliminated.

The first Commission memorandum did not become widely debated as two events influenced the general mood. On the international scene, turbulence on the exchange markets and the loss of confidence in the dollar induced the set-up of the two-tier gold market. In Europe the May crisis in France had attracted attention. Hence, in December 1968, a second Commission memorandum was presented by the Commissioner for Economic and Financial Affairs and EEC vice-president, Raymond Barre. At this time all proposals with far-reaching implications (that is, a European unit of account) were dropped, only to return quickly in the third memorandum, launched on 12 February 1969. This third report, 'Memorandum to the Council on the Coordination of Economic Policies and Monetary Cooperation within the Community', is usually referred to as *the* Barre Report (Commission of the EEC, 1969), as it was the first formal proposal to the Council of Ministers. It was the first attempt of the Commission to suggest extending European integration into the realm of economic and monetary integration. Especially after the completion of the customs union and the creation of the Common Agricultural Policy, there was a strong desire to maintain the integration momentum.[37] At the The Hague Summit in December 1969, the Economic and Monetary Union proposal was finally given approval:

> within the Council, on the basis of the memorandum presented by the Commission on 12 February 1969 and in close collaboration with the latter, a plan in stages [is to] be worked out during 1970 with a view to the creation of an economic and monetary union.
>
> (The Hague Communiqué, 1969, para 8,
> quoted in Commission of the EEC, 1970: 1)

Summarizing, the period between 1958 and 1969 saw a radical change in the position of the EEC Member States in the international monetary system. Where the initial period had been characterized by a shortage of foreign currencies, the 1960s showed a long period of balance of payments surpluses, and large foreign reserves. The position of the dollar and pound, the two reserve currencies at this time, gradually deteriorated. The proposals of monetary integration in the Community were mainly based on external motives. However, at no point during this decade did a plan for monetary integration become a feasible project. This was mainly due to the fact that an international monetary system existed, and because exchange rates were stable until 1967. It was only after the completion of the customs union in 1968 and the EEC exchange rate crisis that internal motivations for a monetary union became more important. Furthermore, the monetary crisis was endangering the only successful common European policy, the Common Agricultural Policy, as it became clear that no actual zone of fixed exchange rates existed in the EEC. All these factors led the national governments to realize that negative integration would be insufficient for further integration.

3.3   The Werner Report and its aftermath (1970–4)

In January 1970 the Council adopted a resolution to establish an economic and monetary union in the Community. The response of the Member States was to present their own views about the ways in which the EMU should be realized. The Member States gave the Commission the task of further elaborating the Barre Plan on the institutional aspects of EMU. In the last week of February 1970 the Finance Ministers meeting discussed the different plans but could not reach an agreement on the precise definition and road to EMU. Nevertheless, similar views were held on two areas: the need to give Europe some form of monetary organization, and the wish to move further after the completion of the customs union, aiming for sustained and balanced growth, by progressing towards a single economic and currency area (Kruse, 1980; Magnifico, 1973).

In March 1970 the Commission responded to the request of the Member States by putting forward a Communication to the Council in which the guidelines determining the principles of EMU were briefly discussed. The Council of Ministers responded by asking a seven-member working group to draft an EMU proposal and report back within three months. Pierre Werner, the Prime Minister and Finance Minister of Luxembourg, chaired the 'impartial' body that studied the possible road to EMU. The Werner Group consisted of Central Bank Governors, the chairmen of the Short- and Medium-Term Economic Policy, Monetary and Budgetary Policy Committees, as well as a representative of the Commission. This composition ensured that each member country was represented in the Werner Group. Virtually every committee member had a high-ranking national position besides holding the official Community position mentioned above. Glenda Rosenthal has suggested that the members were part of the so-called 'economic and financial elite' which had over the past 25 years been discussing economic and monetary integration. 'The individuals in the EEC responsible for policy proposals and decisions on economic and monetary matters knew each other very well indeed by 1970' (Rosenthal, 1975: 102). The Werner Group succeeded in producing an interim report by the end of May, which dealt with the main aspects of establishing an EMU in three stages; that is, 1970/1 to 1972, 1972 to 1975; and 1976 or 1978 onwards. Measures would be taken to coordinate economic policies and taxation, liberalize capital markets, and reach total monetary solidarity. The EMU had two objectives: (i) free movement of goods, services and factors of production (manpower, management and capital); (ii) 'in respect of its relations with outside, it must gradually be transformed into an organic economic and monetary association having an individuality of its own...to enable Europe to contribute usefully to international economic cooperation' (Werner Interim Report, 1970: 3).

How to reach EMU was stated very generally in the report and was open to numerous interpretations. But strong emphasis was put on solidarity, shared risks and common interests:

> EMU must provide for joint framing of the policies *necessary* to the proper functioning of the Community, and hence must postulate joint risks and joint solidarity. ... The factors must be in balance throughout and progress in parallel. Accordingly, the measures to be adopted will need to be decided in the light of a concept of 'common interest' combining and going further than the mere addition of national interests.
> (Werner Interim Report, 1970: 4; emphasis added)

It is remarkable that at this time the Group considered the acceptance of EMU by the social partners of great importance:

> To secure the support of trade unions, business federations and other groupings in the member countries for the measures to institute economic and monetary union, arrangements would have to be

made for regular concertation between the Community institutions on the one hand and the unions, employers' federations and other representative bodies in particular economic and social sectors on the other, the latter to be asked to state their views (the procedural details to be settled later) on the main lines to be followed in economic, fiscal and monetary matters, and on decisions of more direct interest to them.

(Werner Interim Report, 1970: 4)

Although the Group had reached considerable consensus on the contents of EMU, Mr Werner had to admit that the old rivalry between the 'economists' and the 'monetarists' had dominated the discussions:

The solution which we propose takes into account the realities. On the one hand we have a proposal to establish a common monetary policy *vis-à-vis* non-member states in the initial phase. At the same time we feel that real efforts must also be made to coordinate and harmonize economic policies in the initial phase. We are thinking for example of budgetary policy, financial policy and also to some extent of incomes policy. In short, we have come to the conclusion that the greatest prospect for success will come from the parallel application of these widely varying measures in particular to the extent that the measures of monetary and economic policy taken with a view to establishing a monetary union will interact favourably.

(Interview with Pierre Werner, quoted in Rosenthal, 1975: 107–8)

The Werner Interim Report was evaluated at the meeting of the Finance Ministers in Venice in late May 1970. The 'economists', the Federal Republic of Germany (FRG), Italy and the Netherlands, insisted on the integration of national economic policies to precede monetary union. The monetarists, Belgium, France, Luxembourg as well as the Commission, held the view that monetary solidarity would induce the necessary convergence of economic policies. The Council 'solved' the matter by giving the Werner Group a mandate to define the contents of the first stage by September 1970 (Rosenthal, 1975: 108). It would 'prepare a report containing an analysis of the different suggestions and making it possible to identify the basic issues for a realization by stages of economic and monetary union in the Community' (Werner Interim Report, 1970).[38]

The Werner Group unanimously agreed to its final report on 8 October 1970. The Group had combined the wishes of the 'economists' and the 'monetarists', but by doing so it had failed to commit the Member States to anything in the first two years. Only in 1973 would the amendment of the Rome Treaty, and hence transfer of sovereignty, be on the agenda. The compromise package, often referred to as 'parallelism', suggested that the economist and the monetarist paths to EMU could go hand in hand. However, because the two camps departed from opposite assumptions and priorities as to how EMU could be achieved, such a parallel approach could never work. Kruse notes: 'Parallelism merely concealed the irreconcilable differences among the member states' (Kruse, 1980: 73).

EMU had five aims: First, to create 'an area within which goods and services, people and capital will circulate freely and without competitive distortions, without thereby giving rise to structural or regional disequilibrium' (Werner Report, 1970: 9). Second, to increase welfare, and reduce regional and social disparities. In order to achieve these aims the report envisaged the need for consultation of economic and social groups as well as the operation of market forces. Third, to create a monetary union, implying 'a total and irreversible convertibility of currencies, the elimination of margins of fluctuation in exchange rates, the irrevocable fixing of parity rates and the complete liberation of movements of capital' (Werner Report, 1970: 10). Fourth, in EMU only the global balance of payments of the Community *vis-à-vis* the rest of the world would be of any importance. It was hoped that equilibrium would be achieved by the mobility of factors of production and financial transfers by public and private sectors, as is the case within a nation state (Werner Report, 1970: 10; cf. Baer and Padoa-Schioppa, 1989: 53). Finally, to transfer responsibility from the national to the Community level. Monetary policy would be centralized, whereas economic policy-making would in part remain national responsibility. The role of the European budget would need to increase gradually, but would fall short of the size of a national budget.[39]

The Werner Plan consisted of a time-schedule in three stages to reach EMU by 1980. It was concrete about the first stage, which would last three years, but left the timetable for the last two stages completely open. Again, the vagueness was an indication of the compromise nature of the report. On the institutional side, in sharp contrast to what would be proposed nineteen years later, two main organs were envisaged. In addition to a 'Community system for the central banks', a 'Centre of Decision for Economic Policy' (CDEP) was to be created. Economic policies were to be coordinated, by carrying out at least three annual surveys of the economic situation in the Community, which would enable the adoption of common guidelines. Concerning budgetary policies, it was suggested that quantitative guidelines should be adopted on the principal elements of public budgets; that is, on global receipts and expenditure, the distribution of the latter between investment and consumption and the directions and amount of balances. On the fiscal side the Group voiced the need for a progressive harmonization of indirect taxes as well as of those taxes applicable to interest payments on fixed-interest securities and dividends. A European Monetary Fund was planned at the latest during the second stage. It would be the fore-runner of the Community system of Central Banks to be set up in the third stage (Werner Report, 1970).

On 30 October 1970 the Commission had adopted a memorandum which was presented to the Council on 23 November 1970 (*Bulletin of the EC*, Supplement 11, 1970, pp. 11–21). The memorandum accepted the proposals of the Werner Committee, though made two changes which were a result of French and Italian pressure (Kruse, 1980: 75–6). The Commission had omitted reference to institutional arrangements for the eventual transfer of sovereignty, whereas it strengthened provisions for action in the structural and regional fields. At the end of November, when it was discussed by the Council, no agreement could be reached; nor did the final Council meeting in mid-December lead to any joint conclusion. The Dutch and West German delegation stressed that the supranational provisions needed to be installed, which were unacceptable for the French government officials.

In January, at a Franco-German meeting, the West German officials proposed a clause which would ensure 'parallelism' between the economic and monetary provisions in the EMU arrangement. The first stage of both was to last four years; if agreement failed to have been reached on the transition to the second stage, the monetary mechanisms would cease to apply. This 'guillotine' clause was to avoid

> immediate formal undertakings on moving on to the later stages (thus satisfying France), while at the same time removing the automatic element from the monetary measures if insufficient progress was made in coordinating economic policies (thus allaying the FRG's fears).
>
> (Rosenthal, 1975: 111)

On the basis of this compromise, agreement was reached on 9 February 1971 (*Bulletin of the EC*, Supplements 3 and 4, 1971). The Council formally launched EMU on 22 March 1971 (*Journal Officiel des Communautés européennes*, C28 and L73, 27 March 1971, and *Bulletin of the EC*, Supplement 4, 1971). The process had begun, but the irreversible commitments were postponed for three years; a side-effect of the fact that the governmental representatives stood by their national positions until the very last moment, thus making far-reaching agreement very difficult.

Besides the stark division between the 'economist' and the 'monetarist' modes of economic and monetary integration, the problems with coordination in 1971 stemmed from lack of solidarity among the Member States. Member governments were reluctant to sacrifice employment for the sake of price stability or for maintaining an external balance, seeing that this had not worked in the 1960s. Therefore, the chances of success in coordinating them now, without a new supranational body, and without majority rule, were small.

The post-Werner period: international economic and monetary turbulence

During the 1970s it became clear that the 'guillotine' clause did not work. Monetary integration proceeded slowly and followed mainly the scenario of the 'monetarists' – exchange rate agreements, the intervention mechanism and monetary support – rather than coordination of economic and monetary policies. This was no surprise as the aim of fixed exchange rates offered the public the most immediate benefits, and it was the only aim in the EMU plan to which all Member States agreed. Nevertheless, there are many reasons for the failure to achieve EMU during that decade.

Already in the first semester after 22 March 1971 it was apparent that the basis of common interests of the Member States was too narrow. It soon became clear that the gap that appeared at this time was the very same that had existed the decade before while drafting the plan. The French were reluctant to accept any plans leading to the transfer of sovereignty to a European body. The powerful Gaullist groups in France strongly rejected the supranational element of the plans. Their opposition proved to be so strong that the French were obliged to change their policy on the subject of EMU. Hence, the split between France, Belgium and Luxembourg on the one hand, and the FRG, the Netherlands, and to a lesser degree Italy on the other, was complete. Once again a plan for further integration failed to materialize. Again it was due to differences of opinion on which policies to coordinate or harmonize; that is, disagreement about how to proceed towards a 'united Europe'.

In addition to the different interests among the EEC countries, international monetary events catalysed the breakdown of the EMU agreement. In April 1971 a first step was taken, even if only on paper, to reduce the size of the parity bands against the dollar. It would never materialize as the May 1971 exchange crisis made a narrower monetary arrangement impossible. This crisis was a result of several factors: a record balance of payment deficit in the US, resulting in lower interest rates and a capital inflow in Europe. To fight inflation, European central banks were keeping domestic interest rates high. However, it did not have the desired effect as this policy ran counter to US monetary policy. The monetary situation worsened when speculators attacked the Deutschmark. The French had called for a revaluation of gold, and voices in West Germany were calling for a DM float. It was clearly impossible to continue accumulating dollars. West German policy-makers had to decide whether to revalue or float the DM. The Americans were in favour of a revaluation of gold, but the West German government, unconvinced that the DM was structurally Undervalued, decided to float the DM (Brown, 1987). When the Bundesbank called for administrative controls the French, convinced that such a measure was against a common EEC policy, responded by postponing the whole EMU project until at least December, when they hoped the crisis would be over.

The second monetary crisis came on 15 August 1971, when the American president Richard Nixon announced the suspension of the convertibility of the dollar into gold, together with import measures to protect the American domestic economy. The Europeans were forced to choose between allowing the US to continue to run a deficit on its balance of payments, by supporting the overvalued dollar, or accepting a reduction in their national payments surpluses. The American authorities refused to take any more responsibility for the exchange rate of the dollar. It was up to the other central banks to intervene in order to stay within the IMF margins. The consequence was a devaluation of the dollar.

The EEC countries and the Commission were unable to reach an agreement on joint action in response to the American policy change. France refused to accept a revaluation of the franc and proposed a two-tier market system and a more stringent system of capital controls, a system unacceptable to the West Germans. The Italians relaunched their own scheme, and the Benelux countries introduced among themselves a system of 'privot rates', which they had proposed to the other three EEC countries (Tsoukalis, 1977: 115). At this point France accepted a two-tier system and tightened its exchange rate control, while the British at the same time decided to do the opposite.

Thus, a week after the Nixon announcement, the EEC countries had, again, not succeeded in coordinating their response. The EEC currencies were floating against each other, with the exception of the Benelux countries. As a result a complicated system of border taxes and rebates, which were adjusted every week, was installed for the Common Agricultural Policy. Obviously, the EMU plan could not progress any further along the lines set up in March. The EMU objective had quickly proven to be an unobtainable ideal.

It is remarkable that again the division between the 'economists' and the 'monetarists' existed. The Dutch, the Italians and the West Germans (the 'economists') preferred a system of greater exchange rate flexibility. The Belgians, the French and the Luxembourgers (the 'monetarists') were in favour of a two-tier market system.

In December 1971 the Group of Ten most industrialized nations came together to solve the monetary crisis. President Richard Nixon, and the French president Georges Pompidou, acting as an EEC spokesman, agreed on the realignment of exchange rates which included a devaluation of the dollar.[40] The US agreed to abolish the 10 per cent surcharge on imports. The final agreement reached at the Smithsonian Institute in Washington consisted of an exchange rate system with 'central rates' allowing a margin of fluctuation of 2.25 per cent on either side of the dollar parity.

The Smithsonian Agreement was generally seen as a solution to the monetary crisis, and was welcomed by all participants. However, a 4.5 per cent band was still too wide for the EEC Member States as it meant that the principle of common prices in the CAP could be endangered. More important, after the unilateral US decision to break the gold–dollar parity, the European central bankers were reluctant to hold large dollar reserves. Therefore, the EEC countries decided not to make full use of the new margins. Instead, in February 1972 the Council of Ministers decided to limit intra-EEC margins to 2.25 per cent. Following a West German proposal the Council also agreed that exchange rate interventions would be made only in Community currencies. Britain, Denmark, Ireland and Norway, the four candidate-members of the EEC, had all been consulted and had approved of these arrangements, though Britain expressed fears that the EEC margins might be too narrow for the pound. The 'snake' in the 'tunnel' was born.[41]

New EMU proposals?

In January 1972 the Commission made an attempt to relaunch the EMU package decided upon a year earlier.[42] Again it proposed a 'monetarist' method by suggesting a reduction in the margins of fluctuation, and a coordination of economic policies. This might seem an illogical method as the developments of 1971 had made clear the existence of fundamental differences between the Member States, both economic and political, which prevented them from pursuing a common set of monetary and fiscal policies. However, the 1971 turmoil had also demonstrated, more clearly than ever before, that economic policies of the US could negatively affect the objectives of the EEC countries. A logical counteraction to limit these effects was to create an EMU independent of the United States.

Three other factors contributed to the relaunching of the EMU plan. Amidst the failure of the currencies to achieve exchange rate stability there was one success story; the Benelux countries had managed to limit the fluctuations between the Belgium–Luxembourg franc and the guilder to 1.5 per cent. Although this was clearly a special case, due to the small sizes and relative homogeneity of the Benelux economies as well as their history of cooperation, it nevertheless demonstrated to the rest of the Community that, if there is political will, limited exchange rate fluctuations are possible. It articulated once again that the failure to create a monetary union resulted from the lack of common interests to create it. Even though the final result was attractive, the road to reach EMU would not spread the adjustment burden equally between all Member States. Therefore, to relaunch the EMU proposals it was necessary to have common interests and the joint political will to go ahead with the *transition* period. A second factor was a shift in attitudes in the FRG and the Netherlands. Some constructions were made to prevent capital from moving too quickly so as not to put pressure on the currencies. In a sense the two countries moved away from a strict policy of no capital controls. The third factor was that since March 1971 no significant advances had been made in European integration. Furthermore, if the Member States wanted to reach the 1980 target, action in 1972 was indispensable.

Nevertheless, the Council was unable to make a decision on the basis of the Commission's proposals until 21 March 1972. This decision, which showed a fragile balance between the conflicting positions, consisted of five elements: (1) the reduction in size of the intra-Community exchange rate fluctuations; (2) a closer coordination of economic policies, specifically by creating a high-level group with one representative from each Member State to exchange information on national economic strategies; (3) the agreement in principle on the creation of a regional fund to help less developed economic areas in the Community; (4) establishing a common policy on controlling short-term capital movements by ensuring that the authorities in each country could use certain policy instruments;[43] and (5) the Council, not being able to reach consensus right away, promised that it would decide to create a European Monetary Cooperation Fund (EMCF) before the end of the year. In short, the 1972 Council resolution meant a revoicing of decisions taken earlier, and concerning the fluctuation margins of the intra-Community exchange rates, the rules were loosened compared to the statement launched a year earlier. Nevertheless, the resolution was important in that it showed willingness to continue on the road to Economic and Monetary Union.

On 23 May 1972 the snake was enlarged so as to include the British and Irish pounds and the Danish and Norwegian krone. These four countries were applying for EEC membership.[44] The snake soon ran into trouble when, in June 1972, the pound was put under strong speculative pressure. In one week the British authorities used one billion pounds worth of interventions to support the pound. With the prospect of having to repeat the act the British authorities decided to float the pound. The pound left the snake. The sterling crisis was a setback to the exercise of exchange rate stability among the currencies of the 'enlarged' Community. Moreover, it demonstrated that cooperation between the snake countries was very limited. The intervention mechanism did not function on a basis of solidarity. The central bankers in Continental Europe had also intervened during the speculative attack on the pound sterling. These foreign-held sterling balances did not help Britain much, as at the end of the month the Continental central banks converted sterling into gold. Not yet a Community Member, Britain could not even receive financial assistance from the EC, and the snake arrangement had no provisions for either monetary support or cooperation regarding national economic policy.

Following the British pound, the Irish punt and the Danish krone were also floated. The British and Irish currencies stayed out permanently whereas the Danish krone rejoined again on 10 October 1972. In February 1973 Italy left the snake and stayed out. France floated out in January 1974, rejoined in July 1975 and left for good in March 1976. In March 1973 the snake as a whole left the tunnel. By the end of 1977 only half the members of the Community were still in the snake, and in addition various countries had formally or informally pegged their currencies to the snake. Hence it was no longer a purely EEC exchange rate arrangement (Kruse, 1980; Ludlow, 1982; Tew, 1982).

In Paris, on 19–20 October 1972, the Council of Ministers of the enlarged Community met to discuss the next stage of EMU. The main point on the agenda was whether to set up a monetary cooperation fund (EMCF). Again, large differences existed between the two groups: the supranationalists ('economists') and the intergovernmentalists ('monetarists').[45] Both groups repeated their familiar views. The FRG and the Netherlands stressed that until significant progress had been made on economic policy coordination, which in the past six months had been notably lacking, the fund would have no real function. Belgium, France and Luxembourg argued the other way around. However, while interested in the Fund to force upon the members *de jure* monetary alignment, they were still afraid of having to transfer powers to the EEC body. Now this camp was strengthened by the British government who, afraid of losing employment, favoured national control over economic and monetary policy for as long as possible.

By using the convenient, and by now familiar, Community decision-making method – ignoring the difficult policy areas and agreeing only on the uncontroversial issues – an accord was reached. It was again based on parallelism, with modest and carefully balanced advances in the field of policy coordination. A European Monetary Cooperation Fund (EMCF) would be set up and would coordinate the interventions of the central bank under the snake arrangements, organize settlements on a multilateral basis, conduct transactions in a Community unit of account, as well as administer the short-term monetary support mechanisms (Monetary Committee, 1972: 10 and 34–8). But as all of these functions were already performed by the Committee of Central Bank Governors, this decision did not produce any real advance in economic and monetary policy coordination.

The EMCF was indeed set up on 1 June 1973, and the Bank for International Settlements acted as its agent. The BIS performed two functions. On the one hand it managed the snake; on the other hand it executed financial operations in connection with Community borrowing and lending for the purpose of balance-of-payments support for EEC member countries (BIS, 1984: 162–4).

So it is again seen how the Community members could not reach agreement because of the schism between the economists and the monetarists and because they did not perceive their interests along the same lines, thus making it very difficult for them to take far-reaching decisions. Those taken were principally based on national interest rather than in conformation with realistic progress towards economic and monetary union (cf. Kruse, 1980: 193–8).

Probably the most important step forward at the Paris summit was that the three new future members, Britain, Denmark and Ireland, had committed themselves to the Economic and Monetary Union (*Hansard*, vol. 843, cols 791–809: 23).[46] The heads of state and governments showed their determination to proceed with the EMU process by making preparations to start the second stage as scheduled on 1 January 1974. The second stage would be evaluated before the end of 1975 (*Communication of the Commission to the Council*, Com(73)570 def., 19 April 1973; and *Bulletin of the EC*, Supplement 5, 1973; Final Summit Declaration, Paris, 19–21 October 1972).

In February 1973 there was another monetary crisis which was worse than the crisis of June 1972. The dollar came under pressure; the Swiss franc, an important reserve currency, was forced to float, which resulted in a sharp fall of the dollar. The European countries responded by taking measures to combat capital inflows. However, no matter how harsh the measures taken by the monetary authorities, the speculative pressures remained. Obviously these interventions were not sustainable, as they would aggravate inflation, which was at this time rising faster than during earlier crises (OECD, 1972a: 15–25; 1972b: 13–22). Thus, the Finance Ministers decided that the dollar would formally be devalued. The lira left the snake a day later, in circumstances similar to those which had forced out the British pound. Again it demonstrated the weakness of the snake, and showed that the members did not act together when national economic policy objectives coincidentally diverged. When speculative flows reappeared in February/March, the snake countries felt there was no guarantee that any measure would stop the flows. Thus, after the Council in March accepted a compromise reached by France and West Germany (the DM would be 3 per cent revalued, and the franc would rejoin the snake) it was decided to float the snake *vis-à-vis* the dollar. The snake left the tunnel.

This third period of exchange rate turmoil gave EMU a gloomy future. Britain and Italy had decided to stay outside the snake. Even though both countries were formally aiming at joining eventually, it was clear this would not be possible in the short term. The parities were being determined by national interests rather than common policy objectives. Moreover, the EMU discussions could at this time not be continued on the basis of the snake arrangement, because it was not purely EC arrangement. This understanding, however, had not been accepted by the Commission and the national governments. In their view the first stage of EMU had been concluded successfully, with a European monetary arrangement that had survived the collapse of the international monetary system, and had in addition attracted non-EEC participants. The snake had become the symbol of monetary unification, and many could barely make a distinction between the two. This political use of the success of the snake in relationship to the EMU proposals bears remarkable similarities with the way the EMS was treated *vis-à-vis* the EMU plan in the late 1980s and early 1990s.

A second stage of EMU

In a communication to the Council on 19 April 1973 the Commission gave another boost to the EMU objective by relaunching the ambitious 1980 deadline (Commission of the EEC, 1973). As time was passing by, speedy action was needed. The second phase would last three years, from 1 January 1974 until 31 December 1976. In its evaluation of the first stage the Commission regretted the lack of policy harmonization. The second stage would have to reach real communal solidarity, in particular in the field of employment and regional development (Commission of the EEC, 1973: 8, 19). However, it was explicitly mentioned that no new institution with exclusive powers was needed, nor a Treaty amendment (Commission of the EEC, 1973: 28).

Once again the EMU strategy was based on parallelism, leaning perhaps towards the 'monetarists' in emphasizing the integration process via a *de jure* process of limiting the size of the fluctuations. Nevertheless, it also envisaged coordination of economic policies. Five-year plans were to be put into action to assist national authorities in deciding their short- and medium-term policies. In particular, budgetary policies would be watched closely, and strong emphasis was put on the method of financing deficits and the harmonization of policy instruments. Concerning monetary policy, targets were set up for the growth of money supply, interest rates and credit conditions. Coherence among the European currencies would be strengthened by the return of the lira and pound sterling to the snake. Structural differences among the EEC countries needed to be reduced, thus, a common unemployment scheme was planned for the final stage. Also, indirect taxation had to be harmonized, direct taxes coordinated, and national capital markets adjusted to each other (*Bulletin of the EC*, Supplement, May 1973: 10–15).

The proposal was extremely vague about how these aims were to be achieved. It did not mention any institutional changes which countries had to make to join the final stage of EMU. The March 1971 resolution had requested this, and the Dutch and the West Germans had made it clear that they would not start the second stage without all members having committed themselves to the final EMU (De Nederlandsche Bank, 1973: 108–9; Deutsche Bundesbank, 1974: 9–10). The decision-making process based on parallelism had reached its 'natural' limits. The artificial decisions on the easy questions and the side-by-side approach did not solve the deadlock on institutional matters. Which road was to prevail over the other, the monetary or the economic one? Which institutions should be set up, and how much supranational power should they get? These were the fundamental questions that had to be solved to keep going on the road to full EMU, not dissimilar from those which had to be taken almost two decades later.

In June 1973 another monetary crisis emerged. Confidence in the dollar eroded, and the West German authorities responded by revaluing the DM by 5.5 per cent (Deutsche Bundesbank, 1973: 11–14). The snake countries were hesitant to float the snake upwards because they judged their currencies as being at the right parity. Nevertheless after making an agreement with the US authorities it was decided to coordinate interventions. The desired effect, a halt in the fall of the dollar, was achieved, but the snake currencies were affected differently. While the DM remained high, the French franc and Dutch guilder witnessed a downward pressure, followed a month later by a strong demand for guilders. This led to a 5 per cent revaluation of the guilder on 17 September 1973. This is just one of many examples of exchange rate pressure in the months following the float of the snake. All in all the strains were quite predictable as the 'national interests', and thus the policy objectives, of participating countries differed widely.

The Oil Producing Exporting Countries (OPEC) decided on 16 October 1973 to impose limits on production and an embarg on exports to certain countries, for example, the United States, to put pressure on the western countries to solve the conflict between Israel and its neighbours in a way favourable to Arab interests. The resulting oil crisis had an enormous impact on the world economy. The effect on the individual snake countries was more or less the same, as they were all more or less equally dependent on oil, so the tripling in the price of oil affected them all in a similar way (Kruse, 1980: 149–58).

However, it increased the tensions already present between the snake currencies.

A feeling of uncertainty now dominated the scene. Governments were worried about falling outputs (deflation), loss of wealth, what the OPEC countries would do with their accumulated reserves, and higher prices (inflation). And, predictably, by the end of 1973 the snake countries were following three different types of economic policies to combat these problems. All countries were trying to increase exports, preferably to the Arab countries, but West Germany tried to balance supply and demand, the Benelux countries and Denmark were fighting inflation without reducing too much of their economic output, and France was occupied with unemployment, and keeping up levels of production.

The EEC Member States thus all had different priorities and policy objectives, and used different policy instruments to solve their problems. The logical consequence of different national interests was that the second stage of EMU could not be concluded successfully. The deadlock in the process had only been catalysed by the international crises.[47] The formal end of EMU appeared with the start of *a* second stage, as it was cautiously called. No consensus could be reached on the nature of the final stage, the transfer of authority and the relationship of economic policy coordination to exchange rate cooperation. As the Council meeting on 17 December 1973 was unable to reach agreement, EMU was hard to save. Thus, the plan finally broke down after the franc left the snake on 19 January 1974. The strongest advocate of the monetarist approach had failed to adjust policies to stay in the exchange rate system. Now that the snake had lost its symbolic function as an instrument of economic and monetary integraion, EMU died.

3.4   European monetary disillusion (1974–7)

In March 1975 the Marjolin Group, an *ad hoc* body invited by the Commission in 1974 to analyse the problems raised by EMU, presented its evaluative study (Marjolin *et al.*, 1975). It concluded that the endeavours to reach this aim since 1969 had failed completely: Europe had not come closer in this field; if anything, it had moved backwards. The report was very critical and argued that the failure was a result of three factors: (1) setbacks, for example, the international monetary crisis since the late 1960s and the financial crisis resulting from the oil embargo; (2) the lack of political will of national governments;

(3) intellectual short-sightedness, that had led to the acceptance of EMU without having a clear vision of it. The only way out of this negative spiral, according to the group, was to surrender monetary *and*, above all, *economic* policy-making to a Community institution, which should have powers comparable to the national governments. The group concluded that, as there is no wish for such an EMU, it could make no proposals for its creation. It did, however, give some general policy recommendations for successful policy adjustment.

The findings of the Marjolin Group can be seen as one of the last cries for help aimed at saving the EMU project of the early 1970s. Another attempt was made by nine well-known economists in what was called 'The All Saints' Day Manifesto for European Monetary Union', which appeared in *The Economist* on 1 November 1975 (Fratianni and Peeters, 1978: 37–43). This was a plea for the introduction of a parallel currency. The Werner plan in its view had failed because 'it overestimated the willingness of governments to depart from national decision-making because it underestimated the costs associated with a fast resetting of ultimate targets and the policy strategy necessary to meet such targets' (Basevi *et al.*, 1975: 37–8). Furthermore, the Manifesto stressed the need for a gradual process to reach monetary union so as to maximize national political support. Even though the Werner approach entailed a gradual process, its major weakness was its 'non-automatic nature and its reliance on political discretion … as well as it being based on an infinite series of painful compromises' (Basevi *et al.*, 1975: 38). Thus, it concluded that the monetary locking of exchange rates would fail unless it involved monetary reform.

The new proposal was to achieve monetary unification through monetary reform based on the free interplay of market forces. A parallel currency, the Europa, expressed in terms of a weighed basket of national monies, would be introduced gradually. It would be a stable currency which would keep its purchasing power. The European monetary authorities, eventually replacing the national ones, would be independent from political control, comparable to the juridical system.[48] Real economic equilibrium would not be reached via capital and labour mobility. Based on the assumption that there are no unemployment costs in monetary unification in the long run, it was argued that structural policies would serve to correct regional imbalances (Basevi *et al.*, 1975: 43).

The manifesto gave a new boost to the thinking on EMU but did not provide the necessary impetus to revive the attempts made in the first years of the decade. EMU had come to an end, and it would take thirteen years for its revival.

Finally, in a report on the creation of a European Union, the Commission made a very last attempt to revive EMU, but without any success (Commission of the EC, 1976; van Esch and de Bont, 1980). The Tindemans Report (1976) voiced the need to relaunch EMU, if necessary via a 'two-speed' Community.[49] It proposed that it should be possible for some countries, those which had sufficiently converging economies, to go ahead. Others could join in when they were ready for it. This idea circumvented the problem of unanimity voting which often rendered decision-making impossible. Some progress could now be made among those countries willing and able to proceed with EMU.

An evaluation of EMU

It can be concluded that the EEC countries had not come closer to economic and monetary integration in the seven years after The Hague summit of 1969. No major advance was made on any of the aims and objectives of EMU as set out in the Werner Report. Economic policies had not been coordinated, capital markets had not been liberalized, nor had 'total monetary solidarity' been reached. Its two main objectives were also far from being reached. First, the internal market with the freedom of movement of goods, services and factors of production had not been established; secondly, there had been no transformation of the Community into 'an organic economic and monetary association'. In the course of the 1970s economic and monetary decisions were still being made on the basis of diverging national interests.

A number of reasons have been rightly pointed out by the Marjolin Group: unfortunate international circumstances, lack of political will and ignorance about the meaning of EMU. The collapse of the Bretton Woods system and the first oil price shock had produced quite a different economic environment than had been assumed in the Werner Report. Technical adjustments to cope with the changes could have been possible, but as the policy response to the oil shock had differed widely throughout Europe, the necessary economic policy convergence was lacking. More importantly, flexible exchange rates were seen as an instrument of autonomous domestic economic management.

Several points worth mentioning are also made by Kruse in his evaluation of the failure of the EMU project (Kruse, 1980: 200–20). He argues that national governments cannot be blamed for aiming at national interests, rather than working together to create an EMU when national interests seem not to be served by the common endeavour to create an EMU. When, at times, national governments perceived fulfilling the criteria to enhance the EMU project running counter to their national interests – when they encountered divided loyalties – they chose against the EMU objective. After all, they considered EMU to be a means to an end, namely, to increase national welfare. As the 1970s went on, national governments on several occasions regarded exchange rate adjustments, of all the alternatives, as having the smallest welfare costs. Kruse stresses that it should not be forgotten that in 1969 the Member States had not been willing to coordinate economic policies, or formulate a single monetary policy. Even when the international circumstances made it very clear that individual Member States could not control monetary conditions, they still did not cooperate in this field. Quite the opposite:

> governments had been and remained keen to exert an influence on the policies of other member states, but few were prepared to accept the corresponding obligation to modify their policies in line with the wishes of other member states. … In sum, then, contrary to what had been assumed in 1969, progress on the individual elements of economic and monetary unification had not coincided with the interests of the member states as perceived during the first stage.
>
> (Kruse, 1980: 205)

In other words, in Kruse's view the failure of EMU in the early 1970s was due to the lack of change in the behaviour of the national governments. Inherent in this view is that the governments' perceptions of their respective national interest implied aiming at different levels of inflation and exchange rates, hence being able to use the devaluation instrument. This is consistent with the view of the Marjolin Group of 'lack of political will' or 'ignorance about the meaning of EMU'.

A third reason can be added which is embedded in two factors. First, the existence of two incompatible approaches of how to reach EMU, that is, an 'economist' and a 'monetarist' approach. Second, the Community decision-making process implied that the proposals that were agreed upon were vague enough so as to please both camps. The difficult issues had not been settled, hence the problem in the immediate aftermath of the Werner Report.

A last reason is that the Community of the Six that originally agreed to embark on EMU enlarged to the Community of the Nine. This made it more difficult for Europe to coordinate economic and monetary policy, especially because the currency of one of its new members, the

British pound, proved difficult to peg to the other Community currencies. Or to put it in economic terms, the enlarged EEC was not an
Optimum Currency Area (Mundell, 1961; see Chapter 2); the Member
States pursued different monetary objectives (France and Italy, for
example, accepted higher levels of inflation than West Germany and
the Netherlands). Moreover, Europe had low factor mobility due to
large cultural differences, such as linguistic, educational and habitual
differences.

Divergence in national interests: different economic goals

As seen above, the failure of the EMU project was due to the existence
of profound differences between the perceived interests of the Member
States, and consequently their policy choices. Kruse argues that there
seem to have been three factors that led to these differences. First, the
countries gave a different ranking to the importance of the four traditional economic goals: economic growth, full employment, price stability and external payments equilibrium. West Germany, for example,
since the hyperinflation crisis in the interwar period, has taken price
stability as the most important objective. France and Italy, on the other
hand, have traditionally been more worried about full employment,
whereas Britain's biggest concern has been its competitiveness and
free trade.[50]

> That national attitudes are founded on past experiences suggests that
> the ranking of fundamental economic goals changes only very grad-
> ually over time. By implication, then, the differences in emphasis
> between countries are a more or less stable element on the European
> scene acting to impede economic and monetary unification.
>
> (Kruse, 1980: 209)

A second factor allowing for the divergences in national interests,
according to Kruse, were structural differences among the economies of
the EEC members. In France a large part of the working force has traditionally been in agriculture, but this sector has declined. Every year
the non-agriculture working force grew by 1.5 per cent, thus making
economic growth very important. In the FRG, where the average
working week had become shorter, and with a static labour force, lower
growth was required to maintain the full employment prerequisite. In
Britain the social partners, both trade unions and employers' organizations, had a significant degree of market control and used this to maximize their goals (prices and income). The third set of factors leading to

differences in national interests Kruse referred to as 'dissimilarities in actual economic circumstances'. Often countries were in different phases of the economic cycle, so therefore their policy outlook differed accordingly. In Kruse's view this third reason is less important, as it does not reflect a fundamental difference in interests.

This categorization developed by Kruse in order to understand the background of the national interest divergences is useful for the second half of the book, as later chapters will analyse whether or not these differences are still eminent and, if so, what their effects have been on the development of the EMU project. In 1980 Kruse predicted that EMU can be achieved only if three conditions are met (Kruse, 1980: 215). First, national governments need to perceive European unity as serving the immediate national interests of the member countries. Second, EMU has to be considered an objective which the Member States will have to desire for many years. Since this desire implies the commitment to a longer-term objective, rare behaviour for politicians, Kruse states that it is an illusion to think that the short-term economic costs can be offset by the longer-term benefits. To support the integration process the Community thus needs to meet a third criterion, namely to reduce the dissimilarities in the economic goals and structures of the member countries.

4
From the EMS to EMU

The previous chapter has shown that EMU was in the minds of many during the 1960s and 1970s but failed to materialize due to unfortunate international circumstances and divergence in economic policies. This chapter will discuss how the second EMU initiative came about, and what it consisted of. It is subdivided into five main sections. The first section discusses the EMS. The Delors Report is analysed in the second section. The third section discusses the run-up to Maastricht. The penultimate section looks at the post-Maastricht period. The final section summarizes, draws some conclusions and reflects on the eclectic theory introduced in Chapter 2.

4.1 The EMS (1978–88)

One of the most unexpected and therefore widely debated European successes is the European Monetary System (EMS). Certainly after its continued successful existence in the 1980s many have examined the performance of ERM countries with non-ERM European countries in terms of growth, competitiveness, inflation, interest rates, unemployment and so on.[51] Here the discussion of the EMS will be very brief, showing only the process of policy-making, and its basic objectives and instruments, albeit mainly as a step on the road to the second EMU proposals in the late 1980s.[52]

The EMS was first launched by Roy Jenkins, then president of the European Commission, in a speech delivered at the European University Institute in Florence, on 27 October 1977 (Jenkins, 1977). He advocated taking a big step forward to reach monetary union.[53] He advocated a single currency zone, and public finance functions at the EC level, which would function as a political force to obtain economic integration. Jenkins had been inspired by the MacDougall Report (1977) – a report initiated by the EC Commission which discussed the possibility of economic and monetary integration from a perspective of fiscal federalism. The emphasis in the MacDougall Report lay on a unified fiscal system in a monetary union, and concluded that the Community should have a sufficiently large budget for fiscal policy. In the short run this implied a budget of 2–2.5 per cent, whereas it should gradually move to 5–7 per cent of Community GDP. Although the MacDougall Report viewed monetary union as a possibility, it thoroughly evaluated the redistributive effect that could emerge when the fiscal policy aspect was taken into consideration. The Commission president may have interpreted the report as describing the political and economic preconditions for monetary union.

Peter Ludlow stresses that Roy Jenkins may have had two main considerations in mind when launching his monetary integration campaign. First, the Community Member States were not at all cooperating towards further integration. A debate about money could promote a general discussion on problems of unemployment, high inflation and economic divergence. Second, politically the time was right. Not only was he the new Commission president, who had not achieved much during his first six months of his presidency, but other national governments could arguably be interested in reactivating interest in European integration. The Belgians were still frustrated about the lack of interest in the 1976 Tindemans Report and, as they would assume the presidency of the European Council from 1 July 1977, they would need a specific theme. The French had fallen out of the snake several times, and were principally in favour of joining a new European exchange rate system. The FRG, the strongest power in the Community, was thought to be interested only in short-term political projects (Ludlow, 1982: 21–88).

A year later, in April, at the Copenhagen meeting of the European Council, the West German Chancellor, Helmut Schmidt, and the French president, Valéry Giscard d'Estaing, picked up this new effort to regain support for monetary integration.[54] They became the founding fathers of the European Monetary System (EMS), and as the later development towards EMU shows, the Franco-German axis remained important in European politics in the years to come. The two state leaders had been particularly worried about several issues concerning the international economy, uncertainty about oil supplies and other essential raw materials, the instability of the dollar and its destabilizing influence on the exchange rates between the EEC currencies, and the division of the OECD area into three groups – North America, Japan and Western Europe. Thus, in their view it was essential that the Western European countries would be able to cooperate more closely togehter. Through monetary integration, European exposure to external influences could be reduced (Ludlow, 1982). Giscard d'Estaing had given some thought to rejoining the snake, but considered it to be his second-best scenario. His ambition was to create a system more far-reaching than an exchange rate mechanism,[55] though less far-reaching than the Jenkins proposal for a single currency zone.

At the Council of Ministers in Bremen, on 6 and 7 July 1978, the EMS proposals were on the agenda, and from the Bremen Communiqué it became clear that several features of the EMS had already been decided upon.[56] The Exchange Rate Mechanism (ERM) would be at least as strict as the snake. The earlier European unit of Account (EUA) would be replaced by a similar unit, the 'European Currency Unit' (ECU). Like the EUA, the ECU was a basket of EEC currencies and would function as a standard of reference for central exchange rates and a common denominator of claims and liabilities arising from official interventions in EEC currencies. ECU assets were to be created against the receipt of dollars and gold from participants' monetary reserves and, in time, against national currencies. ECU assets were to be used as means of settlements among EEC central banks. However, for the (now obligatory and unlimited) central bank interventions, it was agreed that domestic currencies would be used. A European Monetary Fund (EMF) would form the system's central institution and take over from the EMCF after a two-year transitional period (BIS, 1979: 144). The less prosperous regions were reinsured that, by repeated studying of the economic situation, appropriate action could be taken to strengthen their economies. A last noteworthy new element of the EMS was a 'divergence indicator', which was created to provide some symmetry in the adjustment burden between appreciating and depreciating currencies and an automatic mechanism to enforce consultations before the intervention limits were reached (*Communiqué* Bremen, 7–8 July 1978).

In the following six months the EMS plan was worked out in technical committees and in the Ecofin Council, and the European Monetary System was set up in December 1978.[57] All EEC Member States fully joined the EMS, except the UK which decided to keep the pound out of the Exchange Rate Mechanism (ERM).[58] The 'scheme for the creation of closer monetary cooperation' had a number of formal goals: to create a 'zone of monetary stability in Europe', 'growth with stability' and 'convergence of economic development'. But it was obvious at the time, and even more so during the 1980s, that its main objective was to create a European Exchange Rate Mechanism, and to try to limit the influence of dollar disturbances on EEC economic and monetary policies.

The EMS consisted of phases, as did the earlier EMU plan, and, following a similar fate, the EMS failed to move to the next phase (see also Sumner and Zis, 1982). The start of the second stage was planned for 1981. In this stage the use of the ECU would have been extended, and an EMF would have been fully operating. However, the Member States could not agree on the powers to be given to the new institution. Again the international context did not facilitate matters. This time the setting up of the EMS coincided with the second oil crisis, which led to a deterioration of the balance of payments situation of the participating countries. Hence the second stage was postponed for an indefinite period. Again it was basically the lack of political will to go beyond stage one that led to the abandonment of further integration.[59]

The five periods of the EMS

The launching of the EMS in March 1979 was received with great scepticism. Many, in particular central bankers and most professional economists, thought it would follow the same path as the snake earlier, with regular adjustments and currencies falling out and joining in every now and again. However, against all odds, the Exchange Rate Mechanism of the EMS was very successful until mid-1992.

The achievements of the EMS up to September 1992 can roughly be divided into four time periods (Giavazzi, Micossi and Miller, 1988; Gros and Thygesen, 1992; Ungerer *et al.*, 1983, 1986, 1990). The first period extended from March 1979 to March 1983, in which parities were often adjusted, and the policies and objectives of member countries diverged. The international monetary climate was gloomy, with recession, debt crisis and dollar fluctuations.[60] It was only after 1983, following the earlier recovery of the US, that the Western European economy started to pick up (BIS, 1984).

The second period started in 1983 and lasted until January 1987. The fact that the French government committed itself to the EMS system contributed to the stability of the second period. In this time interval fewer currencies were realigned, and the realignments occurred with a lower frequency. Inflation rates started to fall. However, the cost for achieving disinflation was large: the acceptance of relatively high levels of unemployment in the EMS countries.

The third period started at the last parities adjustment, followed by the Basel–Nyborg agreement in October 1987, in which some reforms of the EMS were achieved (financial services liberalization and the removal of some capital controls). This period ended in August 1992, and is characterized by fixed exchange rate parities, increasing convergence in the achievements of the economies in terms of inflation, interests and economic growth. Obviously, in this period optimism was expressed towards economic and monetary integration.[61]

The fourth period started in August 1992, when increasing speculation forced the UK pound sterling and the Italian lira to leave the ERM. Many other currencies also came under severe downward pressure, which resulted in a devaluation of the Irish punt, the Portuguese escudo and the Spanish peseta. On many occasions the French franc came under attack as well, but at crucial moments it was protected with large interventions by the other ERM-central banks, in particular the Bundesbank. Thus, the French monetary authorities were not forced to devalue the franc.

Finally, a fifth period of the ERM started on 2 August 1993. On that day the ERM could no longer be supported, and the Ministers of Finance decided to widen the bands. It was the greatest change in the formal rules of the ERM since it was set up in 1979; the ERM bands of plus or minus 2.25 per cent were stretched to plus or minus 15 per cent. However, at the risk of over-emphasizing the relative financial calm of the 1994–9 period[62] it can be argued that the ERM currencies have been fluctuating within a relatively narrow band since the widening of the band.[63]

It has often been suggested that the success of the ERM in the second period and third period caused the 1992 ERM crisis.[64] For most Member States the success of the integration process had to be maintained, i.e. completing the internal market, and aiming for an EMU. After 1987 most Member States started to consider it politically important to maintain the rates at their respective levels. They prematurely abandoned the idea that parities were 'fixed but adjustable'. In their view, being able to maintain *de facto* fixed exchange rates would add to the momentum needed to continue along the road towards EMU. It was first revived in 1988 at the Hanover meeting.

4.2   The relaunching of EMU – the Delors Report

The outlook of the completion of the Single Market provided a strong longing for further integration among most of the national governments, but especially among the French and German governments.

Thus, at the Council meeting in Hanover on 27 and 28 June 1988 the Heads of State or Governments stated that 'in adopting the Single Act, the Member States of the Community confirmed the objective of progressive realization of economic and monetary union'.[65] By making this statement the Council was reacting to a proposal put forward at the beginning of March 1988 by Mr Hans-Dietrich Genscher, the West German Foreign Minister (Genscher, 1988).[66] It was decided to set up a committee to study and propose 'concrete stages leading towards this union' to be on the agenda at the June 1989 summit in Madrid. The committee was to be chaired by Mr Jacques Delors and otherwise to comprise: (i) the presidents or governors of member countries' central banks; (ii) another Commissioner (Frans Andriessen, DG I); and (iii) three experts: Mr Niels Thygesen, professor of economics in Copenhagen; Mr Alexandre Lamfalussy, director general of the Bank for International Settlements in Basle;[67] and Mr Miguel Boyer, president of the Banco Exterior de España.

Towards the end of the 1980s the Member States had a variety of attitudes towards a European Monetary Union.[68] At the Hanover summit the British Prime Minister, Mrs Margaret Thatcher, was strongly opposed to a monetary union. She declared that she did not share the 'dream of a United States of Europe with a single European currency' and saw no possibility of a European central bank in her lifetime (*Keesing's*, 1988: 36003). Addressing the UK House of Commons only a few days before (on 23 June) she argued that the creation of a European central bank was possible only if there were a European government rather than twelve national states. 'That being not on the cards, I see no point in having anyone study a European central bank.' In Hanover she spoke more diplomatically, claiming that there was 'not much profit' in pursuing the goal of a European central bank since it was 'so far down the road' (*Keesing's*, 1988: 36307). HM Treasury and the Foreign Affairs Ministry were less sceptical towards the new plans than the Prime Minister.

In West Germany the strongest support for a European central bank was voiced by Mr Hans-Dietrich Genscher. Already in January 1988 he favoured the creation of a European central bank, when Mr Helmut Kohl rejected further plans (*Le Monde*, 16 and 22 January 1988). In a policy speech to the European Parliament on 16 June 1988 he called on the UK to 'accept responsibilities' by joining the ERM.

Although Mr Kohl was more reserved, he said he would favour the creation of a European central bank if it resembled the Bundesbank bsy having a constitutionally independent position, and having price stability as its primary objective. The bank should, however, be set-up only after the completion of the Internal Market (*Le Monde*, 28 January 1988).

The president of the Bundesbank, Mr Karl Otto Pöhl, viewed the set-up of a European Central Bank as a plan for the longer term, as he still had doubts about whether the national governments were ready to give up enough sovereignty to enable its formation (*Financial Times*, 13 June 1988; see also Pöhl *et al.*, 1990. On the Bundebank's attitudes see also Dyson, 1994; Henning, 1994; Kennedy, 1991; Marsh, 1992a). In an interview with the *Süddeutsche Zeitung* on 2 March 1988 he pointed out that:

> the problem is... the fact that over the past nine years the EMS has increasingly developed into a sort of D-Mark zone and not into an ECU zone, as the fathers of the EMS imagined. ... Every currency system needs an anchor. Many EMS members have been keen to use the D-Mark as a standard of stability. ... It would be disastrous if one tried to loosen this anchor.
>
> (Pöhl, quoted in *Keesing's*, 1988: 36307)

The French government was known to be committed to monetary union, openly since January 1988, when it was reported to be in favour of creating a European central bank (*Le Monde*, 12 January 1988). However, it favoured a European bank based on a 'federal coordination between central bank governors' (*The Times*, 25 June 1988, quoted in *Keesing's*, 36307).

The Delors Report

The Committee for the study of Economic and Monetary Union under the chairmanship of Jacques Delors unanimously approved the Report on Economic and Monetary Union in the European Community ('Delors Report') at a meeting in Basle, Switzerland on 11 and 12 April 1988, and it was made public the following week.[69] It outlined in some detail three stages which would lead to the creation of an area with complete freedom of movement for persons, goods, services and capital, as well as irrevocably fixed exchange rates between national currencies and, finally, a single currency (Delors Report, 1989: 17). The following highlights the main characteristics of the three stages.

Stage 1

Completion of the internal market and the reduction of existing disparities through coordination of fiscal and budgetary policies, and supported by more effective social and regional policies. Furthermore, the single financial area has to be completed and, preferably, all Community currencies should be in the ERM and the same rules should apply for all participants. Also to prepare for the next stages, the Treaty of Rome should be amended to set up the future European System of Central Banks (ESCB). The mandate of the existing Committee of central bank governors would be amended so as to include the formal right of proposal or opinion to the Council of Ministers. The Committee was divided on the question of whether a European reserve fund, as a precursor to a European federal central bank, should be created at this or the next stage.

Stage 2

After the new Treaty has come into force the second stage can start, in which the basic organs and structure of economic and monetary union would be set up. This includes the revision of existing institutions as well as the establishment of new ones. This stage is very much a transition period, in which policies are evaluated and further coordinated and consolidated, and coordination should be strengthened. Most important in this stage is the setting up of the ESCB – a federal body of national central banks with a separate new common bank – however leaving ultimate decision-making on economic and monetary policy still with national authorities.

Stage 3

In this stage the exchange rates are 'irrevocably locked' and convertible. National currencies would eventually be replaced by a single Community currency. Macroeconomic and budgetary rules become binding, structural and regional policies would be evaluated and further strengthened. The ESCB would now take up all its responsibility as foreseen in the Treaty, including the formulation and implementation of monetary policy in the Community.

The Delors Report, like the 1970 Werner Report, made a subdivision between the 'economic' union and the 'monetary' union. As was mentioned above in Chapters 1 and 2, this distinction is not quite clear from the terminology used in the economic body of literature on 'integration' (see Section 2.1). Once again this lack of clarity had its origins in the discord between the 'economists' and the 'monetarists', which was discussed in Section 3.3. By emphasizing that economic and monetary union should develop in parallel the report tried to settle the old dispute. The 'economists', the Dutch and the Germans, still insisted on the need to have reached more economic convergence before locking the exchange rates. The other EC countries, except for Britain, supported the 'monetarist' approach which favoured a faster move to monetary integration whereby they assumed that the necessary convergence would automatically result from the operation of fixed exchange rates and a single monetary policy in the EC. The British government wanted neither economic nor monetary integration, as far as a full EMU was concerned, proposing a common currency to be launched in parallel to the existing twelve currencies (see HM Treasury, 1989; see also House of Lords, 1989, 1990).

In the Delors Report the economic union is defined as consisting of four elements: a single market with the four freedoms (persons, goods, services and capital), competition policy aiming at strengthening the market mechanism, common policies improving regional development and structural change and, lastly, macroeconomic policy coordination including binding rules for budgetary policies (Delors Report, 1989: 20).

The monetary union is referred to as a currency area, with either irrevocably fixed exchange rates or, preferably, a single currency. As soon as the capital transactions are liberalized, financial markets are integrated and currencies locked and fully convertible, the national currencies would become increasingly close substitutes. As a result their interest rates would start to converge and would result in a *de facto* single monetary policy. Hence, fixed exchange rates require a common monetary policy. The Delors Report thus calls for the setting up of a new institution in which monetary policy would be decided, that is, decisions on the level of the interest rates, money supply, inflation etc. (Delors Report, 1989: 18–19).

The first stage would start on 1 July 1990, coinciding with the date set at the Hanover summit for the entering into force of full liberalization of capital transactions in eight Member States.[70] The politically sensitive decision of the timetable for the following stages had been left to the politicians to decide upon.

The report was formally presented to the Council of (Finance) Ministers in Luxembourg on 17 April 1989. All but one of the European Member States agreed to the report. Nigel Lawson, the UK Chancellor of the Exchequer, was reported to have said that what EMU envisaged 'would in effect require political union and a United States of Europe', which was 'not on the agenda for now, or for the foreseeable future. ... We cannot accept the transfer of sovereignty which is implied' (*Keesing's*, 1989: 36598). In making these reservations the UK appeared to be completely isolated, as even Denmark's foreign minister had approved the report. Mr Pöhl, president of the Bundesbank, even went as far as finding 'Mr Lawson's comments not entirely understandable' (*Europe Bulletin*, no. 4999, 20 April 1989).

Hence it can be concluded that the central bankers, who until then had been conducting monetary policies, had put forward these monetary decisions to restructure monetary policy-making, and transfer it to a new European institution, a European Central Bank.[71] They, however, left the political decision to the politicians. It soon became clear that the political debate on whether the political implications of EMU were acceptable had only just begun. It had become evident that monetary integration implied making a 'choice of the type of Europe in which the Twelve may or not want to take part' (*Europe Bulletin*, no. 5005, 28 April 1989). The Delors Report was to be discussed at the European Council heads of government meeting in Madrid in June.

The Delors Report resembled the 1970 Werner Report in many respects. It foresaw a parallel strategy, in three stages, of enforcing the 'monetary' as well as the 'economic' union; however, the new report did not envisage a separate supranational institution ensuring economic coordination. It also stressed the need to create central monetary authority – European System of Central Banks (ESCB) – to pursue monetary policies in EMU. Member States would surrender their powers to formulate monetary policy to this new institution, whose primary objective would be price stability.[72]

As at the time of the drafting of the Werner Plan the pressure for EMU was to increase in momentum after the realization of other integration objectives. In 1968 the customs union had been completed, and the Common Agricultural Policy worked successfully, but was put under pressure by currency fluctuations. In comparison, EMU in the 1990s was to ensure full benefit of the completed single European Market. Therefore, to eliminate transaction costs, there was a preference for a single currency, instead of just irrevocably fixed exchange rates, even though the latter was not excluded by the report if a single currency could not be agreed to politically.

The timing of the drafting of the Delors Report is also significant for understanding some political motives. In 1989, when the Delors Report was being drafted, the economic boom of the late 1980s was starting to wear out in Britain.[73] Business confidence had been accelerated by the prospect of the 1992 programme, and the hope was that this new project would keep expectations high, thereby stimulating economic growth (see also Commission, 1985, 1988a, 1988b). The Delors Report therefore sought to continue rapidly with the integration process while the 'Europhoria' still lasted. Also, the 1989–90 political events, the fall of the Berlin Wall, German Reunification, the breaking up of the Soviet Union, and the end of Eastern European Communist regimes, catalysed the revitalization of EMU.[74]

In addition the Community had, for several years, wanted to strengthen its position *vis-à-vis* the United States and Japan; in the late 1980s, before the Japanese bubble economy burst, that country seemed to manage its economy extremely well. In terms of economic growth, productivity, high-technology development and the current account surplus, as well as the capacity to recover from the stock market crash of 1987,[75] it was clear that this country was outperforming Europe and the US.

These international factors were very important to attract and maintain the interest of the European Member States to create EMU in the two-and-a-half year period after the Delors Report until the close at Maastricht of the Intergovernmental Conferences. As will be argued in the chapters that follow, a major reason for trade unions, industry and monetary authorities to want to proceed with EMU is related to their perception of the limited freedom for policy-making and to their way of defining policy objectives. The interdependent, liberal, open world economy restricted the role political actors can play, in their home country, and the role a nation can play in Europe, and in the rest of the world. In other words the prevailing concept in the late 1980s and early 1990s was the perception that there is only one way to answer the challenge posed by global change: identifying common objectives in the European framework. These were to strengthen the role of Europe and its currency in the global economy, and internally to maintain low inflation and to abolish exchange rate uncertainty.

The Madrid Summit

During the run up to the Madrid Summit in June 1989, after the Delors Report was published, a strong negative response towards the monetary integration plans came from Britain, namely from the Prime Minister,[76] the Foreign Secretary, the Trade Ministry and British parliament (*Financial Times*, 19 April, 11 and 17 May 1989). Nigel Lawson, the Chancellor of the Exchequer, however, was more in favour of slow progress in the field of monetary integration, and proposed 1990 as a possible date for the pound to enter the Exchange Rate Mechanism of the EMS.[77] The Bundesbank had accepted the Delors Plan but also voiced some concern; the primary warning being that monetary policy powers might be weakened due to the move towards EMU. Hence, on the eve of the Madrid Summit, Mrs Thatcher found herself isolated in her strong resistance to the Delors Report.

When the Heads of State and Government met on 27 June, a long discussion was held on whether the Delors Report was 'a basis' or 'the basis' of a 'global' process. A compromise was reached and it was decided that the report provided 'a good basis' for further work.[78] Furthermore, to meet some of Mrs Thatcher's complaints of loss of sovereignty it was decided to launch only the first stage of the Delors Plan (in July 1990). EMU had to be viewed from the perspective of the completion of the internal market and in the context of economic and social cohesion. In addition to launching only the first stage, no statement was made on the date of the start of the Intergovernmental Conference, but it was at least affirmed. This compromise made it possible for all twelve Heads of Governments and State to agree to the conclusions of the Summit on 29 June 1989.[79] The single focus on stage one of EMU plan led to a widespread expectation that the United Kingdom would in the future come up with alternatives to stages two and three of the Delors Report, as indeed Mrs Thatcher stated in the UK House of Commons upon her return from Madrid (*Financial Times*, 29 June 1989).

In a first reaction after the Madrid Summit, Delors was 'almost tempted to say that the momentum will now be irreversible'. Thatcher, however, insisted that she had 'conceded absolutely nothing' and denied any automatic link between embarking upon stage one of the Delors Report and moving on to the second and third stages. The *Financial Times* nevertheless described the EC as having 'just passed a watershed in its political history, which is almost certain to be marked by a significant transfer of national sovereignty to EC institutions' (quoted in *Keesing's,* 1989: 36740; on Delors see also Ross, 1995).

It was not necessary to wait long, as on 2 November 1989 HM Treasury published 'An Evolutionary Approach to Economic and Monetary Union'.[80] The British counter-proposal was essentially a competing currencies approach. In this view there was no need for a European central bank. The fear was voiced that the method laid out in the Delors Report might produce a higher inflation rate in Europe – one in which performance approximates more to the average than to the best. The British argued that their plan, on the other hand, would act as 'a powerful stimulus for monetary authorities to adopt policies aimed at low inflation' (*Keesing's,* 1989: 37132). During 1990 a second plan was launched, a so-called 'Hard Ecu Proposal' which built on the earlier plan (Bank of England, 1990; Leigh-Pemberton, 1990a, 1990b, 1990c, 1991a, 1991b). Its official main aim was to introduce a parallel and strong currency, a 'hard ecu', during the second stage of EMU. However, the political objective was initially to obstruct the process of creating full EMU (Crawford, 1993).

EMU remained at the top of the political agenda during the sixteen months between the Madrid Summit and the Rome Summit in October 1990. During the latter Summit it was decided to start the Intergovernmental Conferences in December of the same year. Monetary authorities of the European Member States made their opinion known on various occasions. Of the three countries studied here, France was the most strongly in favour of EMU.

The French Finance Minister, followed a month later by the Foreign Minister, was calling for rapid moves to the next stages of EMU (*Financial Times,* 9 February and 21 March 1990). The French dedication towards this goal had already been shown earlier when the remaining French exchange rate controls were removed six months ahead of the EC deadline (*Financial Times,* 12 December 1989 and 3 January 1990). President Mitterrand made known that he thought that a political union had to be agreed on at the June Summit in Dublin (*Financial Times,* 26 March 1990). Together with chancellor Kohl he pushed for an acceleration of the process of the construction of Europe (*Le Monde* and *Financial Times,* 20 April 1990).

In Germany the reunification process was the main subject of debate. The Berlin Wall had come down in November 1989, and the enlarged Federal Republic of Germany would come into being as of 3 October 1990. In fact, German monetary authorities perceived very soon that the East–West German monetary unification would complicate faster moves towards EMU. For this reason Chancellor Kohl rejected the (Italian, Irish and French) calls for advancing the date of the EC conference on monetary union to July (*Financial Times,* 17 February and 24 March 1990). Other early warnings concerning the negative effect of German reunification were also heard (*Financial Times,* 19 March 1990).[81] However, Kohl changed his position during the spring and by April he agreed that German reunification should not slow down the process of monetary integration, and that a political union should also be constructed.

4.3   The intergovernmental conferences leading to the Maastricht Treaty

At the special meeting of the Council in Dublin in April 1990 it was decided that two Intergovernmental Conferences had to take place in order to amend the Rome Treaty. It was hoped that the new Treaty could be ratified before 1 January 1993. One IGC was to be on Economic and Monetary Union, and one on Political Union (PU); both should start in December 1990 (*Bulletin of the EC*, Supplement 4, 1990). At the Rome Summits (October and December 1990) eleven Member States agreed to the objective of creating an EMU that would closely follow the stages laid out in the Delors Report. Britain stated that it could not accept this approach.

At the start of the IGCs in December in Rome, observers agreed that the *EMU conference* was well prepared. The Commission had circulated a background document (Commission, 1990a) and submitted a Draft Treaty amending the Rome Treaty, central bank governors had outlined draft statutes of the European System of Central Banks, the Commission had made an analysis of the costs and benefits of EMU in a report 'One Market, One Money' (Commission, 1990b) and the Monetary Committee had come up with proposals.

The IGCs went on all through 1991. In Community circles it was heard that the IGC on EMU was progressing rapidly, and that only some difficult decisions needed to be made on politically sensitive questions, notably the timetable, the binding rules on budgetary deficits and public debt, and on macroeconomic performance (inflation, interest rates and stable exchange rates). These five policy areas were to become known in the Maastricht Treaty as the convergence criteria. The difficult question widely debated was how it eventually would be decided which countries could join the final stage of EMU, i.e. how strict the criteria would be applied.

Regarding the IGC on *Political Union* (PU), it was thought that insufficient preparations had preceded the conference. This critique was hardly surprising given that the political integration process had quite a different history, but also because the Franco-German proposal to convene an IGC only dated back to April 1990. Moreover, the concept of PU was less clearly defined (see also Laursen and Vanhoonacker, 1992). In addition, the renewed interest emerged only after it became clear that EMU might be realized. The desire to proceed to EMU followed from the anticipated successful completion of the Internal Market, whereas the urge to create the PU was a result of the ever clearer prospect of creating an EMU.

Most Member States submitted proposals at some point or another. The British evolutionary approach to EMU has been mentioned above. In addition, the British government submitted a proposal for the creation of a European Monetary Fund (*Europe Documents*, 10 January

1991, no. 1682). Shortly thereafter, the French government presented its draft on EMU (*Europe Documents*, 31 January 1991, no. 1686), and the Spanish government made proposals for the second phase of EMU (*Europe Documents*, 1 February 1991, no. 1688), which the British quickly interpreted as being along the same lines as the UK proposals. The Luxembourg presidency took up elements of these contributions and presented a so-called 'non-paper'[82] on amending the Rome Treaty concerning EMU, which served as the basis for a discussion in the context of an Ecofin meeting (*Europe Documents*, 27 February 1991, no. 1693). The last in line were the Germans who responded to the submitted documents with an 'overall proposal' for the IGC (*Europe Documents*, 20 March 1991, no. 1700).

At the summer summit the Luxembourg delegation concluded its half-year EC presidency by submitting a 26-page reference document, 'Draft Treaty on the Union' (*Europe Documents*, 5 July 1991, no. 1722/1723). Next, in September the Dutch government presented a plan (*Europe Documents*, 6 September 1991, no. 1731) which was considered too radical and was rapidly rejected. Some countries, in particular Italy and Spain, but also the European Parliament, feared that the proposal would institutionalize a 'two-speed monetary Europe', and would 'put the others off indefinitely'.[83] Thus, the final text which the final meeting of the IGC would discuss, sent by the Dutch to the Finance Ministries, resembled the Luxembourg Draft Treaty.

The European Trade Union Confederation (ETUC) and the Union of Industrial and Employers' Confederations of Europe (UNICE) each put forward their proposals for EMU, and submitted them to the IGC (ETUC, 1990a, 1991; UNICE, 1990a, 1990b, 1991). The ETUC accentuated that the aim of EMU be to improve the general economic conditions: 'Economic and Monetary Union must not be regarded as an end in itself but as a means of achieving a better life for the Community's citizens' (ETUC, 1990a: 41). Thus, it focused on the objectives of EMU being sustainable development, full employment, economic and social cohesion, in addition to price stability (ETUC, 1990a: 40). It was also emphasized that EMU required a Social Dimension, in which the trade unions hoped to play an important role. Furthermore, it stressed the importance of democratic accountability of the future ECB. It also stressed concern with too-rigid binding rules on national budgetary deficits and public debt (for more details on ETUC see 1990b). In its submission to the IGC it stressed many of these points again, in particular the need to have the Social Dimension be considered an integral of EMU (ETUC, 1991: 1). With reference to the 1977 MacDougall

Report, it pointed to the possible need in future years to increase inter-regional transfer payments (ETUC, 1991: 3). Despite these points of concern it can still be concluded that in broad terms ETUC had accepted the basic concept of EMU which the various national monetary authorities had in mind.

UNICE came forward with documents which declared UNICE's full support for EMU (UNICE 1990a, 1990b, 1991). UNICE stressed the importance of EMU in order to complete the Internal Market. It supported the approach set out in the Delors Report. However, it did not see the need for binding rules on budgetary deficits and public debts: 'UNICE, therefore, does not see a need for centrally determined binding rules on the conduct of budgetary policies, except in the case of serious and persistent imbalances' (UNICE, 1990a: 5). Furthermore, UNICE stressed that EMU would enable the Community to play a more important role in the international monetary and economic system (UNICE, 1990a: 3). UNICE's view of EMU was that in principle all Member States should join. As for the European Central Bank, it supported it being independent and its mandate being to preserve price stability. In November 1991 UNICE submitted a letter to the IGC, in which it reiterated its total support of EMU (UNICE, 1991). In this later statement the objection to binding rules was lifted:

> With regard to budget policy, UNICE insists on the need to set objective criteria to prevent the occurrence of excessive deficits which could compromise monetary stability. To this end it supports the definition of appropriate procedures to correct imbalances which meet the criteria so defined in cases where voluntary coordination turns out to be inadequate.
>
> (UNICE, 1991: 2)

In 1992 UNICE expressly voiced its support of the convergence criteria: 'The convergence process [the formulation of the convergence criteria] within the Community rightly formed the main focus of the treaty discussions at Maastricht' (UNICE, 1992: 1). All in all, the position of UNICE was much in line with the apparent consensus among most monetary authorities in the EC.

The European public opinion in the year in which the IGC was held was in favour of further integration of Europe. According to *Eurobarometer*, an opinion poll held twice a year based on a sample of 12,800 Europeans, in the autumn of 1991, 54 per cent of the interviewees were in favour of a single currency that would replace national currencies in five or six years, whereas 25 per cent were against.

Similarly, 55 per cent agreed to (22 per cent opposed) a European Central Bank with its executive board made up of national central bank governors (*Eurobarometer* 36, November, Commission, 1991c).

The Maastricht Summit

On 9 and 10 December 1991, in the most southern city of the Netherlands, Maastricht, the Heads of State and Government had to conclude the IGCs that had been going on for a year.[84] A well-prepared EMU-IGC was coming to a close. Many proposals had been made beforehand, but an accord on the final text still had to be reached.

A number of surprises surfaced from the Maastricht communiqué where the famous 'package deal' was agreed upon. The most important news on EMU was the decision concerning the timetable for the start of the final stage of EMU, with a single currency to follow a few months later.[85] Not only could EMU start in 1997 when the majority, 'a critical mass', fulfilled the 'convergence criteria', but it would also *automatically* start in 1999 for those countries which fulfilled the following 'convergence criteria', which were put in a protocol to article 109j: (i) inflation rates would have to be within 1.5 percentage points of the rates of the EU's three best performers in terms of price stability; (ii) no excessive deficit should exist;[86] (iii) during the preceding two years the national currency had to have respected the 'normal' fluctuation margins in the narrow band of the ERM, 'without severe tensions'[87] and no devaluations should have been undertaken on the Member States' own initiative in the same period; (iv) the average long-term interest rate in the Member State should not exceed those of the three best-performing Member States by more than two percentage points.

Whether or not the Member States fulfilled these criteria would be decided by the EU leaders at a Summit or Council meeting in 1996 voting with a qualified majority. The European Central Bank (ECB) would be set up by 1 July 1998, or at least six months before a single currency would come into being. Britain was given an opt-out clause for the single currency and monetary policy, as well as for the Social Chapter of the Treaty. The Danish were given the time to hold a referendum. In the case of a notification that Denmark would not take part in the third phase, it would, like Britain, be given an exemption status, in the jargon, a 'derogation'.

4.4   Post Maastricht: a post-mortem?

An outburst of public opposition against Maastricht, by late spring and summer 1992, took policy-makers completely by surprise. Results of two national referenda on Maastricht triggered the emergence of exchange-rate tensions. Danish citizens rejected the Treaty on 2 June 1992, with a narrow majority. The French voters only very narrowly approved it in their national referendum held on 20 September 1992. In late August, however, opinion polls preceding the French referendum suggested a negative outcome (on the French referendum see Criddle, 1993). The negative public opinion on the Maastricht Treaty in the spring and summer of 1992 compounded by other unfavourable circumstances, such as very low interest rates in the United States, resulted in great turbulence on the currency markets. In September it was decided to devalue the Italian lira by 7 per cent. This currency had been under heavy speculative attack following growing fears over the unsustainable Italian budget deficits. On 16 September the British Chancellor of the Exchequer, Norman Lamont, announced the suspension of the pound sterling from the ERM, after it became clear that central bank interventions could not prevent the currency from losing value. The next day the Italians followed the British example, only describing the exit as a 'temporary one'. The autumn, winter and following spring witnessed more devaluations, i.e. of the Irish punt, the Portuguese escudo and the Spanish peseta. Some associate currencies abandoned their peg to the Ecu. The Fins had already decided to float the markka in early September. In November the Swedes and in December the Norwegians suspended pegging their respective currencies to the Ecu.

In May 1993, when the Danish population was given a second referendum on the Maastricht Treaty, after the Danish government was provided an opt-out of the single currency, a majority of the Danish voters accepted the Treaty. The result, however, did not stop the markets from repeating the actions of the year before. Again the summer was characterized by heavy speculations; this time they were mainly directed against the French franc. The Banque de France and the Bundesbank strongly tried to defend the franc, but after desperate interventions the twelve Finance Ministers decided on 2 August 1993 to relax the narrow bands of the ERM. The ERM went from 'bands' to 'boulevards'.[88]

Late July had been crowded with emergency meetings on how to address the ERM crisis. Several proposals were put forward. The DM could be revalued *vis-à-vis* the other currencies, or it, together with the Dutch guilder, could temporarily leave the ERM. However, the Finance Ministers in the early morning of 2 August came up with the widening of the bands for all ERM currencies except the DM/guilder parity which would remain at the old 2.25 per cent.

The exchange rate turmoil and the *de facto* abolition of the ERM posed the question of how the Member States could satisfy the criterion of the Maastricht Treaty requiring countries to stay within the 'normal' bands of the ERM. At first it was believed that the countries would only temporarily maintain the 'boulevards' rather than the narrow bands. This assumption initially was backed up by the evidence that most currencies had remained near the old exchange rate parities in the subsequent months. Yet, since the relaxing of the bands, neither the Ecofin Council nor the central bank presidents had voiced the need to return to narrow bands (*Financial Times*, 9/10 April 1994). At times, moreover, proposals were launched to move to EMU much faster than was envisaged by the Treaty, to put a halt to speculation.[89] However, after currencies again came under attack, in the spring of 1995, it became apparent that waves of speculation should not be ruled out. Since the factual collapse of the ERM Member States have been very hesitant to return to narrow bands very quickly. Regarding the exchange rate criterion in the Maastricht Treaty it has now been generally accepted that 15 per cent bands will be taken as the 'normal bands' of the ERM. The accent has shifted away from worries concerning the exchange rate performance (with the possible exception of the Italian lira that again came under speculative attack in 1994–5, and devalued significantly). From that time onwards it became clear that the two decisive criteria in fact had become those related to performance of Member States' budgetary deficits and public debts. This eventually became clear in the judgement of the Commission to consider eleven Member States to be ready for participation in the third stage of EMU (European Commission, 1998c), which was accepted by the Council in May 1998.

The ratification process in 1992 proved to be much more controversial than any politician had expected when signing the Treaty on European Union in February 1992. At Maastricht it had been hoped that the ratification process would have been completed before the end of 1992. Instead the process dragged on until the end of the next year, when the constitutional court of Germany, the last country to ratify, ruled in late October that the Treaty was not unconstitutional. It came into force the following month, that is, on 1 November 1993.

Ratification proved difficult in various countries for different reasons. Some countries held a referendum on it. Denmark and France were the first, in June and September 1992, with the well-known devastating effects.[90] In other countries, such as Ireland, the discussion centred around the abortion issue, which as always proved to be an emotional issue in that country. Eventually, when the referendum was held, a comfortable majority voted in favour. The Irish 'yes' delivered a sense of relief to the politicians that had carefully negotiated the Maastricht 'package'. In the following months ratification was successfully achieved in the other Member States. The two countries that proved to cause the largest difficulties in 1993 were Britain and Germany.

British politics in 1993 appeared to be completely dominated by the question of ratification and the conditions under which this should take place. The ruling Conservative Party was deeply divided on the issue. In July of 1993 the political situation became very complicated. The Euro-sceptics within the Conservative Party proposed a motion to oppose ratification. Their main worry were the implications the European Union would have on government autonomy, and they were particularly against joining a single currency. The Labour Party, that had been in favour of the Maastricht Treaty but disapproved of the British opt-out from the Social Chapter, put forward an amendment calling for the implementation of the Maastricht Treaty's Social Protocol. When it was beaten by 318 votes to 317 the Labour Party decided to support a government motion of the Euro-sceptics as a way of voicing protest against the government's decision to opt out from the Social Chapter. The motion was rejected. The next day the Prime Minister, John Major, received the support by calling for a motion of confidence 'on the government's policy on the Social Chapter'. The last obstacle was the result of a court case, filed by Lord Rees-Mogg, against ratifying the Treaty. The High Court ruled on 30 July 1993 that the Treaty was in conformity with British constitutional tradition. As the ERM collapsed that weekend, Lord Rees-Mogg decided not to appeal against the High Court ruling, stating that collapse of the ERM made 'one of the main pillars of the Maastricht Treaty nul and void' (quoted in *Agence Europe*, 2/3 August 1993).

In Germany public opinion became concerned with the implications of the signing of the Treaty of Maastricht only during the Summit meetings in December 1991.[91] Public opinion remained very negative about the European Union, and even more about abolishing the DM (*Eurobarometer* 37, Commission (1992); cf. *Eurobarometer* 46, Commission (1997)). Officials in other countries were relieved that the German law did not require a referendum. However, for quite a while it remained uncertain what the verdict of the Constitutional Court in Karlsruhe would be. When its judgement came out in October 1993 some ambiguity remained on the right of the Germans to have the

Court judge again whether joining EMU would violate the German constitution. The Court judgement enables the German parliament, in the future, to make a separate decision on whether or not to join Stage 3 of EMU.

4.5   Conclusions

This chapter has explained the causes behind the relaunch of EMU. It has discussed the EMS, the Delors Report, the Intergovernmental Conferences, and the post-Maastricht period. When the EMS became operational in March 1979 it was assumed it would be short-lived. However, it survived the deep economic recession and the Euro-pessimism of the early 1980s and became well institutionalized in the second part of the decade. Nevertheless, the original plans for a second phase of EMS did not mature. Its success was mainly due to the willingness of participating countries to adopt monetary policies that supported the exchange rate parities as well as the low inflation objective. In the period 1987–92 the EMS became a political symbol of successful European integration. Closer economic and monetary policy coordination indeed emerged during the EMS epoque, but the ERM crisis of 1992 and 1993 showed that an earlier realignment had been necessary and that the countries probably did not adjust their policies enough.

The Single European Act gave a new impetus to the creation of EMU. The prospect of the completion of the internal market implied that the EMU project could be studied. In Hanover in 1988 the European Council set up a committee to study a possible road to EMU. The 1989 Delors Report, written by central bank governors, provided the Community with a path to economic and monetary union, a currency area with a common monetary policy, and free movement of persons, goods, services and capital. This blueprint has been the basis for the amended Treaty agreed to at Maastricht in 1991.

The commitment to the final objective reached momentum at the conclusion of the Intergovernmental Conferences set up to determine the final stages of EMU and to amend the Rome Treaty. The Danish referendum marked the first unexpected downturn of the Europhoria. The run-up to the French referendum showed that things could worsen even further. The crisis culminated when strong speculations put the ERM currencies under pressure, resulting in the fall of the pound and the lira out of the ERM and the devaluation of several other currencies. In addition to these developments the global economy witnessed a severe downturn of the business cycle, leaving the national governments little leeway to solve their problems. The prospect for European monetary integration plans was gloomy. As ERM Members neglected to adjust the exchange rates when necessary, the markets took their toll.

It was however not only lack of policy adjustment that led to the ERM crisis. Several other factors were at work. First, the capital liberalization of July 1990 made capital very mobile across national borders. Second, German reunification worked as an external shock, which boosted inflation and hence interest rates. As this country also provided the anchor currency, these rates were exported to the other EMS countries. Third, the recession of 1992 made it clear that it would be very difficult, and painful, for many countries to meet the Maastricht criteria on budgetary deficits and one on public debts. The analysts thus started to doubt the commitment of some countries to the EMU objective. Fourth, in the summer of 1992 interest rates in the United States were much lower than those in Europe, and the value of the dollar itself hit a record low against the DM. Summarizing, a number of factors contributed to the ERM crisis.

However, the immediate aftermath of the ERM debacle suggested that most Member States perhaps more than before had been committed to seeking a solution to the economic and monetary problems in the context of European cooperation and policy coordination. This is possibly the largest difference between the experience in the 1970s and the 1990s. In both periods the EMU plans were seriously challenged by the appearance of large speculative attacks, an external shock (i.e. the oil crisis and German reunification respectively) and economic downturn. In the 1970s the Member States had divergent responses and aimed at different policy objectives. By contrast, it seems that in the 1990s the Member States still retained their commitment to the EMU objective, even if this implied having to accept short-term sacrifices related to the adjustment or transition period, in which the preparations are made to join EMU.

Let us now return to the analysis made towards the end of Chapter 3 about the failure of the earlier EMU project. Reflecting on the monetary integration process in the 1980s and early 1990s set out above, let us concentrate on the four reasons provided by Kruse. It was mentioned that EMU failed in the 1970s due to four reasons: (1) EMU was not considered to be in the interests of the national governments; (2) lack of change in economic and monetary policy-making; (3) the presence of two incompatible approaches to EMU; (4) the problem of enlargement, in particular, participation of Britain in EMU. Let us discuss these four points in turn.

In contrast to the 1970s, in the 1980s *indeed* did give rise to a number of important changes. First of all, as an after-the-fact interpretation, EMU served the interests of national governments. They signed the Treaty, eventually it was ratified, and the third stage of EMU started on 1 January 1999. Subsequent chapters will examine *exactly how and why* various domestic actors perceived EMU to serve or frustrate their interests. Second, regarding the policy change in economic and monetary policy-making, the 1980s showed a remarkable turn towards cooperation. The crucial catalyst may have been the French turn-around in monetary policy in 1983. But most likely the increasing interdependence and the effects of further financial market integration and other factors have led to the fact that national monetary authorities adopted similar monetary policies. Third, the actual economic circumstances in the core of the EC countries were more similar in the middle and late 1980s than they had been in the 1970s. In part this occurred as a result of the convergence in monetary policy-making, but also as a result of the increasing openness of the national economies and the increasing trade among them. The fourth factor mentioned by Kruse could have still disturbed the EMU process. The EC in the 1980s had been enlarged once again. EMU in the 1990s was to happen with perhaps as many as twelve or more Member States. Interestingly, however, as will be further illustrated in subsequent chapters, the Member States were not anticipating EMU to start with all EC Member States. In fact, throughout the 1980s there was continuous talk of which countries would join EMU from the outset. Notably, the UK government was not terribly keen about the prospect of having to join EMU. The incorporation of strict rules for entry was another way to ensure that EMU would not start off with too many countries that would encompass a groups of countries that would not be able to create a feasible EMU. Thus, it is even more remarkable that eleven Member States eventually entered the third stage of EMU in 1999.

Turning to the conditions that Kruse identified which would have to be met in order to achieve EMU, the following observations can be made. First, he noted that European unity would have to serve the immediate national interest of the individual countries. We can easily conclude that this apparently happened. But we would need to find out why and how. Kruse's second condition was that EMU has to be considered an objective that Member States need to adhere to for a longer period of time. That has happened. Again the question is why and how. Finally, dissimilarities in the economic goals and structures of the Member States needed to be reduced. This has happened because of the European integration process, in particular the internal market and the capital liberalization process, as well as the EMS and increasing monetary cooperation. Let us now turn to the proposed eclectic theory and think a little further about why actors in countries might conceive EMU as serving their interests.

Applying the eclectic theory to the history of EMU

In Chapter 2 an 'eclectic theory' of European integration was presented. How would the history of EMU 'from Delors to Maastricht' fit into the model 'three phases of integration' of the eclectic theory as elaborated above? Before this question is answered a possible categorization is made of the earlier attempts at economic and monetary integration which show how they correspond to the three stages of integration set out above.

In the early 1960s, when Jean Monnet's 1962 Action Programme, which envisaged a European Fund, was launched, the Member States did not perceive a serious external threat. As this necessary condition was not fulfilled Member States did not enter the first stage. Economically the Member States were doing well, and they felt no need to seek national unity and cooperate with neighbouring countries. Therefore they never even embarked on the first stage of integration identified by the eclectic theory.

By 1969 the developing cracks in the Bretton Woods system, and the distorting impact of the dollar on the exchange rates in Europe, provided ample reason to perceive the need for the process of economic and monetary integration. The Member States felt the need to settle their differences to respond to the challenge posed by the external world. Moreover, there was an element present that facilitated embarking on the first stage of integration to create an EMU in Europe. Some economic cooperation had taken place in the 1960s, cumulating in the completion of the customs union in 1968. This meant that the Member States were in some policy areas (customs union, CAP) already well into the first stage of integration. However, in the 1970s the momentum was lost, as not all Member States wanted to cooperate with the countries around them to prevent the collapse of the Bretton Woods system, to handle the oil crisis, to fight inflation and subsequently to fight the recession of 1975. Hence the integration process, which had started up so well, stagnated again. The national aims had outweighed the desire to cooperate with partner countries. The eclectic theory would suggest that the member countries did not really perceive the external threat in the early 1970s to be very serious. On the contrary they believed they could still solve their problems by finding a domestic response, rather than cooperating with partner countries.

The monetary integration drive of the late 1970s was again a response to external factors, most importantly the effects of the dollar on European policies, but also the perceived challenge posed by the strength of both the US and the Pacific Basin. National politicians in Member States again started by thinking that the best solution to these challenges was to settle the differences between Member States and to find a response collectively. Given the failure of the plans (i.e. 1962 and 1969–73) it is surprising that the participating countries actually managed to unite their domestic actors and aim for full cooperation. The example of the French after 1983, the Italians during the whole 1980s, and the British that started to shadow the DM in 1985 are indicative.

The EMS/ERM can be stated to have successfully passed the first stage of the eclectic theory, and moved into the second stage. It became stranded there in 1992–3, when the member countries started the redistributive struggle between them. The German monetary authorities did not want to reduce interest rates, which were too high for the other Member States in recession. Hence, the speculators caused havoc, and finally the system collapsed. Thus, the ERM made it through the first stage of integration of the eclectic theory but collapsed in the second, due to markets' response, dollar weakness and various other factors. Whether it would recover and proceed to develop in the second stage depended on whether the Member States truly believed they needed international cooperation in the field of exchange rates to regain some influence over the global economy. If some countries, however, believed that they could profit from devaluations they would drop out of the integration momentum.

Though not discussed extensively in this study, the Single European Act and the 1992 programme were again a case of the Europeans uniting to face the challenge of the outside world. Surprisingly the actors within Member States were also willing to settle any domestic disputes about negative consequences of the Internal Market programme in order to reach the final objective. As far as the evidence goes, and is discussed by the present study, it seems that this process remains an integrative force in the second phase of integration. Domestic support of the Internal Market is still apparent and cooperation among Member States also is operating with little friction.

The EMU initiative of 1988 and beyond is perhaps the best example of the mechanism of the eclectic theory. Entering the first stage here was facilitated by the '1992 project' which was already operating successfully. EMU could contribute to safeguard that process of integration. In addition, the external threat was perceived to be even stronger by the continuing processes of globalization, liberalization and capital mobility. The collapse of the Communist regimes was used by some to stress that 'capitalism' was the only viable way of running an economy. Thus, it legitimized the processes of privatization, liberalization, etc.

It could be argued that EMU entered the first phase of integration according to the eclectic model in 1989 with its roots in 1987–8. Phase one started when the Member States agreed that EMU was the strategy to unify the partner countries to address the growing challenge posed by the outside world. Some factors that may have contributed to this sense of being challenged were: success of Japan, negative effects of the dollar, the growth of (uncontrollable) financial markets, the increasing interdependence (globalization) more generally, the possibility of the completion of the Uruguay round and, of course, the changes in Eastern Europe which took place in 1989. The domestic society was also aware of this 'danger' and was willing to forget the redistributive struggle in the immediate short term to ensure that the unity was not endangered. The domestic actors were not worried about the distributive effects and emphasized the benefits of the project in their struggle with the political economy, i.e. the rest of the world. The actors did not consider it necessary to understand completely what the final effects were going to be, as long as it was quite probable that the EC as a whole would benefit.

The second phase of integration takes place when a certain degree of integration in the field of economic and monetary integration is reached. This point is when the Maastricht Treaty had been ratified, whereby Delors stage two was started. The characteristics of that period were anticipated to be that some economic benefits of the integration region as a whole would be becoming clear. At the same time, the domestic actors would become more aware of the redistributive effects of EMU for their country and for the societal niche they were representing. The redistributive struggle at the domestic level would stay very limited, but the domestic actors would start to voice complaints for their country as a whole if they perceived the larger cake to be unequally redistributed among the participating countries.

The third phase of integration would start when EMU is fully operational. It was always perceived to be possible that the third phase of integration would be entered by different countries at different times. Those countries who entered phase three would want to discuss the redistributional effects, and would then no longer accept unequal redistribution of the costs and benefits of the enlarged cake delivered by EMU. If the Member States do not perceive this strategy as the right way to combat the global challenge, or if they fear that short-term costs to be borne do not outweigh the potential future benefits, the Member States will not enter the third phase of integration as envisaged by the eclectic theory, or could even drop out later.

Thus, according to the eclectic view presented above, the largest domestic fight about equity concerning wealth distribution is to be expected after EMU becomes fully operational, i.e. for the countries in the fast track, after the year 2002. In the concluding chapter, after having presented and analysed the data in Chapters 6 and 7, the theoretical framework is examined on the basis of the insights generated by examining the data.

This fourth chapter has provided a historical survey of the European monetary integration plans. The next chapter will introduce the method used to discover actors' perceptions of EMU. The results and its analysis are reported in Chapters 6 and 7.

5
Methodology

Chapters 6 and 7 analyse the perceptions of actors in the policy-making process with regard to EMU. As was mentioned in Chapter 1, the data discussed in this study are mainly based on interviews, but supported by 'official' sources (for example annual reports, press releases) as well as by secondary sources including newspaper articles. Before discussing the data provided by the interviews in the next chapter, the present chapter addresses the methodological questions related to the choice of using interviews as the basis of the present study. This chapter is structured as follows. In Section 5.1 a brief justification is given as to why the research is carried out using a qualitative approach rather than a quantitative approach. Section 5.2 discusses the problems related to using interviews as a mode of data collection, and examines the question whether or not those problems distort the aim of the present study. In the last two sections the method used for the present study is described. Section 5.3 discusses the political context in the two periods in which the interviews were conducted. In addition it explains how the respondents were selected. Finally, in Section 5.4 the questionnaire that was used for the interviews with the respondents is provided and the aims of the questions are explained. A very short summary is provided in Section 5.5.

5.1 Qualitative and quantitative research

The question here is not which method is a 'better' research method in general, but which method is better suited to the needs of the particular research project. As this research project concerns the perceptions, attitudes, interests and motives of actors representing various organizations, the choice of the qualitative approach becomes evident. Corbin and Strauss' general definition of qualitative research illustrates this point:

> By the term *qualitative research* we mean any kind of research that produces findings not arrived at by means of statistical procedures or other means of quantification. It can refer to research about persons' lives, stories, behavior, but also about organizational functioning, social movements, or interactional relationships. Some of the data may be quantified as with census data but the analysis itself is a qualitative one.
>
> (Corbin and Strauss, 1990: 17)[92]

The specific information for this research cannot be obtained by analysing statistical data obtained from a large number of respondents, because the information required is known to only a select group of people. Thus a qualitative approach was chosen as research method.

5.2 Interviews: a way to answer certain questions

The qualitative method, particularly when using interviews, helps to discover the answers to certain questions, such as concerning people's attitudes, interests and motives. Such information cannot adequately be obtained by examining existing statistics or collecting data by sending out questionnaires. Usually existing statistics do not give enough precise information about the case the researcher is studying or the variables he/she wishes to consider. Sending out questionnaires may lead to a high non-response, for two main reasons.

First, the respondent is most likely not willing to supply the requested information to 'just anyone' as this information concerns the respondent's personal beliefs and conviction and he/she may want them to remain private or confidential. It is true that if the respondent were adequately informed about the aim of the research, and the integrity of the researcher, he/she might agree to participate after all.

This leads to a second reason why sending questionnaires may lead to a high non-response, that is, the sizeable amount of time required to write down all the requested information. Respondents may not be willing to spend so much time on a questionnaire. Moreover, the respondent may have difficulties writing down in words what exactly his/her attitudes, interests and motives are, or even feel uncomfortable about writing them down on paper.

A person-to-person interview then circumvents these problems as the respondent can speak more freely, and is given the guarantee that he/she may talk 'off the record' and will not be quoted without his/her consent. Finally, an interviewee can freely decide how much time is spent on the interview.

How interviews benefit this research

As the core aim of this research is to understand what the perceptions of EMU are, the qualitative method based on interviews is a logical choice.[93] Interviews were conducted to collect data on perceptions of EMU and on assumed spill-over effects. There are four reasons why respondents were not requested to fill out questionnaires, but instead were interviewed. First, the non-response would be much higher (see above), because the response would require too much time and effort. Second, if the questionnaire were completed, short answers would not give adequate information. Third, talking with the respondent was considered more useful because it allowed asking the respondent *why* certain views were held, and having him or her explain the origins of these views and hypothesize about possible implications of policy choices for the future. Fourth, it was thought necessary to have a complete sample. As the study in any case concentrates on a limited number of respondents, the hope was that all the relevant actors could be interviewed.

The interviews were conducted with representatives of the organizations studied here (that is, monetary authorities and social partners) whose responsibilities included preparing draft documents of their organization's policy towards EMU. In the interview they were asked to give the formal view of the organization with regard to EMU, the organization's policy towards previous monetary integration plans, the view of the organization with regard to the anticipated effect of EMU for the future, the likely effect of EMU on other policy areas, etc. If the organization did not have a view the respondents were asked to surmise what the organization's attitude would probably be, or to give their personal views.

Do we believe what we hear? Ways to ensure reliability

It is usually insufficient just to ask the person 'why' he or she had a certain attitude, perception or motive. Research on understanding attitudes by interviewing shows that respondents want to give a socially acceptable answer (Henerson, Morris and Fitz-Gibbon, 1987). This is especially the case when the respondents feel they *should not* hold the view they hold.[94] Hence one has to beware of the bias that may appear in the outcomes of the interviews. A way to circumvent this effect is by asking additional 'control' questions where a respondent has to apply his or her point of view to a certain situation.

The problem raised above, that respondents might supply an 'acceptable' answer, does not seem to be relevant when interviewing policy-makers because it is their function to represent a certain mode of thought (which on certain issues may not agree with their personal views). Moreover, this problem would also arise when using other methods of data collection.[95]

However, two different problems may arise when interviewing policy-makers. First, they may use the interviewer as a medium to voice a certain view to the outside world. Second, the opposite case, they may not disclose their 'real' attitudes, that is, they are (still) keeping policy choices and policy insights to themselves, and are *explicitly not* mentioning them to the researcher. Again, these problems do not seem to obstruct the aim of the present research. The first problem is inherent in the conduct of a study of attitudes, perceptions and strategies; that is, a researcher, and/or his/her report, may become part of the channels that respondents may utilize to express their views. The second problem seems perhaps more troubling; however, other researchers have found that respondents are pleased to be interviewed. They are willing to give their personal view, as an expert in the policy field, especially where it concerns technical matters, or policy areas which require expertise. The researcher of this study has also found this to be true. Finally, the design of the questionnaire can contribute to ensure that the respondents are indeed expressing their organization's view by 'cross-checking' the answers, for example by asking the interviewees about the answers of the respondents in other organizations and institutions. Hence, without ignoring the problems referred to above, it seems most logical for the aim of the present research to use interviews for collecting the research data.

5.3   The method used for this research

The present research project was inspired by the methods suggested by various leading qualitative methodologists, though it was not designed to follow closely any one of them. Instead it adopted an approach that seemed most useful for the present research question. What it has in common with most qualitative methods is that it started off with a fairly open question, and did not aim at testing a given theory.[96] The leading question was explorative, 'what are the perceptions of EMU ... ', and reflected the desire to make sense of the observation of apparent consensus on EMU in 1989–90. As it was not at all sure that the results of the interviews could be anticipated, the research aim was for a long time kept open. It was only after an initial examination of the data that it was decided that the theoretical insights resulting from the present research would turn out to benefit the 'theories of integration' rather than related theories, such as the theories of bureaucracies, elites, epistemic communities or interest group theories.

Turning to the second aim of this chapter the following section describes how the officials to be approached were selected, what the international context was during the interviews and how the interviews were set up and conducted.

Two periods

The interviews were conducted at two periods in time. The first round was held from February 1991 until mid-May of that year. In this period the first reports on EMU had come out. In October 1990 the Commission communication of EMU[97] came out, followed in early 1991 by the 'One Market, One Money Report' (OMOM), and also the OMOM background reports. The draft statutes of the ESCB circulated in December 1990. In addition, most Member States had released their proposals for a draft Treaty during the course of late 1990 to early 1991.[98] The Intergovernmental Conferences (IGCs) set up to amend the Rome Treaty were well under way in this period. Finally, it is worth noting that at the international political level most eyes were focused on Kuwait and Iraq, where the Gulf war was going on. Thus, one could characterize the period when the first interviews were conducted for the present research as one in which information about EMU was widely available, and most actors had taken a position on EMU. More generally, policies towards the principle of EMU had already been formulated. However, as the IGCs were still going on, actors constantly had to be prepared to respond to amendments with regard to the type of EMU and the rules that could come out of the political debate taking place in the IGCs.

The second round of interviews was held from late October 1992 until January 1993. The Treaty on European Union had been signed in February 1992 and it was to be ratified before the end of that year. However, in the following months there was great uncertainty over the ratification of the Maastricht Treaty. The immediate cause was the Danish rejection of the Treaty on European Union in the June referendum and negative opinion polls in the summer anticipating the outcome of the French referendum that was to be held in September. As a result exchange rates were under continuing pressure, which culmiated in September 1992 with the exit of the pound and (the so-called 'temporary') withdrawal of the lira from the ERM. When the French referendum came out only marginally in favour of 'Maastricht', it did not change the widespread idea in Europe that the Treaty might not be ratified. More importantly, the referendums and the exchange rate turbulence indicated that large numbers of European citizens did not support the Maastricht Treaty, and that financial markets were highly sceptical of the feasibility of the plans agreed to by the governments of the Twelve. Probably the publication of negative economic results in the course of 1992, which indicated the worsening of the economic recession in Continental Europe, contributed to this revived sense of Euro-pessimism.[99] The manifestation of economic gloom just before the internal market was to be completed was widely interpreted as very detrimental to the objective of integration and the stability, growth and welfare which integration meant to produce. Thus, the second period in which interviews were conducted can be characterized as one of scepticism towards the objectives of EMU.

Finding the right person

The interviews were held with those officials in the various organizations who were responsible for the policies concerning EMU. In most cases more than one person was in charge of these policies. In some cases interviews were conducted with more than one respondent successively. However, in most cases only one official of any given organization was interviewed.

To identify which person was in charge of EMU policies an exploratory round of interviews was conducted in November 1990 and officials in several European organizations were asked which persons were responsible for EMU policies in the various organizations in Britain, France and Germany. Officials of several Brussels-based institutions and organizations assisted in identifying the appropriate representatives of trade unions, employers' organizations and the monetary authorities in the three Member States. Officials who provided invaluable assistance in this phase included officials of the Economic and Social Committee, the European Commission (in particular DG II), the European Trade Unions Confederation, and UNICE (the European employers' organization). Moreover, several professors suggested some possible respondents.

The organizations in the Member States were approached, and a verification was made whether the person who had been recommended was indeed responsible for EMU policies. The fact that the research project was welcomed and approved of by several high-ranking officials in Brussels, who were willing to recommend the researcher, proved invaluable to obtain access to the 'right' respondents. One particular sentence appeared to have magical powers: 'I have been recommended by Mr "A" from the European ..., to talk to Mr "B" on the issue of EMU. Would it be possible to talk to him?'

Next, a phone call was made to the potential respondent. The scope of the research was explained briefly, and permission was asked to conduct an interview for a certain date. In 95 per cent of the cases the respondent was willing to cooperate. A date was set, and the questionnaire was sent in advance. This was done to enable the respondents to prepare themselves for answering the questions, and give them enough time to select documentation of policy statements on EMU. It also served as a last check on whether the interview was to be conducted with the right person.

On average the interviews took almost an hour and a half. The respondent would almost always have the questionnaire in front of him or her, and often had prepared a small dossier with policy statements and press releases. It can thus be said that respondents had made preparations (however minor) before the interview. In a few cases the time available to discuss the questionnaire was not sufficient, but when this happened the interview was continued at a later time. Only very few interviews were not completed.

In the second round, a year and a half later, the second interview was conducted with exactly the same persons in all cases but three. When the original respondent had left his or her position (which was the case at the CBI and the French Ministry of Finance) an interview was conducted with the respondent's successor.

The questionnaire in the second round was slightly altered to account for the changes arising from the signing of the Maastricht Treaty, but on the whole it remained the same.

The interviews

All interviews started in the same way. A final check was made to confirm that the official concerned was indeed responsible for EMU policy. The aim and scope of the research were explained and the interviewee was asked if he/she could indicate when he/she was speaking as a spokesperson for his/her institution, and when he/she was giving a personal view. Also it was asked whether he/she could be quoted. Although most respondents initially refused to give permission or disliked the idea of being quoted in person, most did accept the proposal that they should be quoted after having seen the citation in writing before it was published, or be quoted anonymously. The choice of this author was to quote the respondents anonymously.

During the course of the actual interview, in most cases the respondent took a considerable amount of time to answer the first questions, even if he/she lacked detailed knowledge on the position taken by the organization in the 1970s, especially regarding the Werner Report. Respondents would nevertheless go into extreme detail on the historical background of their organization, and supply what they *did* know. In these cases it seemed that they were telling stories to fill time rather than to answer the question. 'Story-telling' in the initial part of the interview was accepted for about ten minutes, before the interviewee was pressed to 'go back to the question'. In the later part of the interview an effort was made to stay close to the questionnaire.

5.4   The questionnaire

In both rounds of interviews a similar questionnaire was used. It was a semi-open set of six (in the first round) or seven (second round) questions. Below the rationale behind the various questions is given; also what was hoped to be learned from the answers and why certain passages were changed in the second round of interviews eighteen months later.[100]

Question 1

The first question (1a) asked about the attitude of the organization towards the earlier EMU plans (the Werner Report and the EMS):

> 1a. With regard to the earlier EMU plans (the Werner Report 1970–1 and the EMS), could you summarize what was the attitude of your organization towards these plans; did you support these plans, or demand any conditions?

This question was posed in order to understand what the historical perspective of the respondent was; whether he/she knew what the institution's policy objectives were in the past, that is, if his or her predecessors were in support of the Werner Report and the EMS or not, and why this was so.[101]

The next three questions (1b, 1c and 1d) were posed with the same objective in mind – checking the respondent's knowledge about priorities, interests and representation in the past:

1b. How did you perceive your priorities at that time, and how did these plans at that time serve your interests?
1c. Could you state what your interest was at that time (Werner Report 1970, EMS 1979) and is at the present moment (1989–90–91).
1d. Has the interest group you represent (or the reason why your institution was founded) changed during this period?

Questions 1e and 1f were included as more general philosophical questions on why EMU was desirable for the institution, and whether or not it was thought that the organization's interests coincided with those of the rest of the country.

1e. How does your function relate to this: more specifically, how does the EMU relate to the interest of your organization or institution?
1f. Could one state that what is in the best interest of your country, is in the best interest of your organization?

After having used these questions in the first round of interviews, this part of the questionnaire was slightly changed for the second round of interviews. Question 1a (1992) only went back to the Delors Plan, and the discussion of the Werner Report and the early phase of the EMS was dropped. It was feared that the respondents would be irritated if the interview started with exactly the same historical question in the second round as it had done in the first round. However, the question referring to the Delors Report was repeated, as it was quite possible that the respondent had changed his or her answer on the policies towards the Delors Report.

1a. (1992). With regard to the earlier Delors-plan, and the One Market One Money report, could you summarize what has been the attitude of your organization towards these plans; did you support these plans, or demand any conditions?

Furthermore, Questions 1b and 1c were merged as they were similar, which resulted in dropping Question 1b in the 1992 version. Questions 1d and 1f remained the same, whereas 1e was reformulated and the part on the 'function of the interviewee' was dropped. Information on the respondent's job profile was given in the brief introductory talk with the respondent, and hence that question could be omitted from the questionnaire.

Question 2

The second question in 1991 referred to the desirability of the EMU; under which conditions it would be desirable, and what its most important aim will be:

> 2a. If we take the Delors report (1989), and the Commission report 'One Market, One Money' (1990) as a starting point, would you agree that this kind of EMU is desirable, wholly or partly or not at all?
>
> 2b. Under which conditions would you totally agree with this kind of EMU?
>
> 2c. If you do not (wholly) agree, can you think of an alternative plan which suits your policies or interests better, and could you explain why the plan would be in your interest?
>
> 2d. With regard to the recent EMU plans mentioned above, what is the most important aim for you?

In the 1992 version of the questionnaire the Maastricht Treaty was compared with the earlier proposals, and again it was asked whether *this kind of EMU* was desirable and under which conditions, etc.:

> 2a. If we compare the Maastricht Treaty with the earlier plans (Delors Report and the Commission's 'One Market, One Money'), would you agree that this kind of EMU is desirable, wholly or partly or not at all?
>
> 2b. Under which conditions would you totally agree with the kind of EMU formulated in the Maastricht Treaty?
>
> 2c. If you do not (wholly) agree, can you think of an alternative plan which suits your policies or interests better, and could you explain why the plan would be in your interest?
>
> 2d. With regard to Maastricht, what is the most important aim for you?

This was a very crucial part of the interview as the respondent had to respond directly to the question, and give reasons why he or she actually was for or against EMU.

Question 3

The third set of questions referred to the assessment of the respondent of the probability that the actual EMU would resemble the type of EMU the respondent desired. In addition questions were asked about the lobbying process to safeguard the features of the EMU that the respondent considered important; whether coordination of similar organizations in other countries would take place; and whether the national cooperation would dominate the international trans-actor level:

3a. Having looked at all the 'pros' and the 'cons', could you indicate how probable it is that the European plans will contain the elements you have just mentioned as being important?

3b. How will you try to achieve this: who do you need to convince that your aims have to be part of the final EMU? (that is, where are you going to lobby?).

3c. Do you think you would be working together with similar organizations in other member states?

3d. Can you indicate whether during the EMU, there is more likely to be a 'national interest' (converging the different interests within the member state) or a 'European interest group' or 'European institutional interest' (interest groups or institutions of the different member states uniting). Can you indicate for which 'questions' or 'policies' this is valid?

The last part of the question in particular needed clarification. Usually it was explained as meaning whether under EMU trade unions, for instance, would more than before cooperate with trade unions in other countries or, alternatively, with the business organizations in their own country. Most interviewees did not mention the questions or policies where increased coordination would take place.

In the 1992 questionnaire the latter part of the question was changed and examples were supplied:

3c. Do you think you would be working together with similar organizations in other member states?

3d. What do you foresee in the final phase of EMU:
   – increasing nationalism (uniting of all national economic actors in each member state);
   – a division of Europe into groups or blocks; a multi-speed Europe;

– there is more likely to be a 'national interest' (combining the different interests within the member state) than 'European interest group' or 'European institutional interest' (interest groups or institutions of the different member states uniting). Can you indicate for which 'questions' or 'policies' this is valid?

Question 4

The fourth question remained the same in both periods.[102] Its emphasis is on the type of EMU that the actor perceives as being most realistic (a repetition question), and he/she is asked to give the implication of EMU for monetary and budgetary policies of his/her national governments. It then goes on to ask about *spill-over* effects to other policy areas, on the people they represent, and on their organizational structure:

4a. How do you think at this moment that the EMU will look when it is completed?

4b. What do you think will be its effect on monetary and budgetary policies (and the freedoms of the governments of the member states to decide them)?

4c. What do you think will be the effect of this EMU on other policies (if you like, in combination with the other plans, that is, the internal market)?
– fiscal policy: what will happen to taxes (direct and indirect);
– social policy: your country as compared to other member states;
– unemployment;
– national social security system;
– economic growth;
– competitive position of your country *vis-à-vis* other countries;
– country-specific shocks;

4d. What do you think would be the effect of the EMU on the group you represent, or your major policy aims?

4e. Would it change anything in the structure of your organization?

It was hoped that Questions 4d and 4e would make the respondent give some self-disclosure on how the dynamics of the integration process would be perceived. It was expected that the respondent would recognize that in both cases EMU would give rise to changes.

Question 6

Question 6 was exactly the same in both periods.[103] It asks about the views on EMU of the other actors (social partners and monetary authorities) in the same country and whether decision-makers take notice of the demands of social partners and monetary authorities:

> 6a. What do you think are the views of trade unions, employers' organizations, multinationals, the Treasury, and the Bank of England towards EMU?[104] Do you think they agree with the EMU plans, as mentioned above, wholly or partly: which demands do they have?
> 6b. In decision-making concerning EMU, how much notice do you think the decision-makers take of the opinions or the demands of the above-mentioned organizations and institutions?

Question 7

The closing question was included to allow the interviewee to add miscellaneous information, or to deal with any questions that had been insufficiently answered:

> Is there anything you would like to add to this conversation on the political implications of EMU?

Additional question in the 1992 questionnaire: Question 5

In 1992 the respondents were asked about the problems of 'Europessimism', the ERM crisis and the ratification problems that had arisen in 1992. A set of questions was added into the questionnaire. The group of questions followed the spill-over Question 4 and was, hence, numbered Question 5. The closing two questions were therefore renumbered Question 6 and Question 7.

> 5a. Why did the period after 'Maastricht' turn out to be a crisis; where did it go wrong?
> 5b. How will your country have to change in order to join the third phase of EMU, that is, institutional changes in your central banking system, and which costs will the government and the people have to carry during the transition period?
> 5c. Do you see an alternative to Maastricht, in other words, is there a way back, or another way?
> 5d. If I were to suggest that EMU or the Maastricht Treaty is a 'Trojan Horse', would you agree?
> 5e. Is it necessary to inform the general public, the people, about the meaning, importance or relevance of EMU?
> 5f. What would be your explanation of what EMU is, and why we need it?

From the first round of interviews and some study into the origins of negative public opinion towards the EMU and the Maastricht Treaty, some assumptions were derived. These assumptions fed into Question 5 which was posed in the 1992 interview. First the respondent was asked what his or her own perception was concerning what factors contributed to the negative mood in Europe concerning the Maastricht Treaty (Question 5a). A more general assumption of the study was that the experts had kept the European integration process too much to themselves, and ultimately had avoided to inform the general public. Thus, the respondent was asked whether he/she thought it was necessary to inform the public (Question 5e).

The research design identified five specific assumptions which might have contributed to the negative sentiments held among the public about Maastricht and the EMU in 1992. First, the public may have been afraid about the possible implications of the EMU process, about adjustments that would have to take place in their country, and how high the costs would be in the transition period to full EMU (Question 5b). Second, the policy-makers had developed the Maastricht package in such a way that it appeared very difficult to stop the process (Question 5c). As the actors in the process had been bureaucrats, technicians and government officials, who negotiated behind closed doors, and used language incomprehensible to the public, some people might have been led to believe that it was a cover-up for something else (Question 5d). Finally, the text in the Maastricht Treaty had become so complicated, and its possible implications so diverse, that no actor could actually explain to a general public in easy and clear terms what the EMU implied, and why it was necessary (Question 5f).

5.5   Conclusion

This chapter has given a background to the method used in the present study. It has indicated why the use of interviews was chosen as a way to collect the data, how the respondents were identified, approached and interviewed, and finally what questions were posed, and why they served to clarify the central research question. It should be mentioned here, however, that the following chapters do not discuss all the questions that were asked to the respondents. It was decided to focus on Questions 1, 2 and 4. The omission of the analysis on Questions 3, 5 and 7 was decided as it would make the present study too lengthy. Moreover, it seemed that Questions 1, 2 and 4 were the core questions. The other questions provided additional insights which operated as 'control' questions.[105]

6
Perceptions of Economic and Monetary Integration

As set out in Chapter 5, the interviews conducted for this research had several aims, such as obtaining the views of the actors on the policies of their organizations towards the Werner Report, the Delors Report and the Maastricht Treaty, as well as obtaining views on, for example, the perceived spill-over effects of EMU on other policy areas, such as fiscal and social policies. This chapter offers a question-by-question report of the replies which the interviewees gave to the questions posed to them in two periods. The first round of interviews was held in the winter and spring of 1991, and the second round was conducted in the autumn of 1992.

This chapter offers a descriptive, comprehensive survey of the perceptions of EMU as held by the various actors subject to this study. It will discuss only the data gathered in the interviews. Additional sources are referred to in notes and references. In the following chapter an analysis of these perceptions will be made and some comparisons will be drawn. Chapter 7 provides both a 'horizontal' and 'vertical' comparison. The horizontal comparison examines the perceptions of the actors across countries (for example, the attitudes of trade unions across the three countries) as well as the dominant views of 'the trade unions' with dominant views of 'the employers' organizations'. The vertical comparison looks at the perceptions of the actors *within* one country (for example comparing the perceptions of all British actors, as well as comparing the 'typical' British view with the 'typical' French view).

The organization of this chapter is as follows. In Sections 6.1 through 6.3 a question-by-question report is given of the responses given in the two interviews. The responses to the questions are reported in a fixed order; that is, the answers of the central banks and Finance Ministries in the three countries are reported first, followed by those of the employers' organizations and those of the trade unions last. In Section 6.4 a short summary of the main findings is given.

6.1   Question 1: History of EMU: why Werner/EMS were (not) desirable – the interests of the organization at that time

1a. *(1991).*[106] *With regard to the earlier EMU plans (the Werner Report 1970–1 and the EMS), could you summarize what the attitude of your organization was towards these plans; did you support these plans, or demand any conditions?*

1a. *(1992). With regard to the earlier Delors plan, and the One Market One Money report, could you summarize the attitude of your organization towards these plans; did you support these plans, or demand any conditions?*

1b. *Could you state the interests of your institution? Has there been any change in the interests of your institution since the earliest monetary union plans (Werner and EMS), up until today. Have these interests recently changed?*

1c. *Has the interest group you represent (or the reason why your institution was founded) changed during this period?*

1d. *How does economic and monetary union relate to the interest of your organization or institution?*

1f. *Could one state that what is in the best interest of your country, is in the best interest of your organization?*

Monetary authorities – central banks and Ministries of Finance on Werner and EMS

The monetary authorities of Britain, France and Germany all argued that the time was not right in the 1970s for EMU. The general idea among officials of central banks and Ministries of Finance was that the original six had drafted a plan that was premature and not workable, as it was a report which tried to compromise between two incompatible schools of thought on how to reach EMU, that is, the 'economist' and the 'monetarist' approach.

The British monetary authorities

Even though Britain was not a member of the EEC during the drafting and adoption of the Werner Plan on EMU, the British monetary authorities *did* discuss the plans. At the time of the creation of the EMS, in 1979, both monetary authorities were convinced that the pound should stay out of the ERM, but the Bank of England was at an earlier stage than HM Treasury interested in pegging the pound to the DM, in order to achieve low inflation.

The Bank of England

The view of a Bank of England (BoE) official on the Werner Plan was that it was not taken seriously in the BoE. Of course, the UK was not yet a Member State of the EEC when the plan was drafted, but it was generally thought in the BoE that an EMU might be feasible in the next century.

The policies of the BoE in the late 1970s were aimed at trying to bring inflation rates down. This was an objective to be reached at whatever immediate cost to the country in the short run, as it would be necessary for future growth and employment. A BoE official explained that in the 1980s the top priority was getting inflation down, the belief being that there was not a trade-off between getting inflation down and unemployment. On the contrary, it was thought that reducing inflation was a necessary condition for sustainable growth and a low level of unemployment. The BoE abandoned the idea of using a domestic nominal anchor after it had become clear that the BoE was not receiving 'the right signals from the markets'. It turned to look for an external nominal anchor, and since 1985 its officials thought that the ERM might offer such an anchor.

> Until 1985 monetary policies were pursued in a purely judgemental way, on the basis of a set of indicators. Increasingly it became accepted in the Bank that membership of the ERM would offer a kind of commitment to an external nominal anchor, that looked to be the solution to our problem. ... So the crucial thing for us was to decide, and to persuade the government I suppose, to join the exchange rate mechanism.[107]

Her Majesty's Treasury

The British Treasury's view on the early European monetary integration plans, including the Werner Report, was that its main objectives were formally accepted, though the Treasury did not agree to the particular interpretation of these plans as held by the Member States of the EEC. That is, the Treasury did not accept that the objective was to create a single currency.

> The British have always accepted the formal objectives of EMU plans but have not shared the particular view of what EMU means in practice. The objective was: price stability, higher growth and full employment. EMU does not mean a single currency.[108]

With regard to the full EMS participation it was argued in the 1991 interview that the Treasury had been saying for ten years that the pound would join the ERM when the time was right, and now they had joined.

When asked why the time had not been right earlier three main reasons were given. Firstly, the existence of North-Sea Oil meant that the pound reacted differently to external shocks than did the other ERM currencies. Second, towards the end of the 1980s Britain was running at a higher level of demand and activity than were the others. This fact, in turn, resulted in high levels of inflation in Britain compared to those countries whose currencies were already in the ERM. Third, as the process of capital liberalization in Europe was almost completed it was considered important for the benefit of all members that the economies would be converging before the pound joined in. The argument was that 'if another major currency came in...with an economy that was not exactly right, this could be disruptive. Not only to the UK but also to the rest of the ERM. So we wanted to join when the economies were converging, which was indeed the case when we joined, as inflation was coming down.'[109]

The French monetary authorities

The officials of the French monetary authorities did not elaborate extensively on their policies towards and interests in the Werner Report. With regard to the EMS they stated they had been very much in favour of its creation. Since 1983 the policies have been directed at becoming one of the best-performing countries in the EMS, in terms of currency stability, low inflation rates and competitiveness. It was argued by an official that in 1983 'France made a choice for Europe'.

The Banque de France

In the 1991 interview a Banque de France (BdF) official argued that the BdF has always been in support of creating some kind of European monetary order as it was thought to favour Europe's interior stability and stable prices, and that it would offer a possibility for successful monetary policies. It had been very supportive of the EMS for that reason.

With regard to the Werner Report it was stated that the main difference between the EMU plan in the 1970s, and the EMS in 1979, is that during the construction of the latter no monetary order existed. France has held a very positive view towards the EMS, arguing that its only goal at the time was to reconstruct a monetary order in Europe after the collapse of the international monetary order, that is, the Bretton Woods system, in the early 1970s.

The French Finance Ministry

The official interviewed in the *Ministère des Finances et du Budget*, the French Finance Ministry (FFM), supplied no specific view on the Werner Plan. He did however stress the difference in economic beliefs held by officials in the Finance Ministry in the 1970s compared to those held today. In the early 1970s the conduct of economic and monetary policies in general, and the role of inflation in particular, was perceived differently from the way it has been perceived since the 1980s. In the early 1970s there were people in the FFM who supported Keynesian policies. There were those who believed that some inflation would benefit economic growth. It was to many still not very clear that it would be in the best interest of a medium-sized European country, such as France, to integrate completely in Europe. This has now been 'fully understood' according to this official. Moreover, he stressed that now it is considered important that Europe is strong and coherent so that it can stand up strong in a world with powers such as Japan and the US. Given this context, the support for Europe is now much stronger than 15 or 20 years ago.[110]

With regard to the EMS he argued that the FFM had perhaps two regrets. First, in 1979 and 1980 the system was not centred around the Ecu, which the French proposed, but functioned via bilateral parities. The institutionalized role of the Ecu in those early years was very limited. A second regret was that the EMS never moved beyond stage 1, which was a possibility foreseen in the original EMS plans, but which never materialized.

The official stressed that in 1983 a large debate took place in France on the question of whether or not the constraints that the EMS posed were an asset for France. The Mitterrand government at the time decided it was beneficial for the country to take part in the EMS and aim for a 'franc fort'. That year France decided to make a choice for a 'monetary Europe'.[111]

The priority of the *Direction du Trésor* (the Treasury department of the French Ministry of Finance) in the 1980s, according to an official, was to conduct economic policies in such a way that inflation rates would be kept down, placing France among the EMS countries with the lowest inflation. It was believed this would also make it one of the most competitive.[112]

The German monetary authorities

The German monetary authorities were in favour of the Werner Plan, but were on the side of the 'economists'. In their view the economic conditions would have to be right before moving towards fixed exchange rates. This attitude also influenced the shaping of the EMS.

The Bundesbank

An official of the Bundesbank explained that his institution was involved in the setting up of both the Werner Plan and the EMS. In both cases they tried to construct it according to the 'economist' principles. Whether or not it was in the Bundesbank's interest for Germany to join the EMS was considered by Bundesbank officials a matter of debate. The widely held view was that it was not the best time to set it up. There was scepticism in the Bundesbank over whether the EMS, as it was planned by Schmidt and Giscard d'Estaing, was going to be workable.[113]

The sceptical attitude was directly related to the timing and the international context of the birth of the EMS, that is, the second oil crisis, high inflation rates in many countries and the American monetary authorities not yet having adopted monetary discipline. However, as it was a political choice made by the German government, the Bundesbank had no choice but to take part in its institutional set-up, and tried to do so in an 'economist' manner. After a critical initial phase the EMS proved to be successful as all Member States were dedicated to ensure that the EMS functioned well. Their goodwill, for example, was demonstrated by the fact that central banks undertook intra-marginal interventions, mostly in DM, which the Bundesbank tolerated.

For the Bundesbank to participate in the EMS implied that conflict *could* arise between two objectives, that is, between the core objective of the Bundesbank, 'price stability', and the objective of the EMS, 'exchange rate stability'. The Bundesbank insisted that at the time they had insisted that, if a choice had to be made, the Bundesbank would not endanger its mandate of securing price stability. The Bundesbank official stressed that the political authorities accepted this.

> The Bonn government agreed that if it really came to the crunch, if the intervention obligations were to impair the monetary policy with the price stability objective in mind, the obligation to intervene would have to give in. In other words, the Bundesbank could in case of serious conflict have opted out of the intervention obligation.[114]

The EMS also served the Bundesbank's interests of securing price stability, in that it ensured that other countries increasingly accepted price stability as a primary objective as well; that is, other countries took the monetary policy of the Bundesbank as their anchor. It was argued that the system as it has evolved has probably helped some countries, such as France, to overcome their inflationary bias. That was considered to serve the Bundesbank's interests as well. 'Obviously, when one country thinks that price stability should be the prime objective it is helpful if other countries also pursue that objective.'[115]

Another reason why the EMS served the Bundesbank's interests was that Member States that relied on 'intra-marginal interventions', had to ensure that monetary conditions were in place to support their monetary interventions so as to make them effective. This implied that the EMS did not lead to 'undue DM liquidity creation' as was the case with interventions at the margin. Moreover, it was argued that the working of the EMS led to a change in monetary behaviour with countries taking the Bundesbank's policy as their anchor (such as France). Thus, over time this led to a change in behaviour in monetary policy of other countries.[116] Nevertheless, the official stressed that the EMS's success was unexpected, 'The bottom line is that the system worked much better than many of us thought.'[117]

The German Finance Ministry

The Werner Report was perceived by a German Finance Ministry (GFM) official to have come about in circumstances very similar to those that gave rise to the launching of the EMU plan in the late 1980s. This provoked raising a question similar to the one posed in the late 1980s. In 1969 the transition period had ended for the creation of the common market. At the time it led to the same type of question being posed as the one in the late 1980s: 'Do we remain in this stage of integration, which basically consists of a "more developed" Free Trade Area, or will we take the integration of the Community a step further.'[118] The question was answered the same way, that is, an Economic and Monetary Union was required.

Three reasons were provided by this official as to why the plan failed to mature: first, the collapse of the Bretton Woods system; second, the shock given by the first and second oil crises; and third, the policy responses to address these difficulties differed strongly from region to region. The core difference between the Werner Report and the Delors Report, in the view of the interviewee, is that the Delors Report responded to a Community that has reached *a higher stage* of integration by completing the Single Market.

Social partners on Werner and EMS

Employers' organizations

The employers' organizations in all three countries had two central lines of argument. First, a single currency has always been considered an ideal that was worth aiming at, even though its timing would be a matter of debate, that is, a political decision. Second, the organizations wanted to refrain from taking political positions. The 'objective' *economic* aims were part of their scope of policy-making.

Officials of two of the three national employers' organizations that were questioned about their policies towards the Werner Plan in the 1970s could not state their organizations' views. The official of the *Confederation of British Industry* (CBI) responded that the CBI did not have a strong view either against or in favour, as it was new ground to them. However, he stated that in retrospect it would have been a plan they supported: 'Looking back, if we could do that, we would certainly be supporters of the Werner Report in its ultimate aim, which is essentially closer integration within Europe and maybe a single currency at the end of it.'[119] A representative of the French *Conseil National du Patronat Français* (CNPF) stated that '[T]wenty years ago nobody believed much in monetary union, even with the Werner Report.'[120]

The official representing the *Bundesverband der Deutschen Industrie* (BDI), however, was very well informed about his organization's attitudes towards the early plans. He explained that the BDI supported the Werner Plan from the start, but warned of the risks of a premature start. It was stated that the BDI posed clear conditions (see also BDI, 1990a). The integration had to proceed on the basis of price stability. It would be necessary to have the various countries meet the necessary conditions. This would imply stronger convergence on the basis of price stability, as that was believed to provide a solid basis for the functioning of integration also in the monetary sphere.[121]

The BDI official stressed that the reason why the Werner Plan failed was due to the oil crises and the turbulence in the international foreign currency markets.[122] At that time the Member States had a different notion of integration; a lot was expected of it, though the countries did not yet have converging policies. The BDI official identified two main differences with the 1970s which provided favourable conditions for the creation of the EMU plan in 1989. First, in the late 1980s monetary policies had slowly become convergent, as a result of 10 years EMS. Second, the countries were now responding to a larger global threat and therefore bound to cooperate.[123]

As regards the policies towards the creation and functioning of the EMS the organizations held different views. The BDI was more sceptical about the set-up of the EMS because it feared that the system would not work, as countries would not pursue monetary policies directed towards low inflation. Of course, eventually it proved to operate well, also as a mechanism for discipline. However, in the view of this BDI official, the EMS's success was in part a result of an international phenomenon, namely the lowering of inflation rates which also took place in countries not participating in the EMS.

The British CBI official stated that it took the business community in the UK some time 'to get tuned in that ERM was a good thing'.[124] It was not until 1985 that it became formal policy of the CBI to support the idea of the pound entering the Exchange Rate Mechanism (ERM).[125] The main benefit of ERM entry would be exchange rate stability. Stable rates were considered paramount for business planning, exports and investments. However, talking in the early 1990s the respondent stressed that inflation rates were still very high in Britain, and that reducing inflation had become the main priority. The CBI was very interested in the experience of the French and the Italians, who went into the EMS with high inflation rates, and had managed to bring them down while participating in it.[126] The official of the French employers' organization, CNPF, again, did not elaborate on their views on the early EMS.

Trade unions

Trade unions in Britain, France and Germany had divergent views on 'Europe' in the 1970s and 1980s. The respondents said that trade unions in those years were not very interested in European monetary integration. If anything, they were sceptical towards these plans. For the trade union confederations in all three countries it seems that the interests of trade unions were long considered to lie at home rather than in Europe.

TUC

In the 1970s the British *Trades Union Congress* (TUC) was opposed to the Common Market. When the Werner Plan came out the TUC thought it was 'pie in the sky'. A TUC official stated that 'there was no way in which you could reach Economic and Monetary Union, indeed even without opposition from Britain, the Werner Report just went nowhere. I think it was a very theoretical debate.'[127] In 1975, when it came to a referendum on Britain's membership in the EC, the TUC advised voting against. When the referendum outcome was 2 : 1 in favour the TUC decided to participate in EC institutions, but they still refused to go to the meetings that the Commission proposed, because they were opposed to the Common Market (see also Brierly, 1987).

This opposition was based on several issues. There were concerns about British industry, and about the size of Britain's contribution to the EC budget, and also issues related to agricultural policy: 'If you read back the debates about whether Britain should join the Common Market, it was almost obsessed by the price of butter.'[128]

Reflecting on this period, the TUC official thought that the discussion at the time was 'rather small-scaled'. With regard to the domestic politics of the second half of the 1970s the respondent gave a personal account of the history. The policy choices were coloured by the experience of high inflation and high unemployment of the 1970s, and the 'obsession' to keep the Labour Party in power.[129] He reiterated the background:

> In the early 1970s unemployment went up to one million, which at the time was seen as catastrophically high. We were also worried about inflation, which went up to 20–25% in 1975. That led us into the Social Contract – voluntary wage constraints with the government. Keeping that show on the road was the major priority. By 1978 we could no longer maintain an agreement with the Labour government on a voluntary incomes policy. In 1979, following a number of strikes in the public services, Mrs Thatcher came to power, with a dominant aim of getting inflation down and nothing else.[130]

This official summarized the main policy aims of the TUC as follows. Until 1975 absolute priority was to reduce unemployment, whereas after 'the hard lesson with the IMF and the Social Contract' it became clear that it was also necessary to direct policies at reducing inflation.

Finally, with regard to the EMS, this TUC official responded that the TUC in theory regarded fixed exchange rates to be preferred above flexible rates, as they were concerned about large capital flows. However, the whole issue was, compared to other issues of economic policy-making, only of minor importance.[131]

French trade unions

The various French trade union confederations were, and still are today, very far apart in their opinions on policy-making in general, and on Europe in particular (see *inter alia* ETUC, 1987; Groux and Mouriaux, 1992; Landier, 1981). Their positions range from much in favour to very much opposed. The *Confédération Française Démocratique du Travail* (CFDT) holds a positive view towards European integration, *Force Ouvrière* (FO) is moderately in favour of the European project, whereas the *Confédération Générale du Travail* (CGT) is bluntly opposed.

With regard to the Werner Report a CFDT official mentioned that the report was abandoned very quickly. She stated that the EMS had had positive and negative effects for the French economy. The CFDT is 'à priori' in favour of the construction of Europe. However, the concerns regarding the EMS and EMU plans are related to the possibility of having 'monetarism', that is, too much emphasis on monetary policy would have negative consequences for employment and growth: '[W]e are apprehensive about the purely monetary aspects, "monetarism", and its consequences on employment and on growth.'[132] The officials of the FO were more reserved about the whole EMU project. The CGT was bluntly opposed. A CGT official explained that the CGT had not written or published a single document or policy statement on EMU. They did not want to contribute to the debate.

DGB

The official of the German *Deutscher Gewerkschaftsbund* (DGB) stated that his organization was very inward-looking in the 1970s and he claimed that the DGB did not even have a position on 'Europe' until the mid-1980s.[133] The interviewee emphasized that in the 1970s the DGB had a much more domestic perspective compared to the late 1980s and early 1990s. 'Europe was not the political theme. We did not have the clearly differentiated positions we have today.'[134]

This DGB official explained that the main difference between the early 1970s and 1990s was that recently the awareness had become manifest that national economic policy-making eventually is ineffective if it is not properly coordinated among European Member States. In the 1970s the Member States had also shared this awareness, but believed that national solutions could be found. A second difference was related to international coordination. In the 1970s this coordination had been apparent, but still happened on a voluntary basis. Due to the Internal Market the coordination has become more obligatory, which creates the possibility for real international economic coordination.

Summarizing Question 1: 'Policies towards Werner and EMS'

Monetary authorities

Not all monetary authorities elaborated in detail on their organization's views on the Werner Report. The ones that did stressed the fact that it was a plan that resembled the Delors Report; it set out to create EMU and envisaged a three-staged plan to achieve it. The reason given as to why it did not materialize was that it encountered unfortunate international conditions which were subsequently met with divergent domestic policy responses.

The event that led to the drafting of the Werner Report was the completion of the customs union. The Bretton Woods system provided a system of fixed exchange rates. In the late 1960s and early 1970s there was the political will to continue along the path of integration but Europe had not yet been struck by the serious economic problems of the 1970s.

The British monetary authorities stressed they had supported the EMU aim, but disagreed that it required the introduction of a single currency. The French emphasized that they welcomed the plan as a part of constructing a monetary Europe. The German monetary authorities supported the Werner Plan, but took an 'economist view'.

The end of the Bretton Woods system, the oil crisis, the recession of the mid-1970s and the diverging responses of national governments to these changes in the economic and monetary circumstances, were seen as the crucial factors contributing to the failure of the materialization of the Werner Plan. The specific problems of inflation and unemployment and the search for separate *national* solutions to these problems fuelled resistance to adjust national policies which would be needed to create EMU in Europe. Clearly, the difference in opinion between the monetary authorities concerning how to achieve EMU and disagreement concerning the necessary conditions that had to be fulfilled before completing EMU were detrimental to the Werner Plan.

The EMS was received with great scepticism. The early success of the EMS was due to the French desire to build Europe, reflected in the dramatic turn-around by the 1983 Mitterrand government from its socialist experiment and the inflation history. The Bundesbank welcomed the neighbouring countries adopting more stringent monetary policies, underlining this by agreeing to support their currencies with interventions when necessary.

Social partners

Employers' organizations were in favour of the principle of EMU for economic reasons, but the British and French were reluctant to take a political stand on which form it would take, or when and under which conditions it would take place. The BDI was more outspoken on the EMU aim, and clarified that adopting an EMU would imply having to think about 'economic' aspects as well. Trade unions had long been oriented towards national interests, and did not perceive European economic and monetary integration as being at the top of their agenda.

With respect to the EMS, the employers' organizations and trade unions were sceptical at first, but as the international environment changed, and countries adjusted policies towards similar aims of combating inflation, and seriously trying to maintain stable exchange rates, the attitude towards EMS changed from scepticism towards favouring the process. Trade unions stated that they, at first, were more focused on national targets.

Comparing Werner with Delors

From the responses to Question 1 a picture emerges about the similarities and differences between the Werner Report and the Delors Report. Six points are discerned about how the plans emerged against a similar background.

1. The completion of the customs union in 1968 favoured the drafting of the Werner Report. In the case of the Delors Report it was the Single Market that was almost completed. In both cases it was thought that integration *had to continue.*
2. The existing monetary order of Bretton Woods in the late 1960s and early 1970s implied that the Member States were already operating in a regime of fixed exchange rates. The same was true in the late 1980s with the ERM providing stable exchange rates.
3. The Werner Report resembled the Delors Report, in that they both had three stages, aimed at a single currency or fixed exchange rates, and politically they tried to merge the economist and the monetarist views. The Werner Report was however too much of a compromise between the 'economists' and the 'monetarists'. The Delors Report came after the countries had come to more consensus concerning the aim of monetary policy and the need for some economic convergence to flank monetary integration.
4. The Werner and Delors Plans were in part a response to frustration about dollar dominance.
5. Global structural and cyclical economic and monetary changes in the 1970s were the immediate cause of abandoning the Werner Plan. These changes were: the collapse of the Bretton Woods, the oil crises, the recession of 1975 and the stagflation of the late 1970s.
6. The final blows to the Werner Report were the subsequent various national responses to these changes in terms of economic and monetary policies, that is, government spending, inflation and interest rate policies. In the case of the Delors Report the turbulent events of 1992 are discussed below, which gave rise to enormous pressure

to abandon the EMU plan. It will be seen below whether the respondents changed their minds and opted for domestic solutions (as they had done in the 1970s), or still acted in concert.

6.2   Question 2: Under which conditions is EMU desirable? Attitudes towards the Delors Report, 'One Market, One Money' and the Maastricht Treaty

2a. (1991). If we take the Delors Report as a starting point, would you agree that this kind of EMU is desirable, wholly, partly or not at all?

2a. (1992). If we compare the Maastricht Treaty with the earlier plans (Delors Report and the Commission's 'One Market, One Money'), would you agree that this kind of EMU is desirable, wholly, partly or not at all?

2b. Under which conditions would you totally agree with the kind of EMU formulated in the Maastricht Treaty?

2c. If you do not (wholly) agree, can you think of an alternative plan which suits your policies or interests better, and could you explain why the plan would be in your interest?

2d. With regard to Maastricht, what is the most important aim for you?

Monetary authorities

All central bank governors of the twelve EC Member States participated in the drafting of the 1989 Delors Report on EMU. Thus, not surprisingly, the respondents of central banks of Britain, France and Germany all agreed in 1991 that the Delors Report was a feasible blueprint. However, they had not commented on the question whether it should be implemented. Especially its timing was to be left to the political bodies to decide. As both the Banque de France and the Bank of England were executive agents of the government in 1991 and 1992 – when the interviews for this research were conducted – one would expect the monetary authorities in these countries to have similar views. This is, however, not the case; for example, the Bank of England is less disapproving of the prospect of joining EMU than is Her Majesty's Treasury.

The Bank of England and the Treasury

In 1991 a Bank of England official explicitly stated that the governor of the Bank of England, Sir Robin Leigh-Pemberton, has always said that the Delors Report presented a workable procedure for moving towards

EMU. The governor did not answer the question of whether one would *want* to adopt a monetary union. That was considered a political decision, on which the governor was not asked to pronounce. One official in a 1991 interview stated:

> The Bank's official view on the question of the desirability of EMU is that we are at the moment not convinced that economically the case has been made, but we have a fairly open mind on it and we could be convinced, and we are certainly not ruling it out.[135]

In the 1992 interview the same official even argued that EMU is very desirable in the longer term. From this statement it becomes clear that the Bank of England principally has a positive attitude towards EMU (see also Leigh-Pemberton, 1992).

Her Majesty's Treasury, however, was in the same period much more explicitly sceptical of setting up an EMU in the short term. In the 1991 interview with a Treasury official the hesitancy of the British government came out much more clearly:

> It is difficult to say for us now that we would *ever* agree to EMU. ... But the important thing for us is, which is different from many of our partners in the EC, who say: 'Yes there will be one day an EMU in the European Community'. We say: 'There *might* be.' We cannot say now that the answer is definitely 'yes'.[136]

The Treasury has clearly taken a more cautious stand towards EMU. Its main fear is that EMU as perceived by the other Member States might move beyond the aims that the Treasury wants; that is, transfer too much power to Brussels. To ensure that EMU stops well before an overly federal set-up, its strategy in the IGCs was to be very much opposed to most initiatives, or very reluctant to accept far-reaching proposals. In any case, the *attitude* set out by the Treasury was certainly more reserved than that of the Bank of England.

In 1991 the Bank of England mentioned three conditions that had to be met in order for it to agree with EMU. It would imply, first, the existence of the Single Market with free capital movements. Second, EMU would need to presuppose only very limited restrictions on fiscal policies.[137] The latter could be sufficiently coordinated by peer group pressure, and not, as the Delors Report recommended, by rigid mandatory rules on fiscal deficits. Third, it was argued that the importance of having a single currency should not be over-emphasized;

achieving low inflation was more important (see also Leigh-Pemberton, 1991c).

In 1992 the Bank of England no longer opposed restrictions on fiscal policies. Compared to the 1991 interview a difference occurred on fiscal policy and the convergence criteria:

> Compared to 1991 a difference in opinion on fiscal rigidities exists. It is still the view of the government that fiscal autonomy needs to be continued, whereas the central bank governors are more of the opinion that we need safeguards – fiscal guidelines – to prevent fiscal policy excesses. ... [T]he compromise reached was acceptable for us, that is, that in the event of fiscal excesses a procedure exists with guidelines rather than definite figures.[138]

In addition it was argued that the currencies should be locked only if the countries concerned are sufficiently alike to allow this or the adoption of a single currency, thereby forming an 'Optimum Currency Area'.[139]

In 1991 the Treasury's views of what EMU would consist of meant that participating countries would have to comply with certain rules, namely: no bail-out and no monetary financing of the budget. However, legal rules on budgetary deficits were considered by the Treasury unacceptable for two reasons. To conduct budgetary policies is a central power of the parliament and 'it would be difficult to know what is always the right fiscal policy, at all times, for all countries'.[140]

In the same interview the Treasury professed the need for economic convergence in several areas before EMU could be set up. The respondent mentioned four areas: 'inflation, interest rates, budget policies, but also unemployment rates in so far as they are an indicator of the flexibility of the economy'.[141] Also, it was considered important that accountability is safeguarded. In the British proposals the ECB – or 'European Monetary Fund (EMF)' as it is called in the Hard Ecu Plan – would have to be politically accountable to the Ecofin Council (see also Bank of England, 1990). This is not the case with the ECB, which was considered unfortunate.

Political conditions were much more difficult to agree to 'because we start with the vision that we are not committed anyway'.[142] However, the reason the Treasury was taking part in the 1991 IGC negotiations was that it wanted to be part of the building process. When it became clear that nothing could stop the eleven Member States from creating EMU – not even British opposition to it – the British authorities decided to take part in its construction, but maintain the right to decide in the end whether or not to join.

> We cannot stand back and say: 'You decide what you want, and then we'll decide whether or not we'll join. We'll be *in there* and make our contribution. And when we come out with a package, we'll say: 'yes', 'no' or 'maybe' – it could be *that* as well.[143]

In October 1992, a month after sthe British pound and the Italian lira had left the ERM, a Treasury official argued that obviously not *only* economic convergence will determine whether British politicians decide whether or not the time is right to join EMU; various aspects of domestic politics and the state of the economy are going to influence the voting behaviour of parliamentarians, hence also whether or not to opt out of the EMU project. Leaving aside its political sensitivity, the decision of whether or not to join the single currency would depend on the perceived costs at the moment of joining. The Treasury official mentioned that they would be looking at two points. First, judging whether the participating economies could operate in EMU without large costs, thereby using the *convergence criteria in the Treaty* (see also HM Treasury, 1992). Second, whether the labour market is sufficiently flexible. The argument being that if adjustment does not happen via labour mobility or exchange rates, it in his view would have to come through wage adjustment. 'If you have an inflexible labour market, where wages do not easily adjust, then there could be problems in a single currency, because you haven't got any other means of making adjustments except unemployment'.[144] Thus it becomes clear that the view of the Treasury on the restrictions on budgetary and fiscal policies changed between 1991 and 1992. In 1991 it opposed strict rules, whereas in 1992 it welcomed the convergence criteria, which include these rules. The final point to be made is that the Treasury insists that labour market flexibility is extremely important for the success of the single currency.

La Banque de France and the French Finance Ministry

Similar to the institutional arrangement in Britain, the Banque de France was still formally under national government control during 1991 and 1992. The BdF was made independent from the government only on 1 January 1994. Thus, here too one would expect similar views between the French central bank and the French Ministry of Finance. In fact, this does indeed seem to be the case, if only because of their very strong 'pro-Europe' sentiments.

When a French Finance Ministry (FFM) official was asked in 1991 whether he thought Economic and Monetary Union was desirable, he responded that the Finance Ministry agreed with the central aims of the Delors Report, namely organizing the single currency and setting up a single independent European Central Bank. The FFM was less accepting of other elements in the Delors Report. First, it disagreed that even more redistributive funds would be needed to support the weaker regions, i.e. the doubling of the structural funds that was agreed to for the completion of the Internal Market would be sufficient. Second, the FFM envisaged that the exchange rate of the Ecu *vis-à-vis* the rest of the world would be decided by the national governments, not by the ECB. Third, the European Central Bank should not be more independent than the Bundesbank.

When asked about the conditions under which it would be desirable to have the EMU, the FFM official held, in addition to the above-mentioned issues, that the EMU should start with all twelve, or at least close to all twelve, countries.[145] The most important aim of the EMU in 1991 was seen as being that of obtaining the single currency, which he was convinced would be part of the EMU plan. More generally, the EMU was considered in 1991 to be a very positive development because countries had already lost independence in monetary and economic policy-making as a result of the capital liberalization and the Internal Market. Thus, the single currency led by an ECB would enable the Member States to regain influence collectively.

Speculating about the effects of EMU becoming operational it was argued that it would be very probable that the EMU would have more important effects than those anticipated 'today' (i.e. 1991). The respondent thought that power would be increasingly transferred to Brussels.

The French monetary authorities made a remarkable U-turn in their formal policies and attitudes towards EMU after the completion of the IGCs in December 1991, on one issue. Whereas during the IGCs they favoured an 'economic government', a supranational organ to conduct 'economic' policies, in 1992, after the signing and the difficulties regarding the ratification of the Treaty, the French authorities claimed there was no reason to transfer economic power to the Community level, arguing that economic policies could be better conducted at a lower level, that is, the principle of subsidiarity would apply.[146]

The BdF was, in 1991, strongly in favour of the Delors Report and totally supported its contents (see also Banque de France, 1990b, 1990c; Lagayette, 1990, 1991). Any critique it had consisted of the treatment of the 'economic union'. In the view of the BdF this blue-print for EMU needed strengthening, very much along the lines of what was originally set out in the Werner Report. It was considered important to deepen the 'economic union'. 'As is stated in the Werner Report, it is necessary to have an economic authority.'[147] The role of this economic 'authority' or 'government' would be to formulate economic policy orientations not only on trade policy, but on policies of taxation, etc. It was to be held responsible for economic policy. It does *not* mean to supervise the ECB.[148]

The BdF's evaluation of the Maastricht Treaty was that its passage on EMU was identical to the Delors Report. Whereas in 1991 comments were still made about the need for more economic steering by a European economic government, the view held now was that EMU as set out in the Delors Report and in the Maastricht Treaty was entirely desirable, and that the principle of subsidiarity ought to apply at the level of economic policy-making:

> This type of EMU is completely desirable, also the economic aspect, which is sometimes neglected. The reason for this is simple: the power over monetary policy may not be dispersed. ... In the economic domain one does not know what to do except that the subsidarity principle applies. That is, there is no reason to move economic power to the European level as it is very well exercised at the national level.[149]

An official of the French Ministry of Finance nuanced this French position towards EMU. She argued that since the signing of the Treaty formal policy has favoured the institutional arrangement, leaning heavily on monetary arrangements, and not, as the French had proposed, on any communal economic policy-making. The French had-made serious concessions in the Intergovernmental Conferences. The official stressed that the problem was not to focus on price stability, but rather the convergence criteria, as well as the absence of more generous social provisions:

> It is not the problem of the price stability, but it may be the problem of the quantitative criteria which were set in the Treaty, the choice of them, the level, the process of decision-making, and the idea of the independence of the central bank. These were serious concessions from the French side. Also, I could imagine that my government

would have wished to have more generous social objectives in the Treaty. But I think the main objective has been met.[150]

In her personal view the Treaty was not adequate on all points:

> If you asked me this question as an official of the Ministry I would answer: 'Of course, this type of EMU is desirable, evidently.' If you asked me personally what I thought, I would answer that 'effectively a number of things are not dealt with adequately in the Maastricht Treaty'.[151]

She argued that these shortcomings relate to the fact that the Treaty did not go far enough. Its institutions, such as the European Monetary Institute, did not have a strong enough mandate. Also, it is not clear how the convergence criteria can be met or dealt with. She considered it as a next step in the integration process. 'For me it is a phase, *une étape*, but not more.'[152]

In other words the French monetary authorities have formally totally accepted the outcome of the negotiations, and have integrated this in their official policy and attitudes towards EMU. However, when asked their personal opinions, one official did not consider the results to be very satisfactory.

The Bundesbank and the German Ministry of Finance

In the 1991 interview the Bundesbank official argued that he considered EMU to be the 'winds of change', thus it cannot be ignored. The Bundesbank was much more sceptical about a fast setting up of EMU than the politicians were (see also Deutsche Bundesbank, 1990a, 1990b, 1990c, 1990d, 1990e, 1990f, 1991a, 1991b, 1991c). Yet it was not against EMU in principle; that is, if every country achieved the economic conditions to join EMU without it costing other countries too much, it would be totally desirable.

> Nevertheless, I would think that if the conditions are right, and if countries are willing, and able to pursue the kinds of policies that will lead to the performances of their economies in macro and micro aspects which allows EMU to operate, then it is totally desirable. I am all for one currency.[153]

However, a great number of problems were perceived if EMU started operating too soon. That would have effects on relative competitiveness, which cannot be offset by big shifts in labour. Moreover, it was argued that 'there is no such labour mobility and no basic solidarity to make it possible for these divergences to be financed, so to say, by enormous financial transfers'.[154]

The Bundesbank did not support the findings reported in the 'One Market, One Money' Report. It was considered to be biased in favour of EMU, thereby underemphasizing the possible costs. The Bundesbank still held the same view 18 months later; EMU is desirable because the politicians want it, though it would still be very costly if the conditions were not fulfilled.

The German Finance Ministry (GFM) more or less accepted the Delors Report as a blueprint for an EMU. EMU was desirable if, in addition to the Delors requirements, three conditions were fulfilled: first, economic policy-making would remain at the level of national policy-making; second, budgetary policies were to be limited in order not to endanger the objective of price stability; and third, more convergence in economic development between the participating Member States had been reached.

An official of the GFM still held these three reservations about the EMU plans in 1992, but had changed his attitude towards the Delors Report and the desirability of EMU when asked the same question the second time around. 'We fully agree to EMU as we have it today. It compares to the earlier Delors Report that was also explicitly accepted by us. The Maastricht Treaty very strongly resembles the Delors Report.'[155]

Social partners on Question 2: Under which conditions is EMU desirable?

Employers' organizations

In all three countries the national employers' confederations perceived EMU as implying strengthening the deregulated single market, introducing a single currency, very small transfer payments and low fiscal and social regulation. In other words, letting the market do the work. They are all very much against tax increases, or more generally, against a 'centralist', strongly regulated Europe.

CBI

The CBI in both the 1991 and the 1992 interview argued that it was very much in favour of EMU. It supported the Delors Report but disagreed that there was a need for an economic union first, before gong into a monetary union (see also CBI, 1989, 1990, 1991).

> We think that if you get one the other will follow. Particularly, if you are successfully completing monetary union, with ERM, narrowing the bands, closer convergence, then economic union will follow. Then there is no need to have binding rules on deficits.[156]

To reach convergence in economic policies, binding rules on budgetary deficits were not considered necessary, nor was the need to have increased regional structural funds to accompany the move to EMU in order to balance out the differences. Economic policies would converge through market forces, which would automatically balance out as investment would move to the low-cost areas of the Community:

> [N]eeds for predetermifned regional structural shifts in funds...we thought were unnecessary. We thought that in time, as economic policies converge, the forms will become more similar. If they don't, then investment will be attracted to the low cost areas of the Community, in which case it would redress the balance.[157]

For the same reasons the CBI opposed the Social Charter. In both periods, in 1991 as well as 1992, the Social Charter was considered an obstacle to greater labour flexibility, which would be needed after the loss of the exchange rate instrument. However, the CBI would like to see the UK be part of the first group of countries to participate in the final stage of EMU.

In the 1992 interview priority was set for convergence rather than the time schedule. Now it was argued that 'closer convergence' takes a higher priority than the deadline or the number of countries that should join (see also Williams, 1992). The *real* convergence (the CBI's definition being: growth rates and economic performance) was an additional criterion that needed to be fulfilled in order to enter the final phase of EMU. The experience in 1992 had shown that the inflation, growth and interest rates in Germany as compared to the rest of Europe were too far apart. It became clear that it was not beneficial to the rest of Europe to have 'German interest rates'. In October 1992, even after the pound had withdrawn from the ERM the previous month, the CBI was still in favour of EMU.[158]

CNPF

In the 1991 interview the respondent argued that EMU was fully desirable, but that it should not start too soon. It would be very costly if it did. Nevertheless, the CNPF did not formally take a position on EMU, as this was considered a political decision (see BDI–CNPF, 1990; CNPF, 1990). It did launch a common statement with the German BDI in support of the EMU objective (see BDI–CNPF, 1990). However, another reason given for not taking a formal CNPF position on EMU was that it was not certain whether all members would agree to EMU; the CNPF members close to the Gaullist Party would not favour a positive stand on EMU.

> The CNPF pays close attention not to hurt the Gaullist movement (RPR).[159] That is the reason that the CNPF has not taken an official position on EMU. There has been a joint document between the BDI and the CNPF, but there is no CNPF document [on EMU].[160]

The respondent, however, did supply three main reasons why EMU was desirable. The first, and foremost, is the aim of price stability; second is the abolition of exchange rates, and third the envisaged budgetary discipline.

Eighteen months later, in the 1992 interview, the CNPF official took a very strong stance in favour of the Maastricht Treaty. Stating that the economic situation was a matter of concern, he stressed that to join an EMU would reduce interest rates, an option currently not available. The argument was that there is not much room for manoeuvre, and that the interest rates were too high.

> The economic situation is a matter of concern, and we certainly have not much room for manoeuvre, and we have interest rates that are certainly much too high. These interest rates would be justified if we had to fight against inflation. But there is no more inflation in France. We know very well that if we lowered interest rates the franc would immediately be attacked.[161]

As there was still a minority within the CNPF sceptical about EMU, the organization as a whole still officially had not taken a position on EMU. Yet when the Maastricht Treaty was put to the citizens in a national referendum, the president of the CNPF stated that the CNPF was officially in favour of 'Europe', and that he would personally recommend the French people to vote 'yes'.

The CNPF official had two concerns. First, the fear that the Delors-2 package would lead to tax increases, which the CNPF would oppose. He was afraid that the European taxes will increase and the French taxes will not decrease, as had been the experience in France with the decentralization; local taxes increased but national taxes did not decrease.[162] Secondly, the fear that the Community would be too open towards third countries such as Japan and the US, as it was thought it had been thus far. He felt more should be done to protect Europe. This was considered a matter of changing the *modus operandi* rather than the text of the Treaty itself.[163]

BDI

The Delors Report was supported by the BDI in 1991, though with some reservations; the three-phase plan to EMU without any timetable was considered unrealistic, as were the political aspects of the Delors plan. The BDI thought they were not thought through adequately. In addition, the political part of the monetary construction was seen as underdeveloped. In 1992 the BDI official stressed that the timetable that was now available might aim for EMU too soon. In the view of this respondent the countries that were to participate in EMU needed to witness real convergence before entering EMU. Taking the German unification as an example, the view of the BDI was that it is necessary to realize that when the devaluation instrument is gone in the final stage of EMU, adjustments will have to take place in the domestic economy. If not, it will give rise to regional or income policies, which will be very costly for the richer areas.

> What will regional, social and income policies look like? These are things that we in Germany at the moment find problematic. We have Länder from East and West Germany together in one country which show strong differences in terms of productivity, and we can conclude from our own observations the meaning regional policy can have, especially when it is needed, but also which role income policy plays if it is needed. At the moment we still have the exchange rate instrument to make adjustments. These, however, will not be available in the future. The adjustment mechanism will have to be dealt with by other factors, ones that lie in the economic realm.[164]

Furthermore, reflecting once more on the lessons of German unification, the BDI would have wanted the Treaty to have been focused not only on monetary convergence but also on economic convergence (see also BDI, 1990a, 1990b, 1991a, 1991b). In 1990 the BDI launched a joint statement with the German trade unions in support of EMU, but explicitly pointing to the need for increased economic convergence and improved democratic legitimacy of the Community to accompany the creation of EMU (BDI–DGB, 1990).

Trade unions

The TUC, the three French trade union confederations and the DGB all held differing views on whether EMU was desirable. All recognized that the room for manoeuvre for trade unions has become very limited in recent years. With the exception of two French trade union confederations – the FO and the CGT – all the trade unions accepted that, no matter how much criticism one may have of the EMU plans of the Community, it is better to participate in the drawing up of the plans than stand outside the process arguing against it. If trade unions merely oppose the process, national decision-makers will definitely not take any notice of the unions.

TUC

In the 1991 interview an official in charge of issues regarding monetary union argued that the TUC did not have a formal policy statement on whether or not EMU is desirable. The official responded that he thought that it was the TUC's judgement that it was 'inevitable'.[165] The TUC official stated that the TUC has been very aware that it is only one player in the game and that it tries to see where influence can be exercised in the political process.[166] EMU would have to incorporate the *Economic* as well as a Monetary Union. However, what the respondent meant by this term was not clear. It did not mean creating a fiscal union, or having more economic coordination, as the TUC considers it important to maintain the conduct of fiscal policies at the national level, especially as the burden of adjustment during the transition and final stage of EMU will fall on the labour market. What the TUC meant by economic convergence was stated as follows:

> But we are looking at what convergence means. What sort of accountability is there of Eurofed? What are its terms of reference? What is the role of fiscal policy in terms of budgetary policy and overall Community budgetary policies, the role of structural funds and regional policies?[167]

When asked what exactly 'Economic Union' means, which elements would be important to realize in an 'Economic Union', he referred back to the terms mentioned under the heading of 'economic convergence', and he illustrated how important the democratic accountability was (cf. ETUC, 1990a):

> democratic accountability (through Ecofin or European Parliament, the former having the preference). The most important thing the British parliament does is control the economic and financial affairs. This is absolutely crucial. We are also looking at the terms of reference of the Eurofed. If it is all central bankers, how about having other interest groups on the board, such as trade unionists and industrialists?[168]

The TUC had not formally formulated any *conditions* that needed to be fulfilled in order for the TUC to favour EMU. It felt that it would not be taken seriously if it took too strong a stand against EMU.[169] Thus the TUC refrained from posing any 'conditions'. Rather, it voiced what could be named 'elements they considered important'. These mainly entailed, according to an official in 1991, that EMU should not pose a 'threat to unemployment or social standards'.

In the 1992 interview with TUC officials it became clear that 'Black Wednesday' had changed perceptions on EMU, though when asked if the TUC perceived EMU to be desirable the official answered that there still was no official policy on whether EMU was desirable, or under which conditions it would/would not be desirable. Yet there was a sense that 'Black Wednesday' had made people in the TUC think that 'some form of closer EMU is desirable'.[170]

However, the Maastricht Treaty would be desirable only if the 3 per cent and 60 per cent convergence criteria had a flexible interpretation. It was feared that the strict application of the rules would be deflationary. On the institutional side the TUC hoped that the European Central Bank would become democratically accountable. The other aims that were considered important were: the Social Chapter; a flexible interpretation of the convergence criteria; obtain other policies such as EC budgetary policies that will aid the system, more regional funds, and the cooperative growth strategy.[171]

When asked if they thought EMU was a good way to obtain growth and employment the TUC official explained his great concern about EMU without the Social Chapter, and argued: 'So at the moment, the British government is able to block most of the social legislation. And you need the Social Chapter to unblock that. So we find it impossible to support any type of Economic and Monetary Union without a social dimension.'[172]

CFDT

Similar to the approach adopted by the TUC, the CFDT has decided to take a strategy on board that a trade union has more influence when it agrees to the general idea of EMU and then makes comments about what could be improved rather than just bluntly rejecting the whole process. The CFDT argued – with some reservations – that EMU as set out in the Delors Report is desirable. The respondent warned against the dangers of 'monetarism', by which the respondent seemed to mean: economic policy being determined by having to achieve monetary policy objectives. The CFDT stated that it supports the proposal by the Finance Minister at that time, Mr Bérégovoy, to create an economic government. It could counterbalance the power of a monetary institution. Policy-making ought to centre not only on monetary targets but also on economic objectives such as employment and the reduction of inequalities between regions and people (see also CFDT, 1990, 1991).

During the 1992 interview the respondent gave a much more positive statement about EMU. It was thought very important that economic objectives, such as growth and employment, would be taken into consideration by the economic and monetary authorities. Particularly employment was the fundamental criterion.

> This criterion seems to us to be indispensable to the construction of Europe, and we believe in Europe. Not only for economic reasons, but also because we want to make a social space, a political space ... solidarity between the European countries. But the priority is employment. Assuming this focus and these objectives, we completely agree with EMU, and we think it is inevitable and good.[173]

The respondent stressed that a European strategy was necessary given the present international context. Given the strong positions of the US and Japan, it seemed clear that there was no solution without 'Europe'.[174]

Summarizing, even though the attitude towards Maastricht and EMU had become more positive in 1992, the fundamental criticism of EMU remained as it had been 18 months earlier; that is, the need for more than just a monetary target, the need for an economic government, centralized European economic policy-making, and the reduction of inequalities in Europe. All trade unions have launched joint statements with their employers' organizations or sister organizations across countries in favour of some sort of EMU.

DGB

In 1991 a DGB official stated that the DGB was in favour of EMU, though it was thought that the *economic* part of it needed to be strengthened. A common economic policy with employment targets and aims for regional equality was necessary.[175] How these policy objectives should be conceptualized or institutionalized remained an open question.[176] The DGB supported the report on EMU drafted by the Economic and Social Committee that some countries could start with EMU and a single currency, and that others could use this European currency as a parallel currency and join in when the time was right (Economic and Social Committee, 1990, 1991).

By 1992 the emphasis had shifted slightly. The condition to favour the 'economic' union was accompanied by the preference for an 'economic government' that would function as a counterbalance to the ESCB. Whether a country fulfils the convergence criteria would have to be judged on the basis of economic policy results and objectives, not by only making a technical judgement.

A new condition mentioned in 1992 was the call for the setting up of a *real* 'political' union:

> The core condition is not an economic, but a political condition: no monetary union without a Political Union. … We believe that adopting a single currency is both an economic and a political act; a sense of sovereignty or identity with a country. It is not only a question of institutions, but rather one of consciousness. The DGB wants the Political Union. Therefore, we have accepted the political 'trick': we now know what EMU consists of, and we give the government time until 1996 to come up with the Political Union.[177]

The official clarified that all in all the DGB accepted EMU as stated in the Maastricht Treaty. The respondent considered it to be identical to the Delors Report except for the timetable and the strict convergence criteria. Yet a political union was necessary. This implied having a federal structure with an 'executive' chosen by the European Parliament (see also DGB, 1989a). The Commission would have to be responsible to the EP, etc. The description resembled more or less the two-chamber model of a national political system. A last condition given was that EMU and a single currency should not start automatically. The national governments would have to make the final decision to join in.

Thus, the TUC, CFDT and the DGB expressed themselves in favour of the creation of EMU. They aimed at influencing the drafting of the Maastricht Treaty by putting their own issues on the agenda. Since the Treaty was signed they have aimed at influencing its interpretation, and are endeavouring at having other policy objectives approved in parallel: the Social Charter, a Cooperative Growth Strategy and so on. The 'costs' of EMU would be considered high if Europe became totally oriented on the market, and neo-liberalism and the market principle determined economic policy-making in Europe. Most trade unions were convinced that focusing solely on 'price stability' would not benefit everyone in Europe, notably not the people who are poor or lose their jobs. This would be particularly worrying in the transition period, stage two of EMU.

Summary of Question 2: Is EMU desirable?

Almost all actors answered the question 'Is EMU desirable?' with the answer 'wholly' or 'partly'. Only the French trade union confederation CGT opposed it completely. Many respondents posed certain conditions under which EMU was desirable. Conditions mentioned by monetary authorities were as follows: an independent ESCB needed to secure price stability, a 'no bail-out rule' as well as 'no monetary financing of the budget' as a necessary guarantee for healthy public finances, and budgetary deficits would have to be reduced. Monetary authorities argued that EMU was desirable as it would offer a stable currency, one single monetary policy aimed at price stability, increased efficiency and so on. The German Finance Ministry linked EMU to Political Union and hoped the integration process would not stop at EMU.

The argument of the employers' organizations very strongly followed that of the monetary authorities. EMU was good for business as it would give stability and thus more efficiency, economic growth, and a larger role for Europe, especially through the use of the European single currency which could provide an alternative to the use of the dollar. Thus its creation was a very important part of why they supported EMU. The employers' organizations wanted, in addition to the conditions posed by the monetary authorities, a market-oriented EMU with a flexible labour market. The EMU project on the whole was considered a valuable project to cope with increased international competition.

The trade unions had a very different type of argument. EMU would offer a response to the challenge supplied by the international competition, in particular from the US and Japan. They were not overly impressed by the potential positive effects of having EMU. However, they realized that they would lose even more ground in the policy-making process if they opposed EMU and the national politicians went ahead and created it anyway. Similarly, not creating anything in the European economic, monetary and *social* context was even less desirable. Thus, they decided to join in the policy-making process to help form EMU. They made their interests known by drafting proposals during the IGCs and in the period after the signing of the Maastricht Treaty. They wanted to combine EMU with the acceptance of a package of social measures, regional and employment policies and a cooperative growth strategy. Not only should the greater wealth of all be the central aim of EMU, but also the *redistribution* of the costs and benefits of EMU was important. They were very sceptical about market forces or monetary policies being able to address these issues adequately. They emphasized the need for democratic accountability of the ESCB. In their view severe risks of EMU would have to be countered by pursuing policies to combat large differences (structural funds, social regulation and a growth strategy). Thus, though they accepted the aim of EMU to be price stability as a condition for growth, they would prefer the convergence criteria not to be applied too strictly, and stressed that common economic policies would need to be adopted to tackle the redistributive problems that might arise from EMU. These issues could only be addressed in part by using the social and regional funds.

6.3   Question 4: The future EMU and its effects

4a. How do you think at this moment that EMU will look when it is completed?

4b. What do you think will be its effect on monetary and budgetary policies (and the freedoms of the governments of the member states to decide them)?

4c. What do you think will be the effect of this EMU on other policies (if you like, in combination with the other plans; that is, the internal market)?

  – fiscal policy: what will happen to taxes (direct and indirect);

  – social policy: your country as compared to other member states;

  – unemployment;

  – national social security system;

– *economic growth;*
– *competitive position of your country* vis-à-vis *other countries;*
– *country-specific shocks;*
   4d. *What do you think would be the effect of EMU on the group you represent, or your major policy aims?*
   4e. *Would it change anything in the structure of your organization?*

Question 4a was posed to obtain a picture of how the respondents at the time of the interview perceived the future EMU. However, in almost all interviews this question had already been adequately elaborated during the discussion of Question 2. Only a limited number of respondents gave new information when answering this question.

Question 4b aimed at understanding to what extent the actors had reflected on how an EMU would limit national sovereignty. This is very obvious in the case of monetary policy autonomy transfer. Indeed, all respondents answered that *de facto* and *de jure* monetary sovereignty would be transferred to the European level. A European monetary authority would be set up that would be responsible for monetary policy; no respondent had any doubt about this fact.

With regard to budgetary policies a large difference was noticeable between the various actors across organizations and across countries. In addition, most respondents also held different opinions in the two successive interviews, concerning the restrictions on budgetary policies at the national level and (limited) budgetary policy-making at the European level.

Monetary authorities

Monetary and budgetary policies

In 1991 the British Treasury strongly opposed restrictions on budgetary policies, though it was understood that some countries would have to reduce their budgetary deficits drastically. The argument was that to avoid the pushing up of interests rates by some Member States, rules on budgets would be necessary, such as a 'no-bailout rule, and no printing of money'.[178] The British Treasury's solution would be to *not* put stringent rules on these levels of debt: 'We do not agree to any legal rules on budgetary deficits for two reasons. It is a central power of the parliament.... Second, it is difficult to know what is always the right fiscal policy, at all times, for all countries.'[179] It was held that, as monetary policy would be conducted at a central level, every Member State would need to maintain sovereignty over especially the area of fiscal policy-making to manage its economy.

By contrast, in the 1992 interview a Treasury official answered that it was good that stringent rules were drawn up for budgetary deficits, as otherwise some countries might borrow too much on the capital market, thereby artificially pushing up interest rates. When reminded that this policy was quite different from the one presented in 1991 he responded:

> You are right to remind me what our policy was before. It was our position that we did not want too strict rules and I think we have come out with a policy compromise which we do accept. The 3 per cent and 60 per cent norms are also well above our own objectives.[180]

Concerning the rules on fiscal deficits the Bank of England's view in both 1991 and 1992 strongly coincided with the Treasury's view on the matter. In 1991 it was argued that there would not be a complete 'fiscal free for all' within EMU. Rather, it would be a process of voluntary consultation of fiscal policy backed up by moral and peer-group pressure. It was thought that this should be sufficient. Thus, the Treasury did not agree with the rules on fiscal deficits.[181] In 1992, when asked whether the respondent saw the 3 per cent and 60 per cent rules as a loss of sovereignty, the answer was: 'Well, there is a loss of sovereignty, unfortunately. ... Ideally we would have wanted all countries to have decided on these targets themselves.'[182]

In France the 1991 preoccupation with budgetary deficits led to exactly the opposite policy choice, that is, stricter rules in order to exercise budgetary discipline: 'On budgetary policy there will certainly be strong monitoring. As you can see in the Treaty, we proposed strong sanctions against countries who do not respect budgetary discipline.'[183] In 1992 an official argued that at some point in time the Community budget will have to play a larger role. 'Budgetary policy, ... you may have a larger amount of the budget at the common level. This is only possible if the institutional side of the Community is more satisfactory. At the moment there is no real will.'[184] The French monetary authorities during the 1991 interview also emphasized the importance of a larger role of *economic* policy-making at the Community level. Sovereignty would be lost at home and would need to be regained at some level of European policy-making. Perhaps some guidelines for the conduct of economic policy-making could be set out. Generally it was thought that the setting up of a monetary authority had to be balanced by the installation of some kind of body of economic policy-making.

In 1992 this idea had been abandoned except for the notion mentioned above that institutional change in the future might give the European Union a larger federal role to play.

The German view in 1991 was again different from the other two. The monetary authorities here were convinced that the ECB would have to be totally independent, and should have only one mandate: price stability. Thus the German authorities did not share the French desire to institutionalize some form of economic policy-making within the framework of EMU. The monetary authorities would conduct a single monetary policy in Europe, and leave the national economic policy-making to the national governments, albeit respecting the limits on budgets:

> Budgetary policy, there we think it is imperative that the excessive deficits will be reduced. It places a high adjustment burden on the Member States that today still have large deficits. Hence, this will limit the room for manoeuvre of national governments, which is good, otherwise it will not work.[185]

From this it follows that the German authorities did not share the British view. They did not think it possible to have one successful monetary policy in Europe if all countries had too much fiscal freedom. Thus, in the view of the German monetary authorities, the binding rules on budgetary policies were a necessary condition in order for them to accept the Maastricht Treaty.

> On the one hand there is subsidiarity, meaning that the individual governments will still have their say. Market discipline will partly take care of reaching a sort of convergence level. But we would not want to rely on that entirely. Thus we need a mechanism, including *possibly* binding rules – you should at least provide for them – otherwise you get too loose an arrangement implying risks to price stability.[186]

This view was still the same in 1992, though now the respondent explicitly excluded the possibility of creating a European fiscal power, arguing that it might run into conflict with a European monetary authority:

> Budgetary policies will follow the principle of subsidiarity and be conducted at the national and regional level. But hopefully it will

not be so diverse that you will have to say that there is no convergence. ... I would not think that it would be desirable if only Brussels were in charge of budgetary policy. The central bank can easily get into trouble if there were a very big fiscal power.[187]

Regarding the effects on other policy areas the monetary authorities held the following views.

Fiscal and social policies

The 1992 programme has already led to some harmonization of the Value Added Tax (VAT). As for other taxes, all monetary authorities argued that they would be harmonized through the pressure of *market forces*. Most of the respondents, not only the monetary authorities, but also the social partners discussed below, explicitly mentioned that these other taxes, in particular direct taxes, would not be harmonized as an act of the EU, but the tendency towards harmonization would be the logical consequence of the Single Market combined with EMU and/or fixed exchange rates. A Treasury official commented on the harmonization tendency as follows:

> Our argument has always been that you do not need any formal arrangement to harmonize tax rates, because market forces will do it for you. Given the rise in mobility, companies and people will have much less tolerance to differences in tax levels. This would mean that there is a constant downward pressure on taxes, which is a good thing. Because, inevitably, in all our societies there is a constant upward pressure on public expenditure. To have another pressure going in the opposite direction, going down, is all together a good thing in the view of the government.[188]

Regarding the mechanism of harmonization of fiscal policy a BdF official described the process as affecting some areas of fiscal policies more than others, though even direct taxes would not be left unaffected:

> Regarding fiscal matters, a certain harmonization is necessary, within the limits of market pressure. Large differences on some taxes will not be possible, such as on VAT, even though limited divergence is possible. ... On direct taxation there will be more margin, but not much. There are many activities which require highly qualified, highly paid individuals who can easily move. ... Thus, there will be a certain harmonization tendency but not towards uniformization, even though the differences will be small.[189]

A Bundesbank official expressed his views as follows:

> In a legal sense there is subsidiarity. Countries will still be able to have their own tax systems. However, given that in a totally unified market, competitiveness is affected by divergence in tax systems, there will be pressures for harmonization, obviously. That does not only apply in the area of indirect taxes, but also in the area of direct taxes and levies and so on. You will have to have harmonization there, otherwise countries will price themselves out of the market.[190]

When discussing the spill-over effects on social policy the Bundesbank official stated:

> The same will apply slowly for the social system. The Portuguese will not immediately want the German system, as it would take away an advantage, for example setting up industries that will not so likely flourish here due to our high level of social security and charges and rules. But in the long run ... it will change, and there will be harmonization.[191]

With respect to social policies, a variety of views were held. A FFM official in 1991 emphasized that social policies would remain the same under EMU. Yet in a 1992 interview a FFM official explained that some change might occur in southern Europe and in the UK. But she thought that there would be little change in the other EU countries, she stated, where the level of social policy is more or less the same. [192] Moreover, change would not come about due to a sensitive public opinion on this issue: 'I personally think that the public opinion will be very, very touchy on this issue, extremely touchy.'[193]

Others thought that the cost of social policy would gradually be affected by market forces, leading to harmonization as well, though at a slower pace than would occur with fiscal policies. Others again, notably the British Treasury, did not make this distinction and foresaw that harmonization through market forces would happen at the level of fiscal policies as well as social policies.

With regard to the harmonization of social policies, a GFM official explained how the costs of an expanding social system had already become part of the struggle for attracting business: 'There already exists a competition to attract industry. If a country wants to pay for an expanding social system with large public funding, then this implies that it will have to make these funds available.'[194] Even though the respondent stressed that it would remain subject to political choice it was clear that the market mechanism would exert pressure. Harmonization of social policy was seen as being able only to come through market forces.

Most respondents stressed that social expenditure, social premiums, increasingly become part of the competitive struggle for attracting industry to a certain geographical area. They generally thought this process via market forces would take place much more gradually than the fiscal harmonization. Moreover, they expressed that policy-making with regard to social policies and national social security systems was considered politically much more sensitive. Nevertheless, they all stressed that it was considered undesirable to make decisions about harmonizing social policies at the European level. To quote a BdF official: 'There remains a total freedom to decide which system one chooses. ... But at the end of the day, it is necessary to remain competitive.[195] Most respondents observed that in a European market, with fixed exchange rates and free capital movements, this harmonization would take place with or without EMU, though it was imagined that EMU with a single currency would provide an easier ground for comparison and hence fuel the harmonization process via market forces. Even if this was the observation, none of the respondents favoured the idea of having social and fiscal policies transferred to the Community level. Even if market forces pushed policies in a certain direction, that would be the preferred option. It would be necessary to keep the levels of fiscal and social policies compatible with competitiveness. As these issues were considered politically sensitive issues, market forces could contribute to help policy-makers to address these issues from the right perspective.

Unemployment and economic growth

The British and German monetary authorities combined the effect of EMU on unemployment with certain conditions or assumptions, in order to have EMU benefit economic growth and employment, whereas the French monetary authorities dared to say that EMU *per se* was 'very favourable' to economic growth, though they were more cautious about the positive effects on employment of EMU. Some, for example the British Treasury, argued that it depended on the level of convergence reached when starting EMU, while others, for example the German monetary authorities, emphasized that the advantages might benefit some areas more than others. The German Bundesbank's estimates in 1991 were that the 'backward' regions would benefit more from EMU than the 'advanced' regions.

Social partners

Monetary and budgetary policies

Employers' organizations in the three countries did not doubt that the future ECB would be politically independent, that a single authority would be in charge of monetary policy in the third stage of EMU, with price stability as its mandate. The trade unions, however, argued that there are more important objectives than just stable money. These elements include growth, employment and minimum social standards. The unions argued that these should be included within the framework of EMU. These issues had all been discussed more or less extensively under the heading of Question 2. Regarding the effects on fiscal and social policy areas, on growth and on employment, the views of employers' organizations and trade unions are described below.

Fiscal and social policies

In both the 1991 and the 1992 interviews the CBI advocated a great need for fiscal freedom, meaning that sovereignty on the conduct of tax policies ought to remain at the level of the Member States. Following an argument similar to that of the British monetary authorities described above, Member States would increasingly need to use fiscal policy for macroeconomic adjustment, for example in the case of a country-specific shock. In 1991 the CBI still believed that the fiscal instrument would still be an important tool to combat a specific shock, but by 1992 it was accepted that the rules on public debt and budgetary deficit as laid down in the protocol to the Maastricht Treaty were necessary. With regard to the potential effect of EMU on fiscal harmonization a CBI official answered in 1992: 'Presumably there will be need for more harmonization of taxes, indirect taxes, corporate taxes. Direct taxes, less importantly. I think we'll end up taxing houses etc., things that cannot move.'[196] The CBI's views on how EMU would affect social policy and the national social security system were not very similar in both years. In 1991 a CBI respondent stated:

> Labour is not flexible. Thus the national social security system is not under pressure as a result of labour mobility. If and when there is higher unemployment, it would be very difficult for a given country to lower unemployment benefits. I do not know where the money comes from to support this.[197]

In 1992 a CBI respondent emphasized the same levelling mechanism would happen with social policies as what was expected to happen with fiscal policies:

> I think, again, it will act as a leveller. If a country is pursuing an independent social policy which involves very high social costs, there will come a point when social legislation is too inflexible, that you are losing competitiveness. If we all have 50 days of holiday and work 6 hours then there is no problem *within Europe* but *vis-à-vis* the *rest of the world* we would be uncompetitive. Thus, it will act to level out.[198]
>
> (emphasis as in original)

The French CNPF in both periods held the view that market forces would automatically adjust the levels of taxes and social premium. Indeed, it was already felt that, regarding monetary policies, even without EMU, the national governments had very little leeway to adopt radically different policies from those of the other Member States.

> On budgetary policy you have a constraint: the convergence criteria. Apart from that, you will certainly have a constraint on spending. For example, in France taxes and social premia are much higher than in Germany. Even though this is not in the Maastricht Treaty there will certainly be a constraint on expenses and on taxes. If you have taxes very different from your neighbour you will have disruptions. But you still have the national choice. There is nothing that says how much money you have to spend on education etc.[199]

The German employers' organization closely followed the other two in foreseeing a downward harmonization trend of fiscal and social policies by market pressures. However, the concern here was that one could end up at the lowest level (downward harmonization), which the respondent did not consider the optimum level. Especially with respect to social policy this was considered undesirable:

> There one has to take care that one does not harmonize towards the lowest standard (as happened with the Euro-standard for automobiles). This counts also with respect to taxes. There are some policy areas where this would be simply unacceptable, such as 'Mitbestimmungsregeln' [the co-determination procedure], environment taxes, and in the sphere of social policy.[200]

Even though the officials of the three national employers' organizations predicted a downward trend on fiscal and social policies, they thought that decisions in these policy areas should not be transferred to the level of the Community. They preferred to have market forces contribute to the harmonization of these policy areas, as these were sensitive areas of policy-making.

In 1991 the TUC feared that EMU would lead to overly strict rules on budgetary and fiscal policies. With regard to taxes the respondent stated: 'I can see taxes moving together.'[201] In the field of social policies it was considered inevitable that EMU would eventually induce harmonization of social systems, even though this would not take place in the short run:

> Our fear is that there will be such a tight monetary policy and such strict control over budgetary policies that nation states will not be able to run their own fiscal policies. The same counts for social policies. It is difficult to think about what is going to happen in the next 10 years, or the next 50 years. Undoubtedly, EMU is going to lead to an approximation of social systems. People in one country are not going to tolerate being worse off than another, and they will be able to make the comparison.[202]

This view was not fundamentally altered by the TUC eighteen months later. Taxes were still seen to be subject to harmonization via market forces, and this mechanism would also affect social policies. This is why the TUC was in favour of the 'Social Dimension'. This was important in order to try to stop countries adjusting by lowering the social standard. It was not thought to prevent it, but to ensure a minimum standard.[203]

The French trade unions held various views regarding the implications of EMU on fiscal and social policies. The CFDT in both the 1991 and the 1992 interviews elaborated on the fact that, compared to the European average, France has a relatively high indirect tax burden, though a relatively low direct tax burden. Thus, with the harmonization of the indirect taxes due to the 1992 process, the government will need higher direct taxes to secure government income. Regarding social polices the CFDT voiced strong concerns about decreased social protection, or, as was formulated in 1992, 'social dumping'.

The German trade union confederation DGB shared the concern of the British and French trade unions, mentioned above, though in 1991 it argued explicitly that the French would have a much greater problem than the Germans, due to the high indirect French taxes. The DGB official envisaged that Germany would also be confronted with a downward pressure on social spending. This respondent's perspective was different from those of the other trade unions. In his view the downward trend on social spending will, in the long run, benefit everyone, not only because the more expensive and not so effective systems will have to compete with the more efficient social systems, but also, as competitiveness becomes very important in the Internal Market, countries run the risk of social dumping even without EMU. EMU thus offers the solution to try to combine efforts; that is, trying to ensure a minimum social level by coordinating social policies.

Unemployment and economic growth

The three employers' organizations were quite optimistic about the effects of the start of EMU stage 3 on employment and economic growth, though they emphasized the need for responsible policies to be pursued by national government with respect to keeping public spending low, and by social partners to ensure a flexible labour market.

In the 1991 interview the CBI warned that unemployment might rise if EMU started too soon, that is, if the countries that were not ready for EMU joined in. With regard to economic growth the CBI thought that ERM and EMU would contribute to a more evenly spread growth over the years.[204] In the 1992 interview the focus had shifted to the effects of the start of the third stage of EMU on various industrial sectors or regions. The official predicted: '[We expect] the same kind of result from EMU as from the Single Market: there will be a net increase in jobs. But there will be structural changes. Some industries will be competitive and able to expand.'[205] With regard to economic growth the official argued that the dynamic of growth would resemble that of the regional distribution of jobs. It was thought that each country has its variance in fiscal policies and also in growth, thus leading to a variance in unemployment.[206] The example of Northern Ireland was quoted, to which vast amounts of resources have been sent, but still unemployment remains high.

The French employers' organization, CNPF, argued very similarly to its British counterpart that the effect of EMU on unemployment and growth primarily depended on the competitiveness of the industry concerned. In the 1991 interview the official argued that EMU would only have a secondary effect on unemployment and growth. In the 1992 interview the official still argued that he did not know whether

EMU would have a positive effect on these macroeconomic indicators.[207] Responding to the next question on economic growth he answered: 'Those two [unemployment and economic growth] are linked. It *should* work. Who can be sure?'[208]

In 1991 the BDI argued that the market should play a larger role in order to solve the economic problems such as unequal spread of unemployment and of economic growth. In 1992 the official argued that with the lack of a national monetary policy, adjustments would take place via the labour market. A number of preconditions were given that would have to be met to enable the market to do its work effectively: 'In order to support the monetary policy pursued, we need a responsible wage policy and financial policy, which does not only imply tax reforms. ... The public debt is the big problem.'[209]

The trade unions' response to how EMU would affect unemployment and economic growth differed greatly. Most respondents predicted that most costs will arise in the transition period, Stage 2 of EMU, when most monetary and financial adjustments will have to be made to have the strongest repercussions on growth and employment and when the benefits will not yet be felt. Concerning the third stage of EMU, some argued that a distinction should be made between general and regional costs and benefits, and argued that some regions might be hit quite severely. The unions also held different views on which regions these would be. Others, for example the French trade union confederation CFDT, held that it was especially this aspect of EMU, positive effects on growth and employment in the medium and longer term, from which it expected the most, and why the union was interested in EMU in the first place.

The view of the trade unions was on the whole more reserved. In 1991 the TUC official interviewed feared that unemployment was going to rise because in his estimate Britain would not be a strong competitor in the third stage of EMU. He claimed to have found his evidence for this in a European publication – either OMOM or the Social Europe Report – in which Britain was shown as a low-wage, but a high-cost country, meaning that Britain's productivity was lagging behind. His estimate was that the effect of the third stage of EMU on economic growth depended on how macroeconomic policies were pursued by Europe. He had some doubts about whether the European Member States would coordinate economic policies towards strengthening growth. In the 1992 interview the TUC official had not changed his view regarding the effects of EMU on unemployment and economic growth, except that now a more pronounced emphasis was placed on EMU not creating economic growth or employment in itself. It would depend much more on the macroeconomic policies pursued in response to the economic cycle: 'It is wrong to say that EMU by itself is going to push things one way or another.'[210]

The CFDT was expecting most from EMU in terms of economic growth and improved employment. In both the 1991 and 1992 interview this was strongly emphasized. In the early interview the respondent made a distinction between the short and the medium term, arguing that negative effects may be seen in the short term, but definitely not in the medium and longer term. In 1992 a similar suggestion was made, only now it was added that staying in the ERM, or accepting overly restrictive convergence criteria, would have very adverse effects on employment and growth.

The German DGB official thought, in both 1991 and 1992, that the most serious problems would be caused by the spread of unemployment across the regions. There would continue to be large variance if structural funds were not directed to equalize the unemployment burden. Considering the effects of EMU on economic growth the argument was very similar to those of the other national trade union confederations, with one exception. The DGB thought that Europe as a whole would benefit from EMU.

> We are living in a global economy. I am optimistic rather than pessimistic. I think that a large European monetary area – if it wants to – is better equipped than Member States currently are to respond independently to influences from the global economy.[211]

With a reminder that according to him the costs lay in the transition period, the respondent went even further in the 1992 interview by claiming that EMU would be 'very positive' in the medium and longer term.

6.4   Short summary of the main findings

The main results of the 1991 interviews are that monetary authorities in the three countries held very similar views with respect to the earlier EMU plans and the EMS, but held substantially different views in that year with respect to conditions under which the EMU was desirable; that is, concerning the restrictions on budgetary and fiscal policies. All monetary authorities agreed to the blueprint set out in the Delors Report. They accepted that the EMU implied having a single monetary authority that would be solely responsible for monetary policy with the single mandate of guaranteeing price stability. Even though France, and especially Britain, faced difficulties in that their central banks would have to become politically independent, the monetary authorities of these two countries did, nevertheless, accept the fact that the new European monetary authority needed to be independent to be effective. In 1991 the British did not want any formal limits on fiscal freedom; the French wanted the limits but wanted them to be compensated for by a transfer of power of economic policy-making to the Community level; whereas the German monetary authorities proposed rules on budgets and no transfer of economic sovereignty.

These matters were settled in the Maastricht Treaty, so that when the second round of interviews was conducted the arrangement could be reflected on, and the respondents asked if they were satisfied. All monetary authority officials explained that the formal policy of their organization or institution was that they were very content with the section in the Treaty on EMU, even though the officials personally criticized some elements.

The British monetary authorities were happy with the Maastricht Treaty as they had secured an 'opt-out' from joining the single currency and from the Social Chapter. They would have preferred not to have the 3 per cent and 60 per cent limits on the budgetary deficits, but argued that these rules were much less restrictive than the objectives that the British had set out for themselves. The difference between the Bank of England and the Treasury became obvious in their general attitude towards EMU. The Bank of England saw EMU as an objective to be included in the long-term strategy of the Bank. The Treasury had grave doubts about whether Britain would ever join EMU.

The French monetary authorities in general were very positive about the EMU passage in the Treaty. They had made some concessions, but the EMU part of the Treaty contained all the elements the French thought were important. It ensured the issuing of a single currency based on price stability. The fact that economic policy-making in the Treaty would have to follow the principle of subsidiarity – that is, would remain at the level of the Member State – no longer seemed to be a problem to the French. When asked her personal opinion an official of the French Finance Ministry argued that a lot still needs to be done on the institutional side, especially concerning the role of economic policy-making, or the role of the Community budget (and of parliamentary decision-making).

The German authorities felt that the Treaty very much followed their proposals, as they had obtained all they hoped for: a politically independent European monetary authority, with a single mandate to secure price stability. Limits had been placed on national budgetary deficits and the timetable would push Member States to become ready to join.

As regards the effects of EMU on other policy areas, the monetary authorities in both 1991 and 1992 shared the view that, once the EMU and the Internal Market were fully operational, national fiscal and social policies would come under market pressure. It would be very difficult to have systems that were very different across national boundaries; moreover, it would be impossible to maintain a system that was not supported by competitiveness and productivity. The French monetary authorities were perhaps the ones that foresaw the smallest change to occur in social policies.

The employers' organizations in the three countries, if taken together as a single group of actors, held the most positive view about EMU of all actors questioned both in 1991 and 1992. In 1991 they emphasized the need for a single currency in Europe for economic efficiency, and a strengthening of the role of Europe and the European single currency in the world economy. They were generally hesitant to accept that any social regulation accompany the move towards the final EMU. In 1992 they welcomed the Treaty and were hopeful about it.

The trade unions saw the EMU as a way of re-enforcing their position in European policy-making. They realized that their voice would not be heard if they opposed the process, and hoped that a constructive contribution would make it possible for them to influence the agenda setting. Their strongest input was on having the Social Chapter included in the Maastricht Treaty, and securing some redistributing funds to regions that might lose out when the EMU becomes fully operational.

In conclusion, monetary authorities and social partners all perceived EMU to be desirable, albeit under various different conditions and aiming at various objectives. Even among sister organizations divergent views are held. This chapter discussed the perceptions of the actors in a descriptive manner. In the next chapter comparisons are drawn between the perceptions of the various sister organizations and the actors within each country. In Chapter 8 some will be drawn which elaborate on the theoretical framework of this study, and finally lessons that can be learnt to understand the process of integration are proposed.

7
Comparing Actors' Perceptions

Chapter 6 reported how the actors responded to the questions posed to them regarding EMU. Building on the material presented there, this chapter draws comparisons. It is divided into ten main sections. The first five sections make a horizontal comparison, the second five sections compare vertically, that is, compare actors within one country.

The first five sections look at actors across borders and make a transnational comparison of the views of similar actors across the three countries. The first four sections focus on four sets of actors: the first section focuses on central banks, the second on Finance Ministries, the third on the employers' organizations, and the fourth on the trade unions. Each section starts with a recapitulation of the actors' perceptions of the Werner Report and the EMS, their positions regarding the desirability of EMU, and stresses the similarities and differences in their views. The fifth section draws a general horizontal comparison and draws conclusions. The vertical comparison is drawn up in sections six through ten. They focus on Britain, France and Germany consecutively. The final section draws general conclusions.

7.1 The central banks

When actors were asked how their organizations perceived the Werner Report and EMS in the past it is striking that almost all actors emphasize the *continuity* of the interests and policy objectives since the 1970s. The main difference between the 1990s and the 1970s was thought to be threefold: first, national economies are in the 1990s much more interdependent and operate in a global economic environment; second, the '1992' Internal Market with freedom of capital movements is now the economic reality of Europe; third, monetary authorities throughout the EU and beyond share the conviction that low inflation is a necessary condition for growth and thus for employment, whereas in the early 1970s some still thought that some inflation might be needed to combat unemployment. In the view of all central bank respondents the success of the EMS was that all participating members accepted the low inflation objective as a leading objective for monetary policies.

When central bankers were asked about the desirability of EMU, and under which conditions it would be fully desirable, consensus was found on most points, though quite distinct views were observed on some features of the EMU project. Consensus appeared on, for example, the aims of the ECB – that is, price stability – the ECB had to be politically independent, institutional provisions[212] were to assure low national deficits, a requirement for joining the final stage would be to have a good performance on several macroeconomic indicators, including inflation rates and interest rates. Consensus also existed on the fact that, unlike the recommendations in the Werner Report, it was now considered unnecessary to create an *economic authority* to flank the ECB, nor did the EC budget have to be substantially increased.

The main elements of disagreement were: first, whether and how limits on budgets should be secured (either voluntary, or via rules); second, what the 'economic union' meant (including the question of the role of economic policies, and whose competence that should be); and third, how to decide when the Member States would be 'ready' to join. Concerning the institutional set-up of EMU virtually no disagreement existed on what an EMU would embody. All central bank officials said they fully agreed with the Delors Report and the EMU provision in the Maastricht Treaty. They agreed that EMU implied creating a single currency and an independent central bank with the mandate to secure price stability. In addition, the biggest change for the British and French central banks – becoming independent from the government but part of the ESCB – was argued by some to strengthen rather than weaken the autonomy of these central banks and thus be desirable.

As for all other areas of policy-making, no arrangements were considered to be necessary. For example, central banks thought that for the conduct of economic policy-making there was no need to set up an economic institution as had been envisaged with regard to monetary policy. The internal market with free capital markets and no transfer of sovereignty over economic policy-making to the Community level would suffice.

There was some disagreement on five points of the Delors Report: the binding rules on budgetary deficits, the possible timetable, the role of the 'economic union' or the 'economic governance', the democratic accountability, and how much need there really was for an extension of regional and social funds. But these were small areas of disagreement compared with the big step that all central bank officials stated that their institutions were willing to accept.

All central bankers interviewed also agreed that EMU would have substantial effects on other areas of policy-making and the macro-economic indicators of national economies. It was argued that the strengthening of the market mechanism in Europe was a positive effect of EMU.

It can be concluded that this whole orientation on the market mechanism was *implicitly* taken on board by the central bankers to be an important positive side-effect of EMU. It was also *implicitly* understood that it would be good for Europe to increase pressures that improve labour flexibility and to reduce public expenditure. As it would be politically too sensitive, and unpopular, to reduce the role of the state, central bankers thought that there was no need to institutionalize Community policy-making; the market mechanism would be the best regulator in these areas.

The three central banks held different views on the overall desirability of EMU. The single currency was not considered to be so important by the Bank of England and the Bundesbank, but very important by the Banque de France. All three central banks hoped that EMU would provide low inflation which they thought was a central benefit of EMU. In addition, to secure these objectives, it was necessary to create the monetary institution aimed at price stability, and make it independent from government politics and from any economic legislator. By doing so they tried to secure the position of the European institution, comparable to that of a 'Constitutional Court', that ultimately stands above the Member States' politics. The central aim of obtaining stable money is the one and only central objective that really interested the officials in all three central banks in both 1991 and 1992.

If we compare the perceptions of central bank officials on the EMU plans in 1991 and 1992 it becomes clear that the British and German central bank officials were much more reserved about the EMU plans than their French colleagues. Comparing the views on the desirability of EMU in the late 1980s and early 1990s with the views on the earlier monetary integration plans of the 1970s, it seems that some (though not very many) interests and policy objectives have changed.

This study also investigates whether actors might have accepted the EMU package because they also had other objectives in mind. A way to evaluate if that was the case was by asking Question 4. The information supplied as answers to this question helps explain how the actors saw the dynamics of the industrial restructuring as part of the desired elements of EMU.

All central bankers predicted that EMU and the 1992 – Internal Market Programme ('EMU + 1992') would intensify the market mechanism in the European Union. This would have an effect on other policy areas, that is, how governments would try to guarantee their income, and how they would spend it. When looking at taxes and social policy spending this would mean that governments would also be subject to competitive pressures. This was, in the view of all central bankers, 'a good thing'; they were strongly in favour of these side-effects of EMU + 1992 on other policy areas. They all foresaw that the market mechanism would force a harmonization trend, a downward trend, on the level of taxes and social spending. This was thought to be 'a good thing' because they would like the role of the state as a regulatory agent to diminish. In order to survive in the global economy the labour market would have to become more flexible, taxes would need to be reduced, competition between various social security systems would rightly lead to more efficient, more effective systems: that is, better quality at a lower price.

Another question that has been addressed in this study is whether the actors perceived EMU as producing the effects typically mentioned by economic theory of integration. The argument is that EMU would increase efficiency through the economies of scale and increased competition. The result would be greater welfare indicated by higher growth and lower unemployment. As to improvement of the economic growth figures, the central bankers viewed the answer to this question as depending on which policies would be followed when EMU was fully operational. The British central bank official gave no clear response to this question. As for employment improvement as an effect of EMU, they were not so sure. It was argued that it would depend on the policies pursued.

7.2   Finance Ministries

The views of national Finance Ministries on the whole resembled the views of their national central banks, although some distinctions can be made between the exact positions taken and their estimations of the 'costs' and 'benefits' of EMU. Even though the central banks of Britain and France were formally an executive agent of their respective Finance Ministries, there were some differences in their views.

From the three views on the early monetary integration plans it is evident that the three Finance Ministries were declaring that they had supported the early monetary union plans in order to reach their aims. The Treasury had dismissed the possibility of having a single currency, but had approved of the monetary integration plans in theory, as long as they offered price stability, higher growth and full employment. In the late 1970s and early 1980s the French Finance Ministry favoured participation in the EMS, which it hoped would facilitate price stability and the move towards increased monetary integration. The German Finance Ministry focused on the Werner plan as a logical next step to the completion of the Common Market, a process which it had strongly favoured. A necessary condition was, however, that the participating countries would be sufficiently converging. That the process of economic and monetary integration came to a halt in the 1970s was considered a result of the collapse of Bretton Woods and the oil crises on the one hand, and divergent policy responses in the various Member States on the other. Further economic and monetary integration has, in the 1970s and 1980s, had very high priority, albeit without endangering the price stability objective.

When the views of the central banks are compared it appears that a large consensus existed between central bankers on the desirability of EMU and its major 'costs' and 'benefits'. When comparing the views of the Finance Ministries we find that, regarding some aspects of EMU, their views were identical; that is, the preoccupation with the fact that monetary policy in Europe would have to be conducted by one monetary authority – an independent European Central Bank – whose aim should be only that of guaranteeing price stability. Another common conviction was that EMU would not need a substantial increase in the EC budget. However, regarding a European economic executive, the three Finance Minstries held divergent views. Finally, a last similarity with the central banks, disagreement also existed among the three Finance Ministries on how limits on budgetary spending should be achieved, and what the role of the 'economic union' was.

Similar to the case of the central banks, the policies of the three Finance Ministries towards the Werner Report and EMS were claimed to be very close to what the views were towards EMU in the 1990s. The British stated that they had already, in the 1970s and 1980s, agreed in principle to EMU and EMS as an objective, but had not agreed to the creation of a single currency. The French favoured the move ahead towards an EMS and EMU; they strongly favoured the move towards a single currency, and had already, with the EMS, proposed strengthening the role of the Ecu. In 1983 they adopted the 'franc fort' strategy. The Germans stressed that in the 1970s the aim of creating an EMU was to increase the benefits of the 'Common Market' that had been completed in 1968. EMU was desirable provided the countries' economies were sufficiently converging.

As was the case with the central bankers' responses, the Finance Ministry officials considered EMU to be desirable as long as it respected the familiar institutional and monetary conditions: monetary policy was to be placed in the hands of an independent European monetary authority with only one mandate – price stability; the no-bail-out rule ought to apply and there should be no monetary financing of the budget; furthermore, budgetary deficits should not be too large; finally, national economies needed to be converging, that is, inflation and interest rates in all participating countries would need to correlate with one another.

Thus far no significant difference between the countries is found in what the central bankers said. Differences between the three Finance Ministries could be found with respect to which rules on budgets were necessary, which countries would be ready and when, as well as why and under which conditions EMU would be desirable for a country. The various Finance Ministries also had different fears about what would happen if an EMU started too soon.

In 1991 the British Treasury – like the Bank of England – had difficulty in accepting the limits on budgets mentioned in the Delors Report. However, 18 months later, once the rules were decided upon and laid down in the Maastricht Treaty, they were accepted by the Treasury. An important precondition, however, to securing adequate functioning of EMU was that labour had to become more flexible, as adjustment would have to take place via the labour market. The Treasury was also very cautious about EMU starting too soon, arguing that the Member States would not be ready in the very short term. As the main cost of EMU was said to be the abolishment of the exchange rate instrument, a premature move to EMU could well lead to high unemployment. This would, in turn, provoke the need for large transfer payments, which the Treasury did not find at all desirable.

The French Finance Ministry, like the Banque de France, on the whole agreed with EMU as it was set out in the Delors Report, and the subsequent section in the Maastricht Treaty. However, unlike the Banque de France it objected to elements in the Delors Report such as the need for larger regional transfers. An important factor mentioned in 1991 was that almost all Member States should immediately participate in the final stage of EMU. In 1992 this requirement was slackened and the time plan in the Treaty was found acceptable, that is, that EMU could also take place with far fewer than all twelve Member States.

The German Finance Ministry saw EMU in both interviews as a way to safeguard market principles in the European Union. To secure the feasibility of EMU it was essential that wages would be flexible, national budgetary deficits low, and economic development converging. In 1992 the German preoccupation moved to the costs of the transition period, and it proclaimed the need for the shortest possible phase 2, given that the convergence criteria in the Maastricht Treaty would need to be strictly applied. A 'new' argument favouring EMU, mentioned in 1992, was that it would reduce a possible fear that other European countries might have of a reunited Germany going ahead alone.

Thus all three Finance Ministries hold very similar views on the institutional and technical features of EMU and the necessary provisions needed to have it operate within the framework of the European Union. They all stress the need for a monetary union. Their fear, however, is that too early a move to EMU would result in the need for transfer payments, which they considered unacceptable. The necessary adjustments would have to follow the rules of the market. What, however, distinguishes the views of the various national Finance Ministries is that they emphasize different elements as being crucial for the setting up of EMU.

The British Treasury emphasises that it supports the *principle* of EMU but dislikes *any* move towards more economic or political integration other than the absolute minimum: transfer of monetary sovereignty, and some rules on budgets. Distortions need not be regulated by a new authority but ought to be overcome by adjustments in the markets, especially labour markets. The way the French see EMU is two-fold: first, EMU makes it possible to regain some power over monetary policy-making by handing over the mandate to a European supranational monetary authority, thereby constricting the role Germany plays in determining monetary policy. Second, it institutionalizes the present monetary policy based on price stability. Finally, the German Finance Ministry is most of all interested in securing the market mechanism in Europe, and extending its rule to all countries of the European Union by creating an EMU that conclusively institutionalizes an anti-inflationary monetary policy in all participating members, that is, all the countries of the EU.

7.3 Employers' organizations

The CBI is interested in EMU provided it does not imply a greater redistributive role for Europe; it opposes the regional transfers, and disapproves of the Social Charter being taken on board to accompany EMU. It sees EMU as favouring price and exchange rate stability, and the lowering of transaction costs. However, the most important point, strongly emphasized in the 1992 interview, was that CBI wants Britain to join the single currency if it is launched. It distanced itself from its government's focus primarily on the political aspects of EMU.

Thus, the main difference between the 1991 and the 1992 interviews refers to the convergence criteria. In 1991 the CBI still opposed rules on budgets, whereas in 1992 the rules were considered important to reach the necessary convergence between the Member States.

Remarkably little difference between the two interviews conducted with the CNPF is found regarding the perceptions on EMU. The main difference between the 1991 and the 1992 interview was that in the latter more emphasis was placed on the need for greater convergence. Possibly this reaction to the strict convergence criteria was only decided upon in the final hours of the Intergovernmental Conferences. The central theme running through the interviews conducted with CNPF officials is that in the organization itself a battle was being fought about the desirability of EMU. This might explain the very positive stance of individual policy-makers in favour of EMU and a single currency.

The view of the BDI is that it favoured EMU as long as it is based on market principles and its participating members had economies that are sufficiently converging. Reflecting on the situation in unified Germany, the concern was over an economic and monetary integration without adequate convergence. The 'economic' component of EMU was considered as important as the 'monetary' component. Thus, for a succesful EMU more convergence between the European economies would be necessary. Several macroeconomic indicators would need to be converging, such as foreign trade, inflation and interest rates, and levels of public debts and budgetary deficits. In addition the role and mandate of the ECB in EMU would have to be identical to that of the Bundesbank in contemporary Germany.

When comparing the three employers' organizations it is clear that all three employers' organizations favour EMU because they see it as a way of improving the business climate in Europe. Their reasons are many. First, the single currency would reduce transactions costs, and make the economic climate across Europe more attractive for business, especially for the small and medium-sized enterprises. Second, a single currency would facilitate international trade with non-European countries. The single currency would probably grow to become a world currency. Third, EMU would institutionalize the 'German' monetary policies in a European framework, which would guarantee low inflation rates and exchange rate stability, though a CBI official was more sceptical about this prospect. The institutionalization of German monetary policies was also the reason the employers' organizations in all three countries believed the ECB should have the same mandate and institutional set-up as the Bundesbank in Germany. Fourth, EMU would have to follow market principles, meaning that the regulatory role of the governments would need to be reduced. All three employers' organizations were convinced that EMU would require – and indeed lead to – less regulation and state intervention than is today the case in many Member States. They did not see the need for increased regulation at the European level. Except for pursuing monetary policies, no supranational authority was necessary. They did not even agree to the adoption of the Social Charter.

There were also differences between the three employers' organizations. The CBI was initially, in 1991, more worried about the apparent need to have limits on national budgetary deficits, even though it recognized the need to have low deficits in EMU. By 1992, however, this was no longer a concern and it took on the generally held view that the limits on budgetary deficits and public debt were indispensable if the necessary convergence was to be reached. In 1991 and 1992 the BDI was the only employers' organization that actively proclaimed the need for constructive action by the European institutions. It realized that an EMU meant more transfer payments. Thus it stressed the need for convergence so that if less developed economies such as Portugal and Greece joined, very large transfer payments would not be required, though some would be unavoidable. In the 1992 interview strong emphasis was put on the need for real convergence. The BDI was critical of the fact that Member States had not taken this aspect very much into consideration during the IGC negotiations. The CNPF also put more emphasis in 1992 than it had in 1991 on convergence as a necessary condition for a country to enter EMU. The CNPF respondent was in general very much in favour of EMU, and did not stress the need for conditions in the same way as the German and British employers' organizations did. However, this view might be misleading as the respondent stressed that an important minority within the organization opposes the move to EMU, making it impossible for the organization as a whole to adopt policy statements favouring EMU.

7.4 Trade unions

Trade union officials claimed that their organization did not have a strong view on the Werner Report and the EMS. At the time they were more concerned with domestic politics. However, regarding the current economic and monetary integration process a clear involvement is displayed. Almost all trade unions in the three countries favoured EMU. The only 'outsider' was the CGT, which stressed that it had not taken a view on it at all, and the TUC did not quite want to put it in those terms.

There are many reasons for the positive attitude of the large majority of trade unions towards the monetary integration plans. Their motives ranged from favouring 'positive integration' to not opposing the EMU plans but hoping to be able to 'reconstructing from within' or 'becoming part of the decision-making process'. An example of the 'positive integration' would be the regaining of power over economic and monetary policy-making at the European level that was felt to have been lost at the national level. An example of 'reconstructing from within' would be lobbying for the Social Chapter, knowing that only a minimal package could be obtained. An example of 'becoming part of the decision-making process' would be submitting proposals to the IGCs and the EP. The trade unions realized that they would not have any influence, and they would be worse off, if they merely voiced opposition to the EMU process. They hoped that once they were accepted as a serious negotiating partner they could persuade the others to adopt policies which would spare workers and trade unions from having to carry too much of the burden of adjustment.

Trade unions did not question the two main objectives that the other actors have stressed, that is, EMU should secure price stability and therefore it needs an independent central bank with only one mandate. Trade unions, however, added that the aim of price stability and the independence of the ECB should not frustrate their main objectives, namely employment, growth and reducing inequality between social classes and regions. In the view of most trade unions it was therefore important that the monetary authority be balanced by an economic authority. This objective was sometimes combined with the need for a political union. All trade unions wanted to aim for various policy objectives at the same time as a package deal. The British stressed the need for Britain to accept the Social Chapter in the Maastricht Treaty, the French wanted an active policy for growth, employment and reduction of inequality, whereas the Germans favoured the development of the 'economic union' and later the 'political union', thereby creating a federal structure for Europe.

The British trade unions were fighting their own battle against their national government. All emphasis in the EMU debate in 1992 moved strongly towards persuading the British government to accept the Social

Chapter. The French and German trade unions were closer in their main objectives of EMU and the contents of their 'packages' that should be adopted side by side with EMU, though for opposite reasons. The French unions were tired of their country being the passive follower of German monetary policies, and envisaged EMU as the ultimate way to become more influential themselves and to restrict Germany's power. The German unions, on the other hand, were worried that the other European Member States would not accept the *de facto* German setting of monetary policy for Europe, especially after reunification. The DGB, by wanting a more federal set-up, would also want to avoid a European monetary union which was being totally deregulated, liberalized and only market-oriented. Hence, a small core moving ahead first and accepting political union would be the desirable option of the DGB.

The surprisingly interesting motive which supports the hypothesis that trade unions want to be taken seriously as a European actor is that none of them, except the CGT, wants to express a firm 'no' to EMU, even if they doubt whether EMU in the short or long run would serve their interests. It appears that their strategy aims at being part of the policy-making process or community; they want to be taken seriously. To reach policy aims it appears that they consider it more effective to make amendments *from within* than to scream 'no' *from outside*. The other interesting result is that trade unions want to look towards Europe to regain the power over economic and monetary policy-making that at the national level has been lost.

A final interesting result of the comparison of the trade unions is that all of them wanted to combine EMU with other policy objectives, two in particular: to diminish the social and regional differences in wealth across Europe, and to have the Social Chapter accepted parallel with the monetary union. A significant number of respondents actually mentioned the fact that Delors was president to explain why they did not want to 'miss the boat' this time. It was thought that Delors would be more susceptible to claims of the trade unions in the field of social provisions and transfer payments.

7.5 Conclusions – the horizontal comparison

The above sections have compared similar actors across three nations by examining the perceptions of EMU held by central banks, Finance Ministries, employers' organizations and trade unions in Britain, France and Germany. It has become clear that every group of actors has broadly similar attitudes towards EMU. The monetary authorities in the three countries voice concerns about EMU's possibly taking place prior to having equal convergence performance in all participating countries. The employers' organizations warmly welcome EMU and are convinced that it will need to operate in the Internal Market, that is, it is necessary that it continues to be based strongly on market principles. These three groups of actors, the two monetary authorities and the employers' organizations, take a liberal market with low state regulation as their point of departure. Lastly, the trade unions fear the negative consequences for workers of the development towards merely regulating *monetary factors*, thereby leaving it to the market mechanism to settle other policy areas. However, they realize that trade unions are not going to be taken seriously if they bluntly oppose the EMU project. Worse still, they fear that they would face an even less regulated market if nothing were to be arranged. They hope that if they can influence the agenda setting of what is decided together with the whole EMU package, this might give them a stronger position.

The above sections have provided a 'horizontal' comparison of the views of actors, that is, those of functionally similar actors, thereby giving an inter-country or transnational comparison of similar actors. In the following sections the 'vertical' comparison is made, that is, the views of the four actors within the three respective countries are analysed.

7.6   The vertical comparison – comparing the actors within each country

So far this chapter has compared how the actors across countries view EMU. The second part of this chapter focuses on the actors within each country. The central aim of this final part of the chapter is to discover what characterizes the perceptions of the four actors in each of the three countries respectively. Finally, when actors voice their perceptions and policies towards EMU a distinction is made between statements in so-called 'national' terms, and 'functional' terms. The latter tries to capture the perspective which characterizes the view of any set of actors, that is, that of 'central banks', 'Finance Ministries', 'employers', 'organizations' and 'trade unions' respectively. Thus the actors' statements are analysed as to when they use arguments typical for the function of organization, and when they use typically national arguments, and when do these overlap?

The remaining part of the chapter is structured as follows. It is divided into five main sections. The first three each discuss the positions taken in the three countries – that is, Britain, France and Germany. They each briefly summarize the attitudes in 1991 and 1992 in each country towards three central issues: firstly, towards the Werner Report and EMS; secondly under which conditions EMU would be considered desirable; and thirdly, the effects of EMU on other policy areas. The final section addresses the question of when a national actor has held a 'functional' attitude to EMU, and when a 'national' attitude.

7.7   Britain

Werner and EMS

The attitudes of the four actors on the Werner Report can be summarized as having been non-existent or having centred only on the theoretical issue. This follows logically from the fact that Britain was not part of the EEC when the Report was published. The Bank of England's view on the Werner Report was that EMU was not taken seriously by officials in the Bank of England, but it was imagined that EMU could happen in the next century. The supranational element of EMU would feature monetary provisions: 'a single currency, a single monetary policy, and a single monetary authority'.[213] The Treasury claimed that it formally accepted the plan, but was opposed to the introduction of a single currency. The CBI respondent mentioned that it did not work on EMU in the 1970s. Lastly, the British trade union confederation, TUC, said that it did indeed discuss EMU but opposed it, as the TUC was completely against the Common Market until 1975.

When the EMS was introduced the British actors were also sceptical about it. The Bank of England was against ERM entry until 1985. Before that date it was thought that the Bank of England could aim at low inflation on the basis of a domestic nominal anchor. In the middle of the 1980s this policy line was abandoned, and it was thought that this 'low inflation' objective might be reached more easily by joining the ERM. A respondent mentioned that it was now necessary to convince the Treasury to join the ERM.

The Treasury gave three reasons as to why it did not favour joining the ERM before 1990: the pound was a petro-currency, inflation rates had been too high, and the process of capital liberalization demanded greater convergence before entering.

The CBI, like the Bank of England, started favouring ERM participation from 1985 onwards. It also had as its primary objective the reduction of inflation rates, because it wanted to combat the high interest rates which were considered undesirable for business. The French and the Italian experience of ERM entry which resulted in lower inflation rates was the *leitmotif* for the CBI.

According to one of its officials, the TUC was, in principle, in favour of fixed exchange rates, though it was very worried about entering the ERM at too high a rate. However, the EMS issue was only a very minor issue on the TUC agenda up to the late 1980s.

What can be concluded from this brief survey on the attitudes of the four British organizations and institutions towards the earlier EMU plan and the EMS is that in this period the actors sought to protect their interests on the basis of *national* indicators. European monetary integration did not play a large role in the policy-making of the four actors. If they evaluated these plans at all they concluded that the time was not yet right – if ever – for Britain, or for a British actor, to take part in it. The first reported change came in 1985 when both the Bank of England and the CBI started favouring ERM entry. The TUC also changed its outlook on Europe during the second half of the 1980s. The Treasury took even longer to favour participation in European monetary integration plans.

Desirability of EMU

All actors reluctantly accepted, or did not accept, the Delors Report, each for different reasons. The Delors Report provided the Bank of England with what it called 'a workable procedure'. Whether or not it should be followed was a political decision which the Bank did not have to make. The Bank of England approved of EMU as it was set out in the Delors Report provided that three conditions were met. First, the Single Market needed to be fully operational, secondly EMU needed to imply only very limited fiscal rules, and, thirdly, the low inflation objective should have priority over the launching of the single currency. The main difference between the 1991 and 1992 interview was that in the later interview the Bank of England no longer opposed the fiscal rules, but, on the contrary, now valued them highly.

The Treasury was much more sceptical about the Delors Report in 1991. It argued that it might never agree to EMU, but was joining the negotiations to influence the outcome of the process. The Treasury wanted to steer the others away from a federal solution, while simultaneously maintaining the British government's right to join EMU if it wished to do so. By 1992 the Treasury was still not at all certain Britain would ever decide to join. What it thought would be the crucial factors determining this decision were domestic politics, the state of the economy, the perceived costs of joining the single currency, and whether the labour markets were flexible enough to cope with the burden of adjustment.

The CBI's view of the Delors Report was very positive. However, like the Bank of England, when interviewed in 1991 the CBI was opposed to the fiscal rules. Again, like the Bank of England, this opposition had been overcome by 1992. The CBI also stressed the need for a flexible labour market to cope with the burden of adjustment if monetary policy-making is to be decided at a supranational level. There was no need to compensate workers or regions for this increased pressure on the labour market; no need for increasing structural funds. Also the respondent did not think it was necessary to have economic convergence before the start of EMU. In 1992 the latter thought was abandoned, and it was now considered necessary to have economic performance, economic growth rates etc. converging before starting EMU.

The TUC was not at all convinced that EMU as set out in the Delors Report was desirable. Rather, it held the view that it was 'inevitable'. The TUC stressed the need for an *Economic* Union as well as a *Monetary* Union; the former term implying the guarantee that employment and social standards would not deteriorate as a consequence of EMU. However, it did not approve of the fiscal rules that were envisaged in the Delors Report for the very same reasons as the other British actors. By 1992 it too had relaxed its protest because it considered the increased burden of adjustment on the labour market too much of a risk. In 1992 'Black Wednesday' had led to a strong movement in the TUC favouring 'some form of closer EMU'. However, because the British government had opted out of the Social Charter, the TUC favoured EMU only if it included a social dimension.

The perceptions of EMU by the British actors show that the British view towards EMU is dominated by concerns about fiscal rules, the realization that the burden of adjustment will fall on the labour market and the question of opting out of the Social Charter. At the same time they were aware of the fact that, if Britain did not participate, 'Continental Europe' might go ahead anyway. Trade unions in Britain had to cope with three actors (two monetary authorities and CBI) who agreed to put the burden of adjustment on the labour market, without requiring any compensation, such as the adoption of the Social Charter. However, the unions decided that the only way to put pressure on the government to adopt the Social Charter anyway, was by pressing for it via EMU.

Effects on fiscal and social policies, unemployment and economic growth

The British interviewees predicted that deciding the levels of direct taxes and social policies would remain the exclusive right of national governments. They could, however, see that market pressures would exert a downward pressure on taxes and social premiums to reduce the cost of labour and to attract business and investment. By striving for competitiveness this downward pressure would appear to result in a downward harmonization trend of fiscal and social policies. The monetary authorities and the CBI thought that it was important to leave the formal autonomy in these policy areas to national governments and to rely on market forces in order to ensure that governments did not endanger the competitiveness of a country. This market constraint was considered a very positive side-effect of further European integration. They opposed any extension of the redistributive task of the Community. The TUC was not very content with the market orientation. It feared that Britain was not internationally competitive. It claimed that Britain was a high-cost country though a low-wage country; hence other countries would benefit from increased competition.

Regarding the effects of EMU on unemployment and economic growth none of the actors claimed that EMU *per se* would be favourable for growth. The monetary authorities stressed that the level of convergence reached before joining EMU would determine the results. The CBI also warned of rising unemployment if EMU started too soon. However, as soon as EMU was fully operational a CBI official predicted a 'net increase in jobs' even though there would be structural changes, that is, some industries would not be able to compete. The TUC foresaw the greatest problems in the transition period, when the benefits of EMU were not provided and adjustment costs would have to be paid in terms of loss of employment and reduced economic growth. In the third stage the costs and benefits of EMU on economic growth and employment would, according to the TUC official, vary strongly across regions and countries. To have a more even spread of the benefits, European Member States would have to coordinate economic policies, which he doubted would happen.

In conclusion, the British actors all seemed to agree that EMU would not by its mere construction create economic growth and jobs. The monetary authorities and employers' organizations were positive about the effects of competition on the results of their domestic economy if EMU were to be started under the right conditions. The TUC was sceptical about the claimed positive effects of EMU, especially about the distribution of the costs and benefits. To improve the situation of the various social groups and regions in EMU it stressed the need for policy coordination among Member States.

7.8 France

Werner and EMS

The French view on European monetary integration in the 1970s was characterized by the fact that some policy-makers still believed that some inflation was good for economic growth. The monetary authorities stressed that even though 'low inflation' had been an objective to aim for, it was only since 1983 that the government had really been committed to a 'franc fort' policy. The employers' organization, CNPF, mentioned that in the 1970s 'nobody believed in EMU'. The trade unions in France were very much divided amongst themselves. The CGT was very anti-European, whereas the CFDT was more cooperative, though in the 1970s the unions as a whole were much more inward-looking, that is, had a more national perspective.

What the data seem to indicate is that in France the attitudes were nationally oriented in the 1970s and early 1980s. It was only in 1983, with the turn-around in the economic policy of the French government, that the French started to take the external environment seriously. By doing so they started to become more pro-European, and started to see European integration as a way of compensating for loss of policy autonomy. The government decided to stay in the EMS and direct its policies towards monetary stability.

Desirability of EMU

The French actors were generally very positive about the Delors Report. Both monetary authorities welcomed it but emphasized, in the 1991 interview, the need to extend the contents of the economic union. They proposed introducing more economic policy competence at the European level which would be conducted by an economic authority. In 1992 this idea was abandoned, and the respondents claimed that the French monetary authorities were satisfied with the clause on 'subsidiarity' that was introduced in the Maastricht Treaty.

The employers' organization CNPF was divided on the issue of EMU. The responsible official was very pro-EMU, but explained it was impossible to put this view forward publicly because the powerful Gaullist fraction in the CNPF was sceptical about it.

The three major trade union confederations interviewed held different views on the Delors Report. The CGT was totally opposed, the FO was moderately opposed, and the CFDT generally agreed to EMU but warned against 'monetarism'. The CFDT strongly favoured the idea of having an economic authority in parallel with the ESCB. It would be responsible for safeguarding economic objectives such as employment and equity. In 1992 the CFDT was not very pleased with the Maastricht Treaty since in its view the Treaty did not envisage more powers for the Community in the field of economic policy-making.

Summing up the French view on the desirability of EMU, it seems that in 1991 all actors favoured a supranational institution which would very moderately parallel the new monetary authority. The 1992 view of the Banque de France and Finance Ministry was that only a very minor transfer in economic policy-making would parallel the complete transfer of monetary policy-making to the European level. The CFDT was less convinced, and was still aiming at extending the powers of the Community to include employment and equity policies. The French CNPF was divided on the issue of EMU and hence refrained from taking a formal position.

Effects on fiscal and social policies, unemployment and economic growth

The French officials held the same view as the British on the issue of the effects that EMU plus the Single Market would have on the policy autonomy of governments when it comes to making fiscal policy (taxation) decisions. Setting the levels of direct taxes and social contributions would remain the sole responsibility of the national governments, though market forces would exert some competitive pressure resulting in a *de facto* harmonization trend. Regarding the effects on social policy the view was slightly different. The French monetary authorities, however, were less convinced than the British that levels of social premiums would be affected as much by market forces as taxes would.

The trade unions, by contrast, were more worried about this harmonization trend via market forces and feared 'social dumping'. As mentioned above, they strongly voiced the need for the Community to commit itself to employment objectives, and to guarantee even regional spread of the costs and benefits of EMU. If nothing was arranged at the European level the CFDT feared large distortions across Europe.

The CNPF thought both areas of policy-making would be affected equally. The CFDT believed that the French would have a more difficult time than other countries as they would have to revise the whole tax system, due to the harmonization of indirect taxes. According to the CFDT, the loss of indirect tax revenue might have to be compensated by *raising* direct taxes in order to finance the level of public spending.

The French monetary authorities believed that economic growth and employment creation would automatically result from EMU. The CNPF voiced a more reserved opinion on this consequence of EMU, stating that it would strongly depend on the competitiveness of the industry involved. The trade unions' idea was that EMU would be most 'painful' in the transition period, but would certainly produce net benefits in the final stage, though the benefits would not automatically be spread evenly.

Summing up the 'French' view on EMU, it can be said that it is generally more positive than the 'British' view. The attitude towards the earlier Werner and EMS plans is more positive, and the Delors Report and EMU as set out in the Maastricht Treaty were given greater support. In addition, even though EMU was thought to affect fiscal policies via market forces, monetary authorities thought that social policies would be less affected by EMU + 1992. Moreover, the French believed that EMU would 'automatically' have positive effects on economic growth and employment.

7.9 Germany

Werner and EMS

The view of all German actors with regard to earlier monetary integration plans has been dominated by the idea that performance on monetary and economic policy indicators should develop in parallel; economic convergence had to be met before embarking on increased European monetary integration – the 'economist' view. The attitude of the monetary authorities towards the Werner Report was generally positive in the early 1970s, but as soon as the international context changed, the plan was put on ice rather quickly. With regard to the EMS all actors in the early 1980s were sceptical about its feasibility. As it proved to operate successfully, the actors started to have more confidence in its development.

Desirability of EMU

The German view of EMU is predominantly an 'economist' view. The idea that economic and even political integration needs to accompany monetary integration is supported by all four German actors.

The Bundesbank was much less enthusiastic about the EMU plan than was the German Finance Ministry. The reason for this lack of enthusiasm was that the Bundesbank did not think it would be possible for all European Member States to reach the adequate level of convergence before the final stage started. Though more generally in favour, the Finance Ministry still mentioned three conditions to be met before it would accept EMU as was set out in the Delors Report: first, economic policy-making needed to remain in the realm of national parliaments; second, strict limits on budgetary deficits needed to be imposed; and, third, convergence in economic development was necessary between those countries that wanted to join EMU. By 1992 the Finance Ministry official was convinced that EMU as envisaged in the Maastricht Treaty was fully acceptable. It was important to the Finance Ministry to have reached agreement on deepening European integration, but also to show the other countries of Europe that Germany was devoted to the European ideal, rather than exploiting its economic power. They thought it necessary to emphasize their political responsibility after German reunification.

The German employers' organization, BDI, supported the Delors Report on three conditions: a credible timetable, more political integration in parallel to EMU and, finally, sufficient economic convergence between the participating countries to avoid having to contemplate the need for transfer payments which might have to be made by an asymmetric spread across regions of the costs and benefits of EMU.

Similarly, the German trade union confederation, DGB, accentuated in 1991 the need to develop the *economic* part of EMU. Upon re-examination of EMU in 1992 the idea emerged that EMU ought to have an economic government, or, more generally, needed to be flanked by the political union.

Effects on fiscal and social policies, unemployment and economic growth

Tax competition was thought to be strengthened by EMU + 1992 market mechanism. The BDI could imagine that both direct taxes and social premiums would be reduced in order to cope with international competition and attract investment to the country. In contrast to the officials of the British and French employers' organizations the respondent of their German counterpart did not believe that outcompeting other regions by reducing social standards and premiums was a very good development. He feared it would result in overly low social standards.

The DGB felt the fear that EMU might lead to a reduction in social spending; in the light of increased competition the respondent considered this a positive development that, in the long run, would benefit everyone. EMU would offer the opportunity to try to ensure minimum social levels through policy coordination.

The monetary authorities were more cautious about how the benefits of EMU would be distributed among the various regions of the Community. It was thought that possibly the weaker regions would develop faster than the wealthier regions once EMU was fully operational. The BDI stressed that the market mechanism should be the main force in correcting imbalances in the labour market. This would be the best solution provided that the labour market was flexible. The DGB was also very positive about the effects of EMU on economic growth and employment in the long run, but foresaw a great uneven regional spread of the costs and benefits of EMU in the transition period. A reason to have an extension of the role of the structural funds was to compensate the regions hit hardest.

The German view on EMU is thus best characterized as being centred on the 'economist' view and, additionally, on combining EMU with Political Union. Notably, the Bundesbank warned against achieving EMU before participants have reached a sufficient level of economic convergence. Furthermore, the actors, trade unions included, had accepted the influence of international competition as a driving force for restructuring society. On the other hand, it has been considered necessary to ensure a good minimum level of social standards – a position that was even expressed by the employers' organization, BDI.

7.10 Conclusions

When do actors 'behave' according to the characteristics of their 'function' and when according to those of the 'country'? It can be stated that the 'national trait' is generally propounded by the Finance Ministry of each country. In Britain the Treasury stresses the need to take part in the negotiations and restrict its outcome to the very minimum while simultaneously arguing the need to perpetuate the possibility of joining EMU eventually. In France the Finance Ministry voices a very strong, almost unconditional, desire to create EMU. Even though it claims there is a need to create some kind of 'economic government', it has not fought for this objective during the Maastricht negotiations. The German Finance Ministry favoured EMU as long as its main objective was price stability, and as long as participating countries' economies

Table 7.1 Attitudes towards EMU

	Pro-EMU		Cautiously Pro-EMU			Reluctant	Opposed
France	FFM	BdF	CNPF[a]	CFDT	CNPF[a]	FO	CGT
Germany		GFM		BDI	DGB	BB	
Britain			CBI		BoE TUC HMT		

[a]The CNPF is divided about the desirability of EMU, which is illustrated in the table by categorizing twice.

Abbreviations: BB (Bundesbank), BdF (Banque de France), BDI (German employers' organization), BoE (Bank of England), CBI (Confederation of British Industry), CFDT Confédération Française Démocratique du Travail), CGT (Confédération Générale du Travail), CNPF (Conseil National du Patronat Français), DGB (Deutscher Gewerkschaftsbund), FFM (French Finance Ministry), FO (Force Ouvrière), GFM (German Finance Ministry), HMT (Her Majesty's Treasury), TUC (Trades Unions Congress).

could 'prove' to be economically converging as expressed by the performance of their monetary indicators. The other German motive was to show the other Member States that Germany was committed to Europe.

Within every country some actors are more in favour of joining the EMU plan while others are more reluctant. After a discussion of the attitudes of the actors within the countries, it is clear that the French are the most positive and the British actors most reserved. In Table 7.1 these attitudes are pictured schematically. The table illustrates that the French actors are on the whole the most positive (if the views of the CGT and FO are left aside) followed by the Germans and lastly the British. Within the three countries there is a spread in support for EMU. This scheme needs to be used with great caution, as it reflects an estimation of the actors' perceptions on EMU. Caution is especially needed as actors do not hold an equally positive/negative view on all issues related to EMU. Likewise, the views have undergone minor changes over time. On the whole it seems true to say that the German and French Finance Ministries pushed the process forwards, whereas the Treasury tried to hold it back. The Banque de France is very positive, whereas the Bank of England, and certainly the Bundesbank, hold more reservations. The employers' organizations seem to be generally more in favour of EMU than the trade unions in their respective countries. The French and the British are more in favour than the German employers organization, mainly because the German employers hold stronger reservations about the conditions under which they would agree to EMU. The trade unions follow the same pattern as the Finance Ministries: the French are the most in favour, the British the most reluctant.

The above analysis has shown a characterization of the actors' perceptions of EMU by adopting a functional or national point of view. It examined three issues: attitudes towards the Werner Plan and EMS, the desirability of EMU, and the spill-over effects of EMU on fiscal and social policies as well as on economic growth and unemployment.

8
Conclusions

What started the present study was the observation that an apparent consensus existed in 1989–90 among monetary authorities and social partners about the desirability of Economic and Monetary Union in a smaller Member State. This led to the core research question for this study: what were the perceptions of EMU of these actors in three 'major' Member States in the period 1991–2 (that is, during the intergovernmental conferences and their immediate aftermath). More specifically, how did actors perceive the potential of EMU to serve or frustrate their policy objectives or interests? In seeking an answer, several questions were posed and examined: which arguments were decisive with regard to the actors accepting or opposing EMU? Which objectives were they aiming for by accepting EMU? And which problems did they think would be solved by EMU?

The study contains four ingredients. First, it includes *an analysis of integration theories* (Chapter 2). There is no single coherent and accepted theory of integration. Nevertheless, there seems to be considerable consensus on the advantages of integration, and to a lesser extent on its disadvantages. Some schools of thought have supplied mechanisms explaining how and when integration takes place. When applied, the outcomes differ strongly depending on whether an economic or a political science perspective is taken. Various economic theories of integration are discussed, such as the theory of Optimum Currency Areas and its more recent critiques. The political theories that are looked into are mainly the neo-functionalist and the intergovernmentalist approaches. Both are discussed and an eclectic approach has been introduced.

Second, the study provides *a history of economic and monetary union in Europe* (Chapters 3 and 4). The historical background helps to understand why and when economic and monetary integration plans rise and fall, fail and succeed. It gives insight into the motivations of national governments for proceeding towards EMU. The attitudes of the social partners and monetary authorities are discussed. It is clear that national interests strongly influenced decision-making towards European integration projects before the mid-1980s. There are some interesting similarities between the conditions that gave rise to the Werner Report in the late 1960s and the Delors Report in the late 1980s. The immediate aftermath of the acceptance of each of the two plans also shows some resemblance, though with two important differences related to national policy decisions and the changes in the global economy.

Third, the study contains *a comparison of attitudes towards EMU* of the four different actors (respectively of central banks, Finance Ministries, employers' organizations and trade unions) across countries, as well as within the three countries (in Britain, France and Germany, respectively). A comparison is made of the perceptions of EMU in two time periods (Chapter 6). Next, a comparison is drawn between the 'functionally' similar actors across the three nations and the comparison of the actors' perceptions within these nations (Chapter 7). The research methodology used for this study is set out in Chapter 5.

Fourth, *the author's theory, an eclectic 'theory'*, is introduced, which provides a framework for understanding the motivations of the actors to accept EMU. It can be viewed as a (partially) amended integration theory (Chapter 2 and this chapter). It is argued that the problems the actors faced in the late 1980s were of a different nature than the problems assumed in the conventional theories, most of which still seem to build on the economic reality of the 1960s and 1970s. European actors were confronted with a loss of power which manifested itself in reduced *de facto* sovereignty. In their view reduced autonomy over policy-making was a result of globalization, deregulation and the success of earlier integration projects. These developments indicate a need to integrate insights from the field of political economy into economic and political science theories of integration.

The remaining part of this chapter is structured as follows. Sections 8.1 and 8.2 return respectively to the economic and the political integration theories. The history of EMU is briefly summarized and discussed in Section 8.3. It is followed by the presentation of the eclectic theory (Section 8.4). Section 8.5 summarizes the perceptions of the actors, Section 8.6 analyses the data, and an application of the eclectic theory is provided in Section 8.7. The chapter concludes by reflecting on the results found in this study (Section 8.8) and offering some indications for further research (Section 8.9).

8.1   Economic theories not persuasive

Several questions were raised in the first part of Chapter 2, which discussed the economic literature of integration. Answers were found in trade theory and the theory of Optimum Currency Areas that predict advantages from free trade, economies of scale, efficiency, and reduction of exchange rate uncertainty. The questions posed were: which benefits and costs are the likely result of economic integration? In particular, what does the economic literature tell us about why an 'economic union' or 'Economic and Monetary Union' would be established? The economic literature review showed that EMU, as it was proposed in the Delors Report and accepted in the Maastricht Treaty, was a European invention. In the relevant economic literature on economic integration several stages are distinguished. The one that resembles 'EMU' most is what was originally named 'economic union', but was later redefined 'complete' or 'full' economic union to avoid confusion with the term used in the Werner and the Delors Reports. Monetary union is an integral part of it. However, to fulfil the criteria of the 'economic union' as defined by the earlier authors (cf. Balassa, 1961; Robson, 1989; Tinbergen, 1965), it would need to have an economic component as well. This set-up would provide for transferring funds via a federal authority. This provision would be necessary in case of adverse effects resulting from the loss of the monetary policy-making instrument. It is clear that this is not quite the same 'economic union' which is envisaged in EMU as was chosen by the EC/EU Member States.

The second concept that resembles part of the EMU project is to be found in the literature on Optimum Currency Areas (OCAs). According to this theory countries which trade a lot with one another, and that still have their own economic policy-making at the national level, may benefit from using a common currency for transactions in a larger economic area. Countries that are eligible for joining an OCA would be countries that are sufficiently alike in their economic structure, and that have the required large interactions taking place between them, as well as high mobility. Economists who have studied this literature and applied it to the EC concluded that the EU was *definitely not* an OCA (see *inter alia* Commission of the EC, 1990b; Eichengreen, 1990, 1993; Sachs and Sala-i-Martín, 1989; Taylor, 1995).

The costs of creating EMU were thought to be particularly high in the transition (the adjustment) period. They were thought to derive mainly from the loss of policy instruments, that is, losing the possibility to raise tariffs as well as the de- or re-valuation possibility. Since the economic benefits of integration are calculated on aggregate, certain regions or sectors probably would suffer considerably as a result of integration. The main reason for this is that EMU will not have a federal budget to offset possible disruptions, as happens in federal states. When EMU is fully operational the distribution of this aggregate wealth will be left to market forces. The EU budget remains very low (between 1 and 2 per cent of total GDP of the EU) and hence it will not be capable of adequately addressing issues of unequal spread of costs and benefits of integration.

Thus, economic theory supplies several reasons why states should proceed towards 'economic union'. However, the main focus is on static effects and on the aggregate benefits. It is difficult to deduce how individuals, sectors or regions will benefit from moving towards EMU if examined separately, or if *dynamic* and *spill-over* effects are taken into consideration. It is also clear, however, that EMU is an invention that has met certain expectations of the Member States. On the basis of this research an attempt is made to see which assumptions the actors within Member States had when embarking on EMU (see in particular Section 8.5). In the next section the political science integration theories are re-examined to see if they offer answers as to why economic and monetary integration would happen, and why Member States and actors within these countries would think EMU desirable.

8.2   Limits of neo-functionalism and intergovernmentalism for understanding EMU

The question raised here was why and how does integration take place? The two main schools of thought that were discussed are neo-functionalism and intergovernmentalism. Both hold different assumptions about why integration happens, who the decisive actors in the process are, and what mechanisms lead to successful or unsuccessful integration. It is now appropriate to recapitulate what their assessment is of the integration process.

The neo-functionalists hold the view that the integration process starts in some policy areas because some actors, whether societal groups or government bureaucracies, consider it functionally practical to settle issues in these policy areas at the supranational level. These issues would concern technical matters that are not politically sensitive areas of policy-making. They are named 'low politics'. An example is social–economic policy. By contrast, 'high politics' refers to issues that are central to the identity of the state and the ideological differences in the domestic political scene, for example, security and defence politics. As soon as integration has successfully taken place in one policy area, it will eventually require integration of other policy areas (spill-over). It seems to have an internal dynamic that is monitored in part by a supranational authority. It is not fully automatic. The actors will notice that the policy areas that were transferred to the supranational level have been looked after successfully. Some policy areas will now be more difficult to handle at the national level in isolation from cooperation with other states and soon thereafter it will prove to be handy to transfer more decision-making capacity to the supranational level. This is the spill-over mechanism.

The intergovernmentalists take the national governments as the dominant and decisive actors. The integration process develops as a logical consequence of interstate bargaining. The larger Member States, in particular Britain, France and Germany, play a dominant role in this interplay. In contrast to the neo-functionalist assumption, societal groups are thought to play at most an indirect role. They can only influence the outcome by lobbying, and persuading their national governments to take their interests into account when defining 'the' national interests. In contrast to the neo-functionalist theory, it is assumed that the integration process does not have any internal dynamic, neither through integration spill-over from one policy to another, nor through the workings of a supranational authority. If there appears to be spill-over, then it is because the Member States decide that they want to embark on further integration because of domestic interests heading in that direction. If the policy objectives of various dominant Member States converge, then one can expect coordination of policies, and eventually perhaps integration. This can happen more easily if national policies and strategies have started to converge, as governments have abandoned earlier policies, and adopted policies of other countries that have pursued such policies with great success. Yet even the globalization process has not been identified as having caused the integration process. It is still argued that the exact outcome of the coordinated policy, or indeed integration, results primarily from the interstate bargaining process.

When examining how these schools of thought view the European economic and monetary integration process it is found that the conventional theories are only partially successful in anticipating the progress of the integration process (see Section 2.3 of Chapter 2). The neo-functionalists would predict that economic policies should be an easy subject for integration; they are considered to fall into the category of 'low politics'. To a certain extent this is actually what happened. The 'economic' part of the development of the Community has kept the integration train moving forwards. Even though on several occasions in the history of economic and monetary integration the EC plans did not materialize, some projects have been unexpectedly successful. The EMS set up in 1979 survived its childhood miraculously, only ran into difficulties in 1992–3. The impact and speed of the completion of the Internal Market, as was set out in the Single European Act of 1985, was perhaps an even better example of the neo-functionalist concept of policy decisions on technical matters being taken at a higher level which eventually would trigger the need for other policy issues to be settled at the supranational level. Finally, EMU was set up to incorporate a monetary policy which would aim at price stability and eventually to supply a single currency. The latter would safeguard the benefits of the Internal Market. These last two integration projects – the Internal Market programme and the EMU project – were considered at the outset to be highly technical matters that could better be arranged at the supranational level, rather than having national politicians conduct individual national policies. These statements all sound very much like neo-functionalist thinking. But there is more to the story.

How would the intergovernmentalists interpret the same facts? Their focus would be on the bargaining of the national governments to safeguard their interests, and whether the domestic policy objectives of the Member States would happen to coincide. The outcome of any bargaining would not contain more than the lowest common denominator or, if it contained more, it would have been a result of the greater bargaining power of the larger states. Hence, referring to the same examples, the EMS was successful because the Member States participating in the EMS had started converging policy objectives. Important contributions to its success were the policy experiences of France (1981–3) and Italy in the mid and late 1980s. These countries discovered that it was necessary to try to keep inflation under control, and during the course of the 1980s they started using the EMS framework to funnel policies to meet the inflation and exchange rate objectives.

The case of the SEA has been seen by Moravcsik (1991) as an exceptional case of countries handing over policy sovereignty to a supranational authority. In this view it is again a logical consequence of policy decisions directed at the same aims. On the other hand the EMU package was perceived much more as a result of bargaining between the Member States, because the actors who took the decisions were the Heads of State and Governments.

Turning back to the discussion of neo-functionalism, the fact is that it can very eloquently explain the dynamics of integration considering only its theoretical concepts of spill-over and the evidence – that is, the renewed move towards European integration. However, neo-functionalist thought does not identify two of the main motives for the renewed interest in integration. What the present study shows is that the move towards EMU is triggered by three causes; in addition to the spill-over effect there are two other causes.

First, the Member States saw EMU as a solution to the problem of lack of national policy autonomy. This lack had resulted from the change in the global economy, rather than from a response to the integration process itself. In preference to fighting each other, they felt that they needed to unite the European interests in order to stand up to the rest of the world, in particular to the Pacific Basin and the United States. This mechanism has been better understood by the intergovernmentalists with what is often been referred to as 'policy objective convergence'.

Second, another result of the awareness that the global economy had changed was that Member States drew the conclusion that their domestic economies were too rigid, making a flexible adjustment to the external changes very difficult. It was politically problematic to address these issues at the national level, as it implied reducing the benefits that industry and labour had received from the state. It was felt that any political actor which would embark on this restructuring of the welfare state would have to try to sell very unpopular measures. By focusing on the benefits of European integration, and by using European integration to legitimize the need for change, it would be much easier to restructure society. It is these two aspects related to the changes in the international global economy that the neo-functionalist theory had not anticipated as having been decisive in creating the momentum for renewed interest in European integration.

Intergovernmentalists failed to recognize that the support of the European economic and monetary integration project by the societal groups made it very easy for the governments to develop the EMU plans. An exception in this regard is Andrew Moravcsik's Liberal Intergovernmentalist approach which *does* incorporate a role for domestic economic interests to affect national government interests and preference formation (Moravcsik, 1998a). However, it does not take seriously the preference formation at the EU level. The current study, however, has showed that employers' organizations and trade union confederations have been very active in promoting the European objective at the European level as well. The umbrella organizations of trade unions and employers' organizations at the European level have played a significant role in getting the message across that they favoured the deepening of European integration objective, albeit under some specific conditions. The support from societal actors served as additional legitimation to national governments for surrendering sovereignty to the supranational level.

What the intergovernmentalists also did not envisage was the fact that the spill-over was indeed taking effect, albeit *in parallel* with the globalization process. It was considered by all actors impossible to turn back the clock. For example, the success of the EMS and the '1992' project made actors want to secure its full benefits by creating the EMU project. The capital liberalization of July 1990 polarized the choice. The Delors Committee decided to let the first stage of EMU coincide with the decision already taken to liberalize capital. Thus, the study disagrees with Grieco's interpretation that spill-over did not occur (Grieco, 1995), when in fact it did. All in all, the European leaders would be either moving beyond the EMS or moving back. The domestic actors in Britain, France and Germany have realized that it is imperative to accept a whole package deal, which has been carefully negotiated, and that there is no easy way back.

8.3 Lessons from history

Despite a number of obvious major differences between the late 1960s and the late 1980s (such as the existence or non-existence of a regime of global fixed exchange rates, the level of economic integration in Europe, the policy culture with regard to economic and monetary policy-making, as well as changes in the global economy), a remarkable similarity occurs between the two periods in which the EMU project was launched in the European Community.

In 1969 in The Hague it was decided to have a group of monetary experts draft a report on how to create an EMU in Europe. The Werner Group that completed the EMU blueprint in October 1970 consisted of members of economic and monetary committees of the EC who represented the six Member States. The reason why this particular point in time gave rise to the idea to create EMU was three-fold. First, it was felt that the integration momentum, which was built up as a result of the completion of the common market in 1968, needed to be maintained. Second, Member States believed that in order to safeguard common European policies, such as the CAP, it was necessary to guarantee stable exchange rates. Third, the institutionalization of fixed exchange rates or a single currency was not thought to be very difficult as the Bretton Woods system had ensured a system of fixed exchange rates. Any pressure on the system was felt to be caused by the United States, in particular the value of the dollar and the US level of interest rates.

Almost two decades later, in 1988, the Hanover Summit called for an EMU blueprint. The Delors Report was completed in April 1989. As had been true for the Werner Report, the Delors Report was written mainly by a group of high-ranking monetary officials, in this case mostly central bank governors, who represented all Member States. The circumstances were very similar to those of two decades before. Whereas in 1968 the customs union had been completed, in the late 1980s the '1992' project to complete the Single Market was well under way. Again it was felt that the integration momentum needed to be maintained. Second, in the late 1980s, as had been the case two decades before with the common market, there was a strong belief that one could only reap the fruits of the Single Market if stable exchange rates, or ideally a single currency, could be achieved. Third, again similar to the late 1960s, the successful operation of the existing system of fixed exchange rates, the EMS (in the 1960s: Bretton Woods), made many believe it would not be too difficult to institutionalize the EMU project.

However, EMU as it was set out in the Werner Report did not survive the difficulties of the early 1970s for four reasons. First, heavy speculation waves took place in the early 1970s, making it very difficult to maintain fixed parities. The devaluation of the dollar in particular proved an obstacle for coordinated response by the Member States. Second, the first oil crisis provided an external shock to the system. Though the EC countries were probably affected more or less similarly, they did not respond to the crisis collectively, nor did they adopt similar policies or aim at similar policy objectives. Third, whereas the 1960s had been an economically profitable period, the early 1970s were economically more difficult, as became apparent from the recession, increasing inflation, and unemployment. Fourth, the Werner Report had been a compromise between the 'economists' and the 'monetarists'. The surging pressure on national economic and monetary policies revealed that insufficient consensus existed between the Member States on how to move forward to reach EMU. The familiar EC decision-making practice of making agreements on uncontroversial issues, and leaving the more difficult issues open, had backfired. In sum, the international context changed, but the Member States were still pursuing policy objectives in isolation.

The Delors Report had a better start than the Werner Report because of the success of the EMS in the mid and late 1980s. The EMS was launched by its initiators in order to tackle a number of international problems: the dollar instability, uncertainty about oil supplies, and the division of the capitalist world into various economic areas.

The EMS plan had a second stage as well, though it never materialized. At this stage the EMS would have probably died like the EMU initiative of the late 1960s and 1970s and the Snake. However, it became successful because participants committed themselves to maintaining the exchange rate parities and reducing inflation. This became apparent in the mid and late 1980s, when parity adjustments became less frequent. In retrospect many stress the importance of the French decision in 1983 to accept the restrictions of the monetary regime, and to direct policies in its support. The '1992' project then added to the momentum which provided the fruitful ground for the creation of EMU. As a result the Member States started to consider the ERM as a political symbol of successful European integration, and tried to avoid adjustments in the exchange rate parities.

In the late 1980s the successful German model of conducting monetary policy (based on price stability) had been accepted by all actors as *the* European model. The discussion of the history of EMU demonstrates that integration plans have been accepted more easily when national policy-making fails, and when it is possible to join a successful partner. The success of these plans then depends strongly on the economic and political conditions at the time when decisions to integrate are made. These decisions are not so much based on a clear understanding of theories of economic integration. Rather, they are based on *ad hoc* ideas with which actors perceive the success of their policies and their own power position.

Now drawing the parallel with the circumstances that led to the early abandonment of the EMU project of the 1970s and the period in the early 1990s, some surprising similarities are found. First, in the early 1990s the external shock was provided by German unification and the end of the Cold War; in the 1970s the Bretton Woods system collapsed and the first oil crisis upset domestic European economies. Second, in 1992–3 heavy speculation appeared against the ERM currencies, again similar to the speculation in the early 1970s. In both cases a low dollar and large Europe–US interest rate differentials worked as a catalyst. Third, both the Delors Report and the Werner Report were drafted during a period of economic boom. The early 1990s, however, were characterized by a deep recession. Fourth, as with the

Werner–EMU, the Delors/Maastricht–EMU had been a compromise, though the split between the various views was not as deep in the late 1980s and early 1990s as it had been two decades before.

Whether the EMU plan will be successful remains to be seen. In any case it has been developed further than ever before, and it appears to be right on track. The eclectic theory presented below suggests that the Member States might in this phase of the integration process have considered this process to be a necessary condition for survival in the global economy. What can be concluded from having studied the perceptions of the actors in the policy-making process, as well as from considering the policy decisions of the monetary authorities in the 1993 period and beyond, is that most Member States appear to have broken with the trend which dominated the 1970s and very early 1980s, namely that national policies were pursued in isolation, and Member States postponed commitment to the integration goal in difficult times. Instead, national policy objectives have been directed towards common goals, and these objectives are not so easily set aside by the appearance of crises. Evidence for this is that the second round of interviews conducted for the present study, which took place during a period of economic recession and severe uncertainty about whether the Maastricht Treaty would be ratified, or whether the ERM would ever recover, did not result in respondents changing their perceptions, or using the negative mood in Europe to voice the desire to strengthen national aims rather than the European monetary integration goal.

The aftermath of the period which was carefully studied in this book, namely the period 1993 onwards, provides evidence of the EMU objective not having been abandoned during a turbulent period. During the 1990s European Member States witnessed a deep recession and at different times strong currency speculation. Yet the EMU objective was not abandoned. In fact many more countries than had been anticipated pursued stringent policies in order to be part of the first group of countries to launch the euro in 1999. However, the results from this book indicate that the fact that political leaders of Member States are still cooperating to aim for EMU is not really surprising. The greater challenge that EMU faced in the second half of the 1990s was societal actors and national governments' response to economic recession. Yet the apparent support for EMU shows the clear commitment to policy objectives underlying EMU. This is the main difference with the situation in the 1970s. Three special cases are Denmark, Sweden and the UK, who seemed to have not wanted to join EMU from the outset. However, in these countries the opposition to EMU seems to have to do more with the political legitimacy of the project than it has to do with the intrinsic changes in policies that it would necessitate or require. It remains to be seen whether these countries will want to stay outside the euro zone or eventually join. At the same time it also remains to be seen whether or not problems occur when EMU is up and running (see also Strange, 1998: 60–77).

8.4 A critique of integration theory: the development of an eclectic theory

As was shown, economic theory and political science integration theory do not adequately explain the renewed interest in EMU in the late 1980s. The economic theories have not been able to give a sufficient economic explanation of why the EC of Twelve or Fifteen would want create to an EMU. According to these theories the present EMU either does not go far enough – that is, it should include more federal, redistributive aspects – or else, if the Member States stop short of the federal objective, it leaves the economists with the puzzle of how *all* twelve, fifteen, or more, could join a single currency, and have all of them benefit from it. As was argued above, economic theory predicts aggregate wealth increase, but does not argue convincingly that the market mechanism can ensure benefits across countries, sectors, political actors or individuals. It can hence be concluded that political motives provide a necessary additional explanation.

The political science integration theories had lost their convincing (predicting) character in the late 1970s and early 1980s, but came back into focus in the early 1990s. The boost in European integration, from the mid-1980s to the early 1990s, had, however, not been 'predicted' and did not follow convincingly from the insights given by the two major integration schools of thought.

Neo-functionalist thought sees the process too much as an a-political transfer of sovereignty, and as a result of the internal European dynamic of handing over policy-making autonomy. The present study shows it is mainly the *perception of the changed external factors* that has convinced actors of the need to increase European integration. These external factors include, for example, the perception of the deteriorating position of Europe in the world *vis-à-vis* the Pacific Basin and North America, the awareness that the dollar has continuously frustrated European integration aims, the realization of the need for restructuring of the industrial societies as a result of changes in international production, trade and finance (see also Verdun, 1998d).

The intergovernmentalist approach refuses to accept the external or the internal dynamic from the process; the neo-functionalists correctly make the latter point. What has been a very interesting conclusion derived from the present study is that the EMU process stands in the middle of a spill-over process. It is a result of spill-over and policy-makers anticipate spill-over from its creation. The first spill-over dynamic is well known. EMU is considered to be the *result of spill-over*, that is, it is a requirement to benefit fully from the Single Market. The second spill-over dynamic is one which can be concluded from the present study. The actors in the policy-making process decided that they favoured EMU for its *perceived future spill-over* on economic policy-making. It is thought that by adopting an 'asymmetrical EMU' the harmonization of economic policy-making will eventually take place via market forces. An 'asymmetrical EMU' was defined in Chapter 1 as an EMU which has a very developed monetary component, including positive integration in the field of monetary policy-making, but a very underdeveloped economic union. The latter does not include positive integration. The coordination that is foreseen in the field of economic policy-making concerns reductions of budgetary deficits and public debts. The other elements were already institutionalized by adopting the Single Market. Adopting this asymmetrical EMU will force a restructuring of domestic societies, stress the need for policies to strengthen a country's competitive position and allow it to cope with the changed international context. More importantly, the political actors will not need to take the full responsibility for this process.

Interdependence and globalization have made it necessary to re-examine how economic questions would fit into the categories of 'low' and 'high' politics as were referred to above. If low politics applies to those policies which Member States believe beyond ideological contention, and which can *better* be monitored at the supranational level, it seems that 'monetary policy' perfectly fits the category. This seems a counter-intuitive result, as 'money' has traditionally been at the core of a people's sense of identity, as well as at the core of national sovereignty – thus crucial for national governments to want to control. However, monetary policy had become a logical candidate for integration because a single currency would increase the benefits of the internal market (*spills over*).

By contrast, this label could not be placed on macroeconomic policy-making, which includes budgetary and fiscal policies, social policies and labour policies. It is widely thought that decision-making in this field should remain the sole responsibility of Member States. Moreover, it would not be considered desirable to transfer competence in this area of policy-making to the Community level in the foreseeable future. Every Member State wants to have the freedom to determine how its GDP is redistributed among its citizens. Evaluating the data of the 1990s the conclusion is drawn that macroeconomic policy-making, social and labour policies – what the neo-functionalists called 'welfare politics' – have become 'high politics'. This stands in stark contrast with what has tradionally been assumed in neo-functionalist theory (Haas, 1958, 1964), or for that matter in the intergovernmentalist critique of neo-functionalism.[214]

The intergovernmentalists took the view that the European integration process is an extension of international bargaining. To a certain extent the data here provide evidence for this idea. For example, the French government and domestic actors want EMU because it will restrict German hegemony over monetary policy-making. However, it has been found in the present study that the loss of policy-making autonomy was also a driving force behind the urge for economic and monetary integration. Yet an analysis merely of the intergovernmental bargaining process cannot fully appreciate the underlying motives for EMU.

To understand why there has been renewed interest in EMU, it should be recognized that the world economy has changed. National economies have become more than ever interdependent, and geographical borders cannot protect the producers from competition from elsewhere. If national policies are out of line with neighbouring countries, capital and production will move across the border, or even switch continents. As the welfare state in Europe has developed over the years, labour costs have risen, and competitiveness has been lost *vis-à-vis* the rest of the world. In the 1980s and 1990s Europe's growth has been sluggish compared to the boom of the 1960s. Job creation in Europe remains low, and major industries have declined at the same time other economies in the world have had a much better performance. As a result countries are fighting to attract production and to create an attractive business climate. As the countries have become more and more interdependent individual countries only have limited tools available for attracting business; national policy autonomy has been lost.

These circumstances are quite different from what was assumed conducive to integration in the theories discussed above. Yet there is a renewed interest in integration which is therefore a result of a different process. The actors involved (social partners and monetary authorities) were hoping to give a boost to economic growth. It is interesting that the mid-1980s witnessed a first upswing after a major recession in the early 1980s. The common denominator of the European countries was not being able to compete adequately with the rest of the world.

In this situation the European countries decided to integrate; form a block together to solve the problems. Following economic theory of integration, creating the Internal Market was envisaged to increase aggregate (European) wealth. As soon as the integration 'momentum' had been created, it had to be maintained. Further economic and monetary integration was needed; EMU was the ideal candidate.

Accepting a common currency or irrevocably fixed exchange rates requires a single monetary policy. This implies a total transfer of monetary sovereignty to a supranational institution such as a European central bank. Now, why would it be possible that actors in major European Member States agree to this significant transfer of sovereignty in the late 1980s? Below it will be seen how the eclectic integration theory explains this.

In this globalized world, divided into three strong economic blocs (and others that are not related to one of these three blocs), the leading economy in Europe was Germany. It enjoyed great international success and its currency was strong. An exceptional feature of the politics of the German economy was its stringent monetary policies. The independent Bundesbank had one clear mandate: securing price stability. As a result of the dominance of Germany in the world and the dominance of its monetary policies in the EMS, a future European monetary union had to have German monetary policies at the heart of the new system, and with a monetary institution operating as the Bundesbank.

In sum, integration theories must include more factors than they have included thus far. The actors in the policy-making process in middle-sized nation states, such as Britain, France and Germany, have lost much of their *de facto* sovereignty due to developments in the global economy. Thus, economic and monetary integration was embraced to solve problems of loss of sovereignty at the national level, for it was hoped by the various actors that they would regain it at the supranational level.

In Chapter 2 a framework was set out to explain why actors within countries would agree to postpone the domestic concern about redistribution, and unite in order to proceed towards integration. Three stages were identified as to how the process would move on. The results of the present study support the dynamics set out in that chapter. Instead of repeating the three stages laid out there, the mechanism will be illustrated by the following example.

Suppose that actors and elites within a country consider the challenge from the new global economy to be an attack on its existing domestic economy. They thus respond to it as they would respond to a state of war. In phase one the national authorities and the societal actors make a dramatic appeal to the population to unite and fight the enemy. Everyone is requested to work and cooperate to reach this goal. Nobody makes a problem about working conditions or pay; it is all done to save the country. The permanent threat of the state of war silences other demands.

In phase two the war has ended, the enemy is defeated. The country is disrupted completely. The goal of phase one is fulfilled, everyone is praised for his/her contribution. But again an appeal is made to everyone to cooperate in reconstructing the country. Now, the 'fear' element of the war is gone. Slowly people start to see the benefits of their work and gradually start making demands. These are still silenced by the need to consolidate first.

In phase three the country has successfully been reconstructed. There is no fear of war, nor the idea that special effort has to be made to get the country up to par. Everything in the country can function normally again. Hence, the traditional questions of power and redistribution are back at the top of the agenda.

What is pictured with this illustration is the mechanism of actors and elites in a country feeling threatened by an external factor, and being willing to compensate for it by temporarily postponing their internal differences and in particular redistributive matters. This example will illustrate the way to use the framework for understanding the findings of the research to which the discussion now is directed. In Section 8.7 the findings are applied to the eclectic theory.

8.5 Actors' perceptions of EMU

Chapters 6 and 7 of the study examined what answers the actors gave to questions in interviews concerning their perceptions and interests towards EMU. A number of questions were examined: what are the specific interests/policy objectives of the various actors subject of this study, and how does EMU serve their interests? What policies do they pursue towards EMU? Under which circumstances do they favour EMU? How can further integration serve their interests? This section briefly states how the actors perceived EMU, that is, the perceptions of the central banks, Ministries of Finance, employers' organizations and trade unions.

EMU was perceived by the central banks to benefit their policy objectives. They favoured a number of its aspects. The Bank of England was determined to keep the door open for eventual participation in EMU. The Banque de France favoured it to secure a European influence in the global economy and to regain some ground on the Germans. The Bundesbank was sceptical of EMU but agreed with it as long as it would copy the German model. If that were the case the Bundesbank would have managed to have its domestic policy choice institutionalized in the EU. Given the fact that the DM had grown in importance as a global currency, the Bundesbank considered it a merit of EMS and EMU if other countries were to adopt monetary policies similar to those of Germany.

In other words, given the changes in the global economy the central banks see EMU as a way to safeguard domestic policy choices. These can be addressed better by creating a European-wide framework, such as EMU, than by depending on national policy choices and bargaining between European Member States.

The Ministries of Finance have held views similar to those of their national central banks, though with distinct differences. HM Treasury was generally more reserved than the Bank of England. The Treasury did not want to rule out the possibility that EMU might never come into being, whereas the Bank of England perceived it as something of the near future. The Treasury, however, still chose to participate in the negotiations in order to put the brake on the push forward to further integration, and to ensure that the other Member States did not move in the direction of a federal goal.

The Ministère des Finances has been very much in favour of EMU, though not quite as much as the Banque de France. Its main benefits have been perceived as institutionalizing the *de facto* exchange rate regime, and introducing a single currency. Its point of reference has been that at present France has not been very influential on a global scale. More particularly, it has been concerned about the fact that in Europe France's monetary policy decisions have been dominated by those of Germany, notably the Bundesbank. By creating EMU, France has hoped to regain power on both the global and the European level.

Finally, the German Bundesfinanzministerium was much more positive towards EMU than was the Bundesbank. Its official stated that integration, that is, economic, monetary and political integration, was its core aim. This intention to integrate became even stronger after the fall of Communism with all the consequences for Central and Eastern Europe and the rest of the world.

All three Finance Ministries called for the assurance that EMU would operate in a fully fledged market economy, and that economic convergence between Member States would be strengthened. The main fear was that EMU would lead to transfer payments to weaker regions.

The employers' organizations in the three countries have also stressed the need to create EMU, and in particular to create the single currency. However, they would be opposed to having the EMU plan be accompanied with policy creation or positive integration in other fields of policy-making (such as fiscal or social policy). Hence, they have been very satisfied with the outline of the present EMU, which has an asymmetric nature. Most importantly it has left coordination of economic policy-making and achieving economic convergence to the Member States and market forces.

The CBI in 1991 was worried about the fiscal rules, but accepted them in 1992. The CBI considered it very important that Britain would join EMU if it came into being. It would be most costly if the rest of Europe went ahead, and Britain decided to stay out. The little hesitancy that the CBI had against EMU was related to the fear that if EMU did not benefit all participants, then transfer payments would be necessary. This is why CBI officials stated that the convergence criteria (including the debt and deficit criterion) were good provisions. They would keep the economically weaker countries initially out of EMU, which would then reduce the risk of having to pay compensation if they did not equally profit from monetary integration.

The French CNPF members were divided amongst themselves. The Gaullist members of the CNPF were opposed to the plan, mainly because they disapproved of the transfer of sovereignty to a European Central Bank. By stark contrast, the advocates of EMU within the CNPF were strongly in favour. Similar to the view held in the Ministry of Finance, they saw it as a way to make France via Europe again a powerful actor. In addition, their perception was that German policy and German industry were the main beneficiaries of the *status quo*. Hence, EMU was very important to those members in favour of it.

The German BDI took a slightly different view. It did not regard EMU as a sensible idea unless there was a willingness to go beyond what was formally proposed. The economic component needed to be strengthened, in order to avoid the risks of having to make transfer payments to regions or sectors that would be affected negatively. It was more important to have reached sufficient convergence and solidarity before entering the third stage of EMU than to start strictly on time. The view of the BDI clearly reflected the fear of having to repeat at the European level what had happened at Germany's reunification.

Most trade unions in the three countries were positive about participating in the EMU process. The exception was the French communist trade union, the CGT, which was fully opposed. It had particular motives. Next to the French CGT, the TUC had the most cautious attitude towards EMU, mainly because its national government managed to opt out of the Social Protocol of the Maastricht Treaty. The TUC's main objective was to influence the policy-making process, by contributing to the debate rather than opposing it even if the proposals did not serve their interests. Its main interest was to try to push the debate on EMU towards discussing the Social Protocol and convince the British government to adopt it. The TUC officials explained that they could not accept the Maastricht Treaty without the Social Protocol. After the pound had just left the ERM, in 1992, the TUC was more sceptical about the convergence criteria than it had been in 1991. This resulted mainly from the frustration that the British government immediately relaxed monetary policy after having dropped out of the ERM. The years of accepting policies to secure monetary rigidity seemed wasted.

In France the trade union confederations had different views on EMU. The CGT, as mentioned, was completely opposed, the FO was opposed to some parts of EMU, and in favour of others. The analysis in the present study has focused mainly on the CFDT rather than the CGT and FO. The CFDT was generally open to the plan. It was convinced that France's future lay in Europe. EMU was considered a necessary tool to support the main aims of the CFDT. Its main reservation concerned 'monetarism'. The fear was that monetary objectives would have supremacy above all other economic objectives such as fighting unemployment, and a more equal spread of wealth across social class and regions. Still, this was not a reason to oppose EMU, because the *de facto* choice would be between the dominance of the Bundesbank or of the European central bank.

The DGB was more positive about EMU than the TUC or the CGT, but more reserved than the CFDT. Though very much like the TUC it decided that it was more important to participate in the debate than to oppose the whole process and risk having an even worse outcome as a result of not having contributed to the negotiating process and/or leaving things as they were. The reason why it favoured EMU was the realization that ultimately national economic policy-making will fail to be effective if it is not coordinated with that of other European countries. Its main aim, however, was to strengthen the 'economic' component of EMU. In 1992 it was thought that EMU would not be acceptable to Germany if the political union remained underdeveloped.

On the basis of this study, the 'prevailing view' in the three countries would be sketched as follows. Though the 'British view' was not unitary some trends can be distinguished. All British actors wanted, first, to secure that if others went ahead they wanted to be able to choose to enter EMU, and second, they wanted a safeguard against the rest of Europe moving ahead to a federal goal. With regard to the EMU proposals the British actors were, initially, very sceptical of the fiscal rules, but they accepted them after the Treaty was signed as they realized that it provided a mechanism that would keep the less-well-performing countries out of EMU. It would protect them against having to accept a transfer union, or having to harmonize other policy areas measures, which they fully opposed.

In comparison, the French view was by far the most uniform and the most pro-European (that is, if the CGT and the Gaullist members of the CNPF are excluded). The French hoped to achieve two aims. First, as they had come to realize that the role of France in the world was very marginal, they wanted to regain influence in the global setting by strengthening Europe, creating a single currency, and by playing an important role within Europe. Second, they wanted to contain German influence, especially in the monetary sphere. EMU was a way to gain back some power.

The German view on EMU was that EMU ought to institutionalize the successful principles of the EMS and the monetary policy choice of the European monetary authorities to aim at price stability. However, it was absolutely crucial that this EMU would not take place with members that did not have converging economies. The long-term motive to have EMU is that it would contribute to four German aims: strengthen the market economy in Europe, ensure that further European integration would not significantly increase transfer payments to weaker regions, improve economic convergence between the Member States, and eventually establish political integration. The integration objective was very important in the light of the changes in the tri-polar world, particularly after the collapse of Communism.

Summarizing, the actors in all three countries saw EMU as an answer to changes in the global economy, as well as a way to compensate for the loss of national autonomy, but also to facilitate achieving a variety of domestic aims. The framework against which the decision was made was the success of the EMS. Hence it was thought that no serious policy adjustments in the monetary field were needed, and a large potential of gaining influence in the global economy lay ahead.

8.6   Analysing the results

To understand why integration takes place, the findings of this study can be analysed by distinguishing between the actors' use of 'economic' and 'political' arguments. In addition, the process of integration can be analysed by examining the results at three different levels: the geopolitical (or global) level, the domestic level and the level of the actors. Table 8.1 has schematically set out the results (see also Verdun,

Table 8.1   The motives for adopting EMU mentioned by the majority of the respondents

Economic motives

Related to Monetary Union	*Related to Economic Union (strengthening the Single Market)*
Price stability	Reducing transactions costs
Exchange rate stability in the EU	Increasing benefits through economies of scale
Single currency	Increasing competition by strengthening market principles
Regarding sovereignty at the European level	Increasing trade through reduced exchange rate insecurity
	Increasing efficiency/productivity

Political motives

Related to domestic politics	*Related to geopolitics*
Legitimation of the adoption of 'German-type' monetary policy by institutionalization and centralization at the European level	Strengthening the *political* role of the EU *vis-à-vis* the rest of the world
Legitimation of the need to restructure the national welfare state	Strengthening the *monetary* role of the EU *vis-à-vis* the rest of the world
EU does not become a federation – no transfer-union	Having the Ecu/euro as a world reserve and trade currency
Slow progress of economic integration in other policy areas	
Integration of the nation-state in Europe	

1996). Table 8.1 has been already incorporated in Verdun (1996). (Unfortunately, however, in the original publication the first item on the left-hand side in that table under the heading 'monetary union' incorrectly stated 'public stability' instead of 'price stability', as is correctly reproduced here.) This scheme tries to grasp the consensus of the actors by focusing on the main economic and political motives for promoting the creation of an EMU. Part of the economic motives fall under the heading 'Monetary Union' with four central objectives. The actors agree that a European monetary policy has as its core objectives price stability and exchange rate stability in the EU as well as a single currency. These three objectives require as fourth an institutionalized single monetary authority which directs policies to achieve these goals. Under the heading of 'Economic Union' economic motives are highlighted which strengthen market forces in general and the Single Market in particular. It is clear that no central economic authority was thought to be necessary to enforce these aims. On the contrary, policies in this field should be left to the nation-states, and the 'testing' of the efficiency of policies will be done by market forces.

The second main category highlights political motives. In the domain of domestic political motives it was found that actors felt the need to legitimize two trends. First, the trend that requires adoption of 'German type' – that is, anti-inflationary – monetary policy-making. Secondly, the trend that requires the restructuring of the welfare state. Although all actors anticipated that the present 'generous' welfare provisions in EU Member States could be an obstacle to labour flexibility and international competitiveness, addressing these issues was seen as being politically very difficult. Thus, it was considered attractive to rely on market forces for eventual harmonization to restructure the national welfare state. A third motive related to domestic politics is that actors stressed the need to ensure that the EU refrained from taking on a substantial redistributive role. A fourth motive in this category was the need to make *only* slow progress in other areas of policy-making; anything more would not be politically possible or desirable at the moment. However, as mentioned before, it was recognized that other areas of economic policy-making (such as fiscal and social policies) would be affected by EMU and the working of market forces. The fifth and final motive related to domestic politics was the need to ensure the integration of the nation-state into Europe. What is meant here is that Member States have considered it very important, for political reasons, that their country is firmly integrated into Europe. This point is placed in this category rather than in the category related to geopolitics, because it refers back to the individual nation-state, rather than Europe as a whole. The last category, 'geopolitics', seeks to portray the role of Europe as a whole within a wider world. Motives in this category centre on how respondents viewed European unity as a necessary prerequisite for gaining influence in the global economy. Europe would have a more important voice in monetary and political affairs, as well as increased bargaining power, by having a single currency that could be used in international trade and as a reserve currency.

What the scheme does not include is the level of the actors. This study has disclosed that the actors were experts in the monetary field; they had a similar educational background and had ample experience in working on monetary policy issues and European integration. They were very well informed about what the economic literature had to say on the costs and benefits of economic integration and had often read the Commission reports (e.g. the 'One Market, One Money' Report). They participated in international meetings, usually knew their colleagues in other Member States, and were generally well informed about the view of actors in other countries.

It is interesting that many of the respondents have tried to isolate monetary affairs from adjacent policy areas. They held similar views about how low inflation would contribute to economic growth, and they generally accepted the idea that an independent monetary authority would be more able to guarantee low inflation than politicians. It is also remarkable that they all perceived EMU to have a long-term effect on social and fiscal policies. They perceived market pressure to force some level of harmonization on these policy areas. Some actors (monetary authorities and employers' organizations) were more excited about this prospect than others (trade unions). Thus, it can be stated that the integration process benefited from the actors in the policy-making process holding similar views. In addition, all actors favoured participating in the process and they favoured contributing to the creation of an EMU, even if this implied that the final package deal would not fully serve their aims.

8.7 Applying the eclectic theory

It is now time to apply the three stages of integration as set out in the eclectic theory of integration to the findings of the present study. The core idea of the eclectic theory is that actors within countries may temporarily settle the differences between themselves, especially the redistribution issue, in order to fight for survival. In their search for allies in other countries with whom to cooperate they are also willing to settle possible differences. It may be useful to keep in mind the illustration that was set out in Section 8.4 above, where a comparison was drawn with a country at war. Stage one resembled the 'war economy', stage two referred to 'reconstruction' and in stage three a country was 'back to normal'. Its explanation of why integration takes place depends strongly on the perception of actors within a country that they are not going to gain anything if the country does not unite within, cooperate with allies and respond to the challenge posed by the 'enemy', in this case the perceived changed global economy. The domestic actors are willing to make temporary sacrifices in order to ensure that they benefit from integration. Hence, in stage one domestic actors have postponed the domestic struggle for redistribution. As long as it is assumed that the actors within the country are going to find a strategy to fight external challenge, domestic support will be there. The assumption is that remaining outside the process will definitely harm the actors and citizens within the country. In the eclectic theory of integration this is considered the first stage of integration. Five reasons for why the commitment to EMU developed are stated below.

1. The EMS had been successful in the 1980s because all participants eventually agreed to the aim of monetary stability, that is, low inflation and stable exchange rates between the members. The experience of four major countries and the coordinated effort of the smaller countries were crucial. Germany was a country which witnessed economic prosperity throughout the decades. It had also managed, without interruption, to maintain low inflation rates already in the 1970s but also throughout the 1980s. It never had to devalue against other currencies. This country became an example that many countries eventually started to follow. Second, the lesson learnt by France in 1983 also contributed importantly to the success of the EMS. In 1983 the French government abandoned overnight the Keynesian demand-led policies and adopted policies aimed at low inflation. Monetary policies were directed to reach this objective throughout the 1980s. Third, the experience of Britain again showed how difficult it was to conduct policies in isolation. That country had between 1979 and 1985 tried to maintain low inflation by merely focusing on domestic indicators. When this failed it was decided in 1985, unofficially, to shadow the DM. Fourth, the Italians successfully reduced their rate of inflation by joining the

ERM. Fifth, the Benelux countries, Denmark and Ireland managed to keep their exchange rates within the ERM narrow bands.

2. The '1992' project to create a Single Market induced the genuine belief among producers, consumers, employers, employees and governments, that fixed exchange rates and preferably a single currency were needed to reap the profits from its completion. This view was accepted by all actors, though they held different perceptions about the costs they would agree to incur in order to reach this aim. The SEA had already voiced this logic in its document. The central banks very quickly drafted the Delors Report, and the Finance Ministers had already done substantial work on EMU before the start of the IGCs. The employers' organizations favoured the single currency and refrained from entering the debate on political issues. Even the trade unions grasped their opportunity to manifest themselves in the debate. They generally favoured EMU to support the Single Market and decided that this was the time to add to the agenda the issue of the Social Dimension and related issues of unemployment, the democratic deficit, the more equal spread of wealth across the regions and the attempt to institutionalize collective bargaining principles at the European level.

3. The liberalization of capital flows in July 1990 and the financial innovations that had been developed during the 1980s made it very difficult for the ERM to survive if speculative attacks on ERM currencies were to occur. In 1991 when the Maastricht Treaty was negotiated everything was still quiet in the financial markets. The turmoil started as a result of a multitude of factors: the recession in Europe of 1992–3, the publication of the convergence criteria and the subsequent realization of what they would imply for certain countries, the Danish 'no' in the referendum on the Maastricht Treaty, opinion polls predicting a 'no' in the French referendum, followed a month later with a 'petit oui'. As the EMS had become a political symbol of successful European integration, no agreement could be reached on an early adjustment of the ERM parities. More factors compounded the troubled state of the ERM: the inflationary effect of German reunification and the resulting high inflation rates in the rest of Europe, large interest differentials between the United States and Europe, a low value of the dollar, and finally, of course, the fact that the pound and the lira could not stay in the ERM and many other currencies were forced to devalue. Hence, countries in 1992 could choose to accept that EMU was dead, or that they would have to put in extra effort to keep it alive.

4. In order to maintain a healthy competitive position in the global economy it was felt that the European societies needed restructuring. The role of the public sector would have to be reduced through privatization and deregulation. In addition the actors agreed that, in order to safeguard communal monetary policies, government public debt and budgetary deficit should not be 'excessive'. They decided that the adjustment mechanism would increasingly have to operate through market forces. In particular labour markets had to be made more flexible in order for this mechanism to operate successfully in the market place. It is ironic that the British are most opposed to joining EMU; their society is most advanced in this process of restructuring and they would very much favour a European economy which would be strongly based on market principles and would have more labour market flexibility. In any case, it was seen that the European integration goal, and thus also EMU, which implies that Member States have decided voluntarily to bind their own hands, would provide the necessary discipline. But, more importantly, it is hoped it would provide the *legitimation* of addressing these difficult domestic issues. Again, whether or not this will be successful is another matter which I have dealt with elsewhere (Verdun, 1998a, 1998c, 2000b; Verdun and Christiansen, 2000).

5. The Member States have identified as their main competitors in the fight for survival the actors outside Europe. The Member States in isolation realize that they cannot influence what is happening in the global economy. Due to the globalization process the world has become an even more open and interdependent world than ever. With more countries starting to be successful in the world economy the European Member States feel that they are losing out. Hence, the integration of Europe, by first creating a European Single Market, followed by a European monetary institution and a single currency, is an attempt at creating an actor that integrates the European interests. Member States deeply hoped that by combining efforts the result would be a supranational institution and a European single currency that would be able to have an influence in this new global political economy.

After the EMU plan has been set out, the countries that are on their way to join in are, according to the eclectic theory, entering the second stage of integration which in the analogy with the war economy was named 'reconstruction'; the actors within the country feel that they have now successfully won the war; that is, their country is participating in the EMU process. The domestic actors' hope is that 'Europe' will ultimately serve as an instrument to cope with the outside world, for example that EMU and a single currency will reduce the strong influence of the US and the Pacific Basin. On the domestic level it will still be considered necessary to set aside the internal redistribution struggle, but the domestic actors believe that the country is on the right road.

Not all countries have successfully entered stage 2 of the eclectic theory. Those who do are those that are sure to become members in the fast track to EMU. Countries that are still trying to become part of EMU eventually, such as Greece, and countries that have applied for membership to the EU feel they are still, in this metaphor, fighting the war, and are still in stage one. A number of other countries, such as Denmark, Sweden and the UK, seem to have developed a problem within stage one. These countries appears to be fighting a metaphoric 'civil war' rather than 'uniting to fight the foreign enemy'.

In the third stage, when integration is becoming complete, the actors within a country start to rediscover the issue of distribution of wealth. For the countries that have successfully entered EMU this issue will arise after EMU has become fully operational. It is likely that, if EMU affects some countries, regions or groups of individuals much worse than others, they will not be silent about it just to serve the greater whole (which is what happens in stages one and two). Rather, it is to be expected that the redistributive battle will start.

8.8   In conclusion

This study has embarked on the difficult task of exploring different perceptions of EMU and making sense of its findings. It has tried to generate insights into why monetary integration occurs, by understanding the motives of the various societal actors and monetary authorities in three major Member States. It compared the similarities and differences between the actors, between and within countries, and it tried to make a picture of the 'typical' attitude to EMU in the four functional organizations, as well as of the 'typical' attitude of the actors within each of the three nations. It also examined whether or not the perceptions of EMU changed after the completion of the 1991 Intergovernmental Conferences, and found very few differences.

This study explored whether an analytical framework for integration is offered by the conventional theories of European (economic) integration and political science. It concluded that the economic theories could not explain why all twelve or fifteen EU Member States would want to join an 'asymmetrical EMU'. The political integration theories did not identify all the factors that gave rise to renewed interest in European economic and monetary integration. The study suggested that, to understand the process of integration, it is necessary to make the analysis at three different levels: at the global level, the domestic level and the level of the actor. It proved worthwhile to examine at which point economic and at which point political motives were used, as motives in both the realm of economics and of politics were put forward by the actors.

After the perceptions of EMU have been studied at some length the conclusion is drawn that the actors in the policy-making process in 1991–2, be it the British monetary authorities, the French employers' organization or the German trade unions, all wanted to move forward; that is, to participate in the process of economic and monetary integration. They were all very familiar with the economic theory of economic integration, and had usually read the Commission reports. They were thus aware that the 'asymmetrical EMU' presented an inherent risk of either having to accept great disparities between countries or regions in Europe, or having to increase transfer payments to prevent these disparities from occurring. Each actor and each country had its own specific assumptions concerning why the asymmetric EMU was nevertheless a good thing, and how these pitfalls were to be avoided.

For two reasons all actors thought that the 'asymmetrical EMU' was the correct next phase of integration. First, EMU would not institutionalize much more than what was already happening in the context of the ERM, capital liberalization and the 1992 project. Second, except for the surrender of monetary policy-making to a supranational authority, no transfer of sovereignty would take place. Harmonization of fiscal, social and labour policies would have to come about via market forces.

EMU was thought to be likely to benefit global and domestic objectives. European actors felt that they were losing terrain *vis-à-vis* the US and the Pacific Basin. EMU would give the twelve countries of the European Community/Union a larger voice and larger political weight internationally. The hope was that it would make the European single currency a leading global trading and reserve currency, making Europe less dependent on the US dollar, and more generally on policy decisions taken by the US. Second, it also served all countries' and actors' domestic aims. German actors wanted to promote the integration goal, French actors wanted to contain Germany's power and regain some itself, and British actors wanted not to be left out from the integration plans, and wanted to keep the others from the federalist solution. The monetary authorities wanted to institutionalize the monetary decisions made earlier, but wanted to avoid creating a 'transfer union' or additional policy harmonization; the employers' organizations saw EMU as a way to institutionalize a liberal market economy and the trade unions grabbed their opportunity to set the European agenda for social, regional, employment and redistributive issues. They also thought that they could improve their national position by cooperating rather than obstructing the integration process.

The illusion that the actors seem to hold is that nobody will be held responsible for EMU's results. This is a highly debatable assumption. If large economic disruptions occur, the European Union and its Member States will have to find an answer. The legitimacy problems that the EU has been facing in the second half of the 1990s are evidence of this fact (see also Patomäki, 1997). Moreover, in 1997 the popularity of the new euro was at its lowest point. Fortunately for EMU enthusiasts, support improved in 1998 (European Commission, 1997, 1998a, 1998b; see also Verdun, 1999d). But problems still exist and may surface if the euro has no clear politically responsible body (for further discussion of these issues see Verdun, 1998a, 1998c, 2000b; Verdun and Christiansen, 2000).

If this study had to advise the Member States, its recommendation to them would be that they should start reserving financial resources for the 'costs' of EMU. *They should be aware that EMU could cost them more than they have been willing to accept.* If aggregate benefits of EMU are really significant, then these costs should on the whole not be too high for the Member States. It is naive to assume that one can only integrate monetary policy and leave harmonization of related policy areas to market forces, and be convinced that the domestic and European actors as well as national governments will be happy with the outcome. The belief is held here that EMU will eventually necessitate more integration of economic, fiscal, social and labour policies. To maintain political stability there will be a need for larger transfer payments than is provided for by today's structural funds, including the cohesion fund which was established in 1992. It will need to be made clear who may be held politically accountable over the consequences of the euro, and what is the basis of the legitimacy of the project, if costs and benefits are unevenly spread across the euro zone.

8.9   Recommendations for further research

This comparative case study of perceptions of EMU in three countries has offered some interesting insights into why integration happens, and has provided some suggestions for amending the existing European integration theories. A future study could perhaps focus specifically on perception formation, and aim at obtaining a better understanding of what makes actors perceive certain external effects as being detrimental or favourable to their interests.

A three-country and single-policy area study inevitably risks having a certain bias. In order to gain fuller understanding, its results would need to be examined in more depth. Ideally a future study would focus on more countries, and on other areas of policy-making. The policymaking processes of Greece, Italy, Portugal and Spain would undoubtedly provide interesting case studies.

It would also be very interesting to scrutinize the conclusions reached in this study regarding the perceived effects of EMU on 'other policy areas', and examine *exactly how* EMU affects these policy-making areas. In a similar vein it would be useful to analyse how the 'E' of EMU needs to be developed to cope with the likely future problems that may occur once EMU has become fully operational and the euro banknotes and coins circulate. Are the monetary authorities, employers' organizations and European Commission correct to assume that Europe does not need a federal government, nor a larger redistributive role, nor a larger EU budget? In any event, it is rather doubtful that the Member States will be satisfied for very long with letting market forces determine the outcome of policy harmonization in the field of economic, fiscal, budgetary, social and labour policy. It is quite possible that in the years to come actors and governments will find themselves considering the need for expanding the European integration process into these policy areas as a perceived useful response to globalization and financial market integration.

Notes

1 This book does not aim at contributing to the rapidly growing literature which assesses and defines the nature and novelty of the phenomenon of 'globalization'. For the purpose of this study it suffices to use the vaguer definition. As will be seen in subsequent chapters, none of the actors studied here has a clear definition of globalization in mind when discussing policy-making or perceptions of EMU. Yet, the actors do have an intuitive sense of what it means. Thus, whether or not, and if so to what extent, globalization is really happening, how 'new' it is, and what *precisely* it consists of, will not be discussed here. The interested reader can refer, among many others, to Axtmann (1996, 1998); Dunning (1993); Germain (forthcoming); Helleiner (1994); Hirst and Thompson (1996); Jones (1995); Scholte (forthcoming).

2 The policies of the newly elected socialist government headed by president François Mitterrand aimed at boosting the economy by increasing government spending. This 'redistributive Keynesianism' led to higher rates of inflation in France at a time when German monetary authorities were pursuing a restrictive monetary policy. The result was large speculative attacks on the franc, and a flight into the DM (see for a discussion of Mitterrand's policies in 1981–3 see Hall, 1986: 192–226).

3 In 1988 the size of the Community budget was approximately 1 per cent. In comparison, the gross federal expenditures, as a percentage of total expenditure of the federal states mentioned, are: United States: 70.8 per cent; Canada: 63.9 per cent; Germany 63.9 per cent; Austria 69.1 per cent and Switzerland 29.6 per cent (Lamfalussy, 1989: 109, in: Delors Report, collection of papers).

4 Some misunderstandings might emerge from the usage of these traditionally held labels in this context. 'Monetarist' in this sense simply means that the monetary pegging of the exchange rates should come first (that is, before economic convergence). In this context it is not used to refer to Milton Friedman's influential mode of thought, also referred to as 'monetarist'. The 'economists' stress that economic convergence should precede monetary integration.

5 The Stability Pact was first launched in November 1995 by the German Finance Minister Theo Waigel ('Stabilitätspakt für Europa', *Auszüge aus Presseartikeln*, no. 75, 7 November 1995. See also *Financial Times* interview with the German Finance Minister in *Financial Times*, 11 December 1995). After a year-long discussion it was finally adopted by the European Commission in October 1996.

6 The Euro-X Council was adopted in a Resolution at the Luxembourg Council in December 1997 (*OJ* C 35 2-2-1998). It is based on the articles 109 and 109b of the EC Treaty. It has subsequently been referred to as the 'Euro 11 Group'.

7 Emphasis added.

8 This term should not be confused with a different usage of 'asymmetry' in the literature on European monetary integration, namely the one widely used with reference to the dominance of the DM and German monetary policy in the EMS (cf. Fratianni and Von Hagen, 1990; Giavazzi and Giovannini, 1989; de Grauwe, 1988 and Smeets, 1990).

9 The Delors Committee that drafted the 'Delors Report' consisted of the twelve Member State central bank governors, three independent experts, an EC Commissioner, and had Commission President Jacques Delors as its president. They were asked by the Heads of States and Governments of the Member States to draft a blueprint for EMU (see also Chapter 4).

10 Italy, Spain, Portugal and Greece still gained substantially more from seignorage, i.e. in 1988 these figures were respectively, 1.13 per cent, 1.36 per cent, 2.23 per cent and 2.75 per cent (Commission of the EC, 1990b: 120–1). In the period 1979–86 these countries still had revenues ranging from 6 to 12 per cent (Drazen, 1989; see also Dornbush, 1989; Grilli, 1989; and Spaventa, 1989).

11 A similar argument can be made for revaluations. However, countries that are economically highly intertwined with each other are generally more worried about devaluations than revaluations.

12 Other 'costs' that were mentioned referred to an imperfect introduction of EMU. Fear was it would be created either too speedily or too slowly, and/or with countries whose policies were insufficiently converging. This is why there was call for the creation of an independent ECB whose mandate it would be to guarantee price stability, and why there would be criteria for entry to EMU (see *inter alia* Cohen, 1989).

13 Commission of the European Communities (1990b). The background studies are found in EC Commission (1991). The 'One Market, One Money' Report was also published in a commercial edition: Michael Emerson *et al.* (1992). A shorter, more accessible appeared as well: Michael Emerson and Christopher Huhne (1991). This popular edition was made available in all Community languages.

14 The convergence criteria were decided upon in the Monetary Committee. They were partially based on the average performance of Member States in 1990 (see Commission, 1991b). But in part it was also the outcome of political negotiation within the Monetary Committee, especially with regard to the debt and deficit criteria (see Italianer, 1993; Monetary Committee official, interview with the author, autumn 1996).

15 For a discussion of the use of the cohesion funds in EMU, see *inter alia* Britton and Mayes (1992).

16 The eclectic 'theory' does not try to predict or prescribe. It merely tries to give an explanatory framework for the observed puzzles of actors' attitudes towards European economic and monetary integration (see for the role of 'theory' in the discipline of International Political Economy, Strange, 1994: 9–12).

17 The concept of *spill-back* has subsequently been used as meaning the destruction of integration (cf. Haas, 1968; xxix, and 1971; Hoffmann, 1966: 902; Schmitter, 1971: 242, 264).

18 This special role for a supranational institution is also recognized by the so-called 'new institutionalists' (cf. March and Olsen, 1989). The

supranational aspect of the Community was already recognized at an early stage by a legal scholar Joseph Weiler (1981).

19 It is hard to imagine that this assumption of rational state behaviour holds in complex processes in which a national state preference is the result of a multitude of domestic pressures. Moravcsik heroically accounts for the rational state behaviour by linking two types of general international relations theory into his framework: a theory of national preference formation and a theory of interstate strategic interactions (Moravcsik, 1993b: 482; on the EMS see Moravcsik, 1998a and 1998b. For his overall rational choice treatment of the European integration process see Moravcsik, 1998a).

20 Trade and investment policies are not dealt with. The explanation of why social and labour policies are examined was provided in Chapter 1. The assumption is that, when the EMU process is fully operational, monetary policies can no longer be used for domestic adjustments. As strong emphasis was placed on the need to have the adjustments in the labour market, the study also examines attitudes towards the role of social and labour policies in economic policy-making. Other authors have also stressed the need to examine the role of collective bargaining (Hall, 1994), social policies (Lange, 1993), and the 'stability' attitudes of a country (Busch, 1994a) for examining the implications of fixed exchange rates or EMU. Rudiger Dornbusch (1991) has stressed that adopting fixed exchange rates (and thus an EMU) implies shifting the adjustment burden to fiscal institutions and wage policy.

21 See also Cameron (1992).

22 For a discussion of France and the EMS in the 1980s see *inter alia* Bordes and Girardin (1992). For a general discussion on monetary policy in the 1980s in France and Germany see Goodman (1989, 1992).

23 Moreover, in later work Smith and Sandholtz stress that 'Germany was a vital source of leadership and of initiative on behalf of monetary and political integration' (Smith and Sandholtz, 1995: 248). In this recent publication they stress also the importance of the *EC institutional structure*. 'He [Chancellor Kohl] was able to push for a Treaty on EMU despite the reluctance and scepticism of the Bundesbank. ... The EC's institutional structure for amending the Treaty of Rome empowered Kohl – and the heads of state in general – during the intergovernmental, treatymaking phase' (*ibid.*).

24 These and several additional papers were reprinted in Eichengreen and Frieden (1994).

25 Reflecting on the German Reunification experience, Willy Friedmann (1992) has made a plea for strict convergence requirements.

26 Earlier comprehensive studies of the first EMU project are Tsoukalis (1977) and Kruse (1980). The process of creating the EMS is found in Ludlow (1982), see Chapter 3 below. A new forthcoming book by Dyson and Featherstone (1999) promises to provide a rich analysis of the intergovernmental negotiations leading up to the 1992 Maastricht Treaty.

27 The word 'theory' is used here with great caution (see note above).

28 The domestic economic activity here is also secured, or purely the aggregated economic growth, knowing that, when the area gains as a whole, there will always be something in it for everyone. The problems at this level are mainly for the larger participants (in the case of the EU these are

Britain, France, Germany), and for (smaller) participants with a very different economic structure, or national policies. Central and Eastern European countries applying for EU membership, examples of the latter, may find they have to pay a very high price in terms of loss of economic activity if they decide to carry the large adjustment costs necessary in order to be able to qualify to join EMU.

29 This 'fall back' may or may not be considered a good or bad thing, depending on one's normative position on integration.

30 In the 1950s *three* European Communit*ies* were created: the European Coal and Steel Community (ECSC), the European Atomic Energy Community (Euratom) and the European Economic Community (EEC). As they shared the same institutions the three communities together were referred to as *the* European Communities (EC), or in everyday usage 'European Community'. When the Treaty on European Union – the Maastricht Treaty – came into force on 1 November 1993, the notion of 'European Communities' formally was replaced by 'European Union' (EU). However, the three original treaties, incorporated in so-called 'pillar one' of the Maastricht Treaty, were now officially named 'European Community'.

31 In 1960 it formed, together with six other European countries, the European Free Trade Association (EFTA). The seven member countries of the EFTA were: Austria, Denmark, Norway, Portugal, Sweden, Switzerland and the UK.

32 Between the drafting of the ECSC and the Euratom and EEC, negotiations took place in 1951–2 for a European Defence Community (EDC) and a European Political Community (EPC). The EDC Treaty was even signed in May 1952. However, the two draft Treaties failed to mature because of French opposition in its National Assembly.

33 The 1992 Maastricht Treaty stipulated that the Monetary Committee would cease to exist at the start of the third stage of EMU. An Economic and Financial Committee with more or less the same mandate would replace it. This has meanwhile happened, i.e. on 1 January 1999.

34 This section draws heavily on Tsoukalis (1977); see in particular pp. 52–73.

35 In 1974 the Short-term Policy Committee, the Medium-Term Economic Policy Committee and the Budgetary Policy Committee merged into a single Economic Policy Committee (for a discussion see Rosenthal, 1975 and Haas, 1976).

36 The farmers were protected from sudden changes in the exchange rates through the usage of the so-called Monetary Compensatory Amounts (MCAs) or 'green currencies'.

37 See for a comprehensive chronology of events: *Bulletin of the EEC*, Supplement 4, 1971, pp. 12–15.

38 Decision of the Council of 6 March 1970, in: Annex 2 of the Werner Report (1970).

39 The Group itself summarized the characteristics and most important consequences of EMU as follows:
   – the Community currencies will be assured of total irreversible mutual convertibility free from fluctuations in rates and with immutable parity rates, or preferably they will be replaced by a sole Community currency;

- the creation of liquidity throughout the area and monetary and credit policy will be centralized;
- monetary policy in relation to the outside world will be within the jurisdiction of the Community;
- the policies of the Member States regarding the capital market will be unified;
- the essential features of the whole of the public budgets, and in particular variations in their volume, the size of balances and the methods of financing or utilizing them, will be decided at the Community level;
- regional and structural policies will no longer be exclusively within the jurisdiction of the member countries;
- a systematic and continuous consultation between the social partners will be ensured at the Community level (Werner Report, 1970: 12).

40 The US dollar devalued 10 per cent on average. Against the dollar the European currencies went up: DM 13.6 per cent, BF 11.6 per cent, HFl 11.6 per cent, FF 8.6 per cent, Lit 7.5 per cent and £ 8.6 per cent (Source: Tsoukalis, 1977: 117).

41 The 'snake' refers to the European smaller band of currency fluctuations, whereas the tunnel is the band of 4.5 per cent.

42 For this and the subsequent section I have benefited from the accounts and research reported in Kruse (1980) and Tsoukalis (1977).

43 This directive was in reality a formality, as the national authorities were already able to use the policy instruments referred to.

44 All except Norway joined the EEC in 1973. Norway had to withdraw its application after the negative result of the 26 September 1972 referendum on membership to the Community, and withdrew from the snake in November 1972. Sweden became a associate member of the snake, whereas Austria and later Switzerland, informally linked their currencies to it.

45 In Rome, on 12 September 1972, the Finance Ministers had already discussed the creation of the monetary cooperation fund. Here too, the usual split between the economists and the monetarists dominated the meeting.

46 This point is worth remembering for the discussion of the British attitudes towards the EMU plans, as will be discussed in Chapters 6, 7 and 8.

47 This is an important conclusion to keep in mind for the evaluation of EMU in the late 1980s and 1990s. As will be discussed in Chapters 6 and 7, many officials stressed that EMU never came beyond its formal adoption in 1971, and that it was never taken seriously. In addition respondents in the interviews identify the oil crisis together with the end of the Bretton Woods era as the primary reason for abolishing the EMU project. Reflecting on this history of EMU it is suggested that was the *lack of common interests* that led to the deadlock and, subsequently, the suspension of European monetary integration plans until 1978 (EMS) and again until 1989 (Delors Report).

48 In voicing demand for currency with low inflation and an independent monetary authority, the 'All Saints Manifesto' resembled the proposals made in the Delors Report fourteen years later, although the later blueprint did not envisage a parallel currency.

49 Leo Tindemans, the Belgian Prime Minister, chaired the *ad hoc* committee. As the report did not receive much response, the Belgians, when it was their turn to chair the EC, sought to re-open the debate.

50 France redistributed wealth to the government and business via inflation; see David S. Landes (1969). It was only in 1968, after the customs union was created and French markets opened up to foreign competition, that the control of inflation became a priority objective of economic policy.

51 Some authors have argued that even though the EMS countries developed along the same line in terms of economic growth etc., their growth rates were not necessarily better than that in the non-EMS countries (de Grauwe, 1989).

52 The interested reader can refer to the following excellent analyses of the EMS: Coffey (1984), De Cecco and Giovannini (1989), Commission (1982, 1989), Dornbusch (1988), Fratianni and Von Hagen (1990, 1992), Giavazzi and Giovannini (1989), Giavazzi, Micossi and Miller (1988), de Grauwe (1988), de Grauwe and Papademos (1990), Gros and Thygesen (1998), Ludlow (1982), McNamara (1998), Ostrup (1992), Smeets (1990), Thygesen (1993), Ungerer (1989), Ungerer *et al.* (1983, 1986, 1990), Walsh (1994) and Weber (1991).

53 The specific historical–political background in which Jenkins decided to make monetary union a central theme of his presidency is described by Ludlow, using appropriate anecdotes, in his well-documented study on the EMS (Ludlow, 1982: 37–62).

54 Actually, the Commission had responded three weeks after Jenkins's speech. On 17 November 1977 it came up with an initiative to revive EMU as a means of achieving economic stability and growth in the Community. The document, 'Communication on the prospect of economic and monetary union', gave an analysis of the reasons for the EMU failure in the early 1970s, and provided a path to reach full EMU. It included: an action programme aiming at convergence of national economies over a period of five years, the creation of a single market, and the development of policies to solve structural and social problems in the Community (Commission of the EEC, 1977).

55 Giscard d'Estaing had apparently given this view during the dinner meetings at the Council in Copenhagen, 7–8 April 1978 (Ludlow, 1982: 90). In an interview Helmut Schmidt is reported to have said: 'I'm not so much thinking in terms of enlarging the snake, but of something which goes a little beyond the present snake' (interview with *Business Week*, 26 June 1978, quoted in Ludlow, 1982: 90).

56 The framework of the new system was laid down in an annex to the Council's Bremen communiqué, issued on 7 July 1978.

57 Resolution of the European Council of 5 December 1978 on the establishment of the European Monetary System (EMS) and related matters (Commission of the EC, 1979a, 1979b).

58 The eight countries participating in the ERM were: Belgium, Denmark, the Federal Republic of Germany, France, Ireland, Italy, Luxembourg and the Netherlands. The Bank of England participated in the ECU-creating mechanism, and the pound was part of the ECU. Italy joined the ERM with wider margins, ±6 per cent instead of the ±2.25 per cent band which was adopted by all other ERM members.

59 An aggravation of this problem was the fact that in 1980–1, in Germany and France, elections were coming up. Both Helmut Schmidt and Giscard

d'Estaing were unwilling to make EMS an electoral issue (Tsoukalis, 1983: 132).

60 When the European Community was to celebrate its 25th anniversary on 25 March 1982 the press was full of reports mentioning: 'deadlock', 'stagnation', 'crisis' and 'disintegration' (Dankert, 1983: 3). The general mood in Europe was gloomy and it was thought that European integration could not help to solve the problems that were related to the recession.

61 The ERM was enlarged during this period. It witnessed the first entrance of the Spanish peseta on 19 June 1989, and the British pound sterling on 8 October. Both currencies joined the wider band. In early January 1990 the Italian lira devalued slightly and joined the smaller band of ± 2.25 per cent.

62 For example, from December 1994 to the spring of 1995 the Italian lira and the British pound came under renewed pressure. They were still out of the ERM, but the effect of the downward pressure on these two currencies, which happened at a time when the dollar was at an 'all time low against the DM' implied that pressure was felt on the ERM currencies. The Spanish peseta and Portuguese escudo were most hit, and were devalued in the spring of 1995.

63 Of course the ERM changed its nature altogether with the start of the third stage of EMU on 1 January 1999. From that date onwards eleven countries are formally part of the euro. At the European Council meeting in Amsterdam, in June 1997, it was decided that the old EMS would cease to exist on 1 January 1999, and would instead be replaced by a new Exchange Rate Mechanism, referred to as ERM-2 (*OJ C 236*, 2-8-1997).

64 For a discussion of the ERM crisis see *inter alia* Busch (1994b); Cameron (1994); Sandholtz (1996); Talani (1998) and Temperton (1993).

65 Conclusions of the Hanover European Council, 27–28 June 1988, quoted in Delors Report (1989). It should be noted that no formal statement was made on the question of the possible establishment of a central bank.

66 Earlier, in late 1987, proposals for the creation of a single European currency and a European central bank had been put forward by Mr Edouard Balladur, then French Minister of Finance. They were next discussed at the Franco-German economic council meeting on 21 March 1988.

67 In January 1994 he became the first president of the European Monetary Institute, the institution called for by the Maastricht Treaty to be the predecessor of the European Central Bank.

68 For interesting accounts of, and attitudes towards, EMU in these early years, see *inter alia* Brown (1990), De Cecco (1989), Driffill and Beber (1991), Franklin (1990), Goodman (1992), Hasse (1990), Kloten (1987), Lebègue (1991), Louis (1989), Weidenfeld (1989).

69 Committee for the Study of Economic and Monetary Union (1989) 'Report on economic and monetary union in the European Community'. Hereafter referred to as 'Delors Committee' and 'Delors Report'.

70 On 13 June 1988 the Council of Ministers finally agreed after prolonged debate to remove all barriers to the free movement of capital within the EEC, effective from July 1990 (Greece, Ireland, Portugal and Spain being given until January 1992). However, in response to fears of France and the United Kingdom about a loss of fiscal sovereignty, the measure included provisions allowing member governments to impose special restraints on capital movements in times of emergency. The agreement added to the

pressure on the United Kingdom to participate in the exchange rate mechanism of the EMS. During the meetings leading to the 13 June announcement the UK had insisted on the deletion of a clause which would have necessitated all Community currencies (thus also the pound) to enter the ERM by 1992.

71 A finding consistent with Dyson, Featherstone and Michalopoulos (1995).

72 The other tasks were: to support the general economic policy set at the Community level by the competent bodies; to be responsible for the formulation and implementation of monetary policy, exchange rate and reserve management and a properly functioning payment system; finally, to participate in the coordination of banking supervision policies of the supervisory authorities (Delors Report, 1989: 26).

73 Due to its strong trading relationship with the US, as well as the fact that its currency is a petro-currency, the United Kingdom is usually the first country to feel the changes in the business cycle. Other West-European countries tend to follow the trend shortly thereafter.

74 Authors differ about the role of German reunification and the end of the Cold War in determining the outcome of the EMU process. Some are convinced that the EMU negotiations were well under way, and most issues were settled even before the Berlin Wall came down (cf. Thiel, 1995). Others stress that the German reunification provided Germany with the necessity to show the other EC/EU Member States that it was committed to Europe (Artis, 1994; Garrett, 1993; Sandholtz, 1993a). As will be demonstrated in Chapters 6, 7 and 8, the present study supplies evidence for the latter argument.

75 Three months after the world-wide stock exchange crash, the Nikkei index was back to its pre-crash level, and an 'all-time high' was to follow shortly. The other OECD countries adjusted at a much slower pace.

76 After agreeing to the objective of creating EMU reached at the Hanover Summit, Mrs Thatcher started an offensive against EMU in September 1988 with her famous speech at the Collège d'Europe in Bruges. She opposed the idea of transferring sovereignty, and proclaimed cooperation between interdependent sovereign states *(Keesing's,* 1989: 36491).

77 His differences with the Prime Minister on the full membership of EMS led him to resign on 26 October 1989.

78 Curiously enough when the 'conclusions' of the Madrid Summit were made public, the Delors Report was not mentioned. Only a few days later the Committee of Permanent Representatives observed this 'substantive error' *(Europe Documents,* no. 5048, 1 July 1989).

79 See for the conclusions of the Madrid Council, *Bulletin of the EC,* Supplement 6, 1989.

80 Shortly afterwards the CBI published 'European Monetary Union: a Business Perspective' (CBI, 1989).

81 The newspaper heading was 'Former West German Chancellor warns reunification may slow down single market plans and monetary harmonization'.

82 'Non-Paper. Draft Treaty Articles with a View to Achieving Political Union.'

83 The President of the European Parliament, Mr Enrique Baron Crespo, stated this in his speech to the interinstitutional conference (quoted in *Agence Europe,* 9/10 September 1991, no. 5563).

84 For other useful accounts on the path leading up to the Maastricht Treaty see Artis (1992); Bini-Smaghi, Padoa-Schioppa and Papadia (1994); Fratianni, Von Hagen and Waller (1992); Henning (1994); Italianer (1993); Thiel (1995).

85 The question of when exactly a single currency would be launched during the third phase remained vague for quite some time. In the newspapers after the Maastricht summit, the third stage and the single currency were often perceived as being the same thing, as, for example, the leading article of the *Financial Times* stated: 'Single currency by 1999 despite UK objections' (*Financial Times*, 10 December 1991). The official conclusions of the Maastricht summit referred to the prospect of a single currency by 1 January 1999 and the establishment of a procedure for transition to stage III by 1 July 1999' (*Bulletin of the EC*, 1991–12: 7). Elsewhere in the same Bulletin it was formulated as follows: 'The main feature is the *establishment* by 1 January 1999 of a single currency administered by a single, completely independent central bank' (*Bulletin of the EC*, 1991–12: 17). The formal text of the Treaty on European Union did not make clear when a single currency would be launched: 'At the starting date of the third stage, the Council shall, acting with the unanimity of the Member States without a derogation ... adopt the conversion rates at which their currencies will be irrevocably fixed and at which irrevocably fixed rate the Ecu shall be substituted for these currencies, and the Ecu will become a currency in its own right' (Treaty on European Union, 1992: 43–4).

This issue returned in 1994 and 1995, and the European Commission proposed that a single currency be launched as soon as possible after the third stage had become operational, probably three years later. It was also still subject of debate whether the single currency should be launched in phases, and have it circulate in parallel to national currencies, or whether to have a 'big bang'. By July 1995 the support for the 'big bang' had died down completely, as its main protagonist, the Bundesbank, started favouring a gradual introduction of the single currency (*Financial Times*, 22 July 1995). Finally, during 1995 renewed debate focused on the *name* of the single currency. The Germans, who had never liked the 'Ecu', put the issue on the European agenda. Their proposal was to have any name that resembled an existing currency, i.e. 'Euro-mark', or 'Euro-franken' or just 'Franken'. In the autumn of 1995 the favourite was the 'Euro' (*Financial Times*, 6 October 1995).

86 Nor should monetary financing be used to balance the budget.

87 During the drafting of the Treaty the normal bands were plus or minus 2.25 per cent or 6 per cent. Since August 1993 these are plus or minus 15 per cent (see discussion above, Section 4.4).

88 Expression used by the *Financial Times* editor Lionel Barber during the 1995 biennial ECSA conference, Charleston, South Carolina, May.

89 For example, in April 1994 the French government started to relax their opposition to the 'variable geometry', when the European affairs minister, Alain Lamassoure, stressed the need for a core group to move ahead in creating the monetary union (*Financial Times*, 16/17 April 1994).

90 The narrow 'yes' of the French referendum was felt to be a difficult outcome, though everyone was convinced that a French 'no' would have given a final blow to the Maastricht Treaty.

91 A Bundesbank official expressed the sudden change in public opinion as follows: 'The people in Germany did not understand that EMU meant giving up the Deutschmark. Nobody told them, until the *Bild Zeitung* did, and *Der Spiegel*, three days before the signature under the Maastricht Treaty. Before that the public did not care, listen, or read. These are, of course, somewhat sophisticated matters. You should have heard our drivers, asking me: "What does that mean? Do you really think we should give up the Deutschmark?"' (Bundesbank official, 1992, interview with the author).

92 Two authors made an important contribution to the qualitative methodology literature in their classic *The Discovery of Grounded Theory* (Glaser and Strauss, 1967). For their more recent work on the qualitative method see Glaser (1978); Strauss (1987); Corbin and Strauss (1990). Their 'grounded theory' provides an inductive method to theory-building on the basis of qualitative data analysis.

93 Elites are often studied by conducting interviews (cf. Dexter, 1970; Higley, Deacon and Smart, 1979; Higley, Lowell Field and Groholt, 1976; Hoffmann-Lange, 1987). For the way to conduct research interviewing see *inter alia* Dexter (1970), Mishler (1986), Moyser and Wagstaffe (1987). See Deutsch *et al.* (1967) for an example of a political science scholarly work which conducted interviews to understand elite opinion.

94 Sometimes the opposite happens, that is people want to give a controversial answer. In the case of EMU one has to be aware that it is possible respondents *may not* give an honest view about their perceptions of EMU. They could possibly camouflage anticipated negative effects or exaggerate either the negative or positive effects of EMU.

95 For example, the data collected through opinion polling, or statements made in press releases, television or newspaper interviews, and even primary sources such as an annual report, may also aim at providing 'acceptable' or 'non-controversial' views.

96 This, again, is a very legitimate way to start a qualitative research project, see Maso (1989).

97 The 21 August 1990 document on the 'meaning' of EMU (Commission of the EC, 1990a).

98 Draft Treaty proposals came successively from: Germany, Britain, Spain and France. *Agence Europe* January and February 1991. See also Chapter 4.

99 The recession in the UK already started in 1991.

100 The questionnaire was based on the one used for a study of attitudes of EMU in the Netherlands (Verdun, 1990). Some questions were dropped and others added.

101 The perceptions of these early monetary integration plans are not central to this study. However, as the Werner Report in a number of ways resembled the Delors Report, the views regarding this early plan help explain why in the 1970s the time was not ripe for EMU. Questions on the EMS were posed to understand the evolution from the Werner Report to the Delors Report.

102 With the exception of the sub-question concerning 'country-specific shocks', which was added to the questionnaire in 1992.

103 Due to the fact that an additional 'Question 5' was inserted in the 1992 questionnaire, the question discussed here is labelled 'Question 6', though in fact in the original 1991 interview it was listed as the fifth question.

104   The actor interviewed was omitted from this listing; that is, when talking to the Bank of England, questions would be posed about the trade unions, the employers' organizations and the Treasury.

105   The interested reader may want to refer to Verdun (1995).

106   As mentioned in Chapter 5, Question 1a on the history of EMU plans was posed only in the 1991 interview.

107   Bank of England official, 1991, interview with the author.

108   HM Treasury official, 1991, interview with the author.

109   Treasury official, 1991, interview with the author.

110   French Finance Ministry official, 1991, interview with the author.

111   French Finance Ministry official, 1991, interview with the author (author's translation).

112   French Finance Ministry official, 1991, interview with the author (author's translation).

113   Bundesbank official, 1991, interview with the author.

114   Bundesbank official, 1991, interview with the author.

115   Bundesbank official, 1991, interview with the author.

116   Bundesbank official, 1991, interview with the author.

117   Bundesbank official, 1991, interview with the author.

118   German Finance Ministry official, 1991, interview with the author (author's translation).

119   CBI official, 1991, interview with the author.

120   CNPF official, 1992, interview with the author. For an interesting account of the history of the CNPF see Brizay (1975). For a historical background on French organised business, see Ehrmann (1957).

121   BDI official, 1991, interview with the author (author's translation).

122   For a historical account of the power of the German employers' organization see Simon (1976).

123   BDI official, 1991, interview with the author (author's translation).

124   CBI official, 1991, interview with the author.

125   See Eberlie (1993) for an interesting account on the CBI's approach to influencing policy-making in the EC.

126   CBI official, 1991, interview with the author.

127   TUC official, 1991, interview with the author.

128   TUC official, 1991, interview with the author.

129   TUC official, 1991, interview with the author.

130   TUC official, 1991, interview with the author.

131   For a background on British trade unions, see among others ETUC (1986) and McIlroy (1988). For the trade union reaction to Margaret Thatcher's policies, see Marsh (1992b). For the British trade unions' reactions to European integration see *inter alia* Rosamond (1993) and Wendon (1994).

132   CFDT official, 1991, interview with the author (author's translation).

133   For a historical account of the German trade unions see, *inter alia*, Cullingford (1976) and ETUC (1984).

134   DGB official, 1991, interview with the author (author's translation).

135   Bank of England official, 1991, interview with the author.

136   Treasury official, 1991, interview with the author.

137   See also Leigh-Pemberton (1991a, 1991b).

138   Bank of England official, 1992, interview with the author.

139 Bank of England official, 1992, interview with the author.
140 Treasury official, 1991, interview with the author.
141 Treasury official, 1991, interview with the author.
142 Treasury official, 1991, interview with the author.
143 Treasury official, 1991, interview with the author.
144 Treasury official, 1992, interview with the author.
145 FFM official, 1991, interview with the author.
146 EMU was discussed by French Finance Ministry officials and the wider academic and policy community at a conference in June 1990 (see Ministère de l'Economie, des Finances et du Budget, 1990).
147 Banque de France official, 1991, interview with the author (author's translation).
148 Banque de France official, 1991, interview with the author (author's translation). See on the French government's view on these issues, Ministère de l'Economie, des Finances et du Budget (1991).
149 Banque de France official, 1992, interview with the author.
150 French Finance Ministry official, 1992, interview with the author.
151 French Finance Ministry official, 1992, interview with the author.
152 French Finance Ministry official, 1992, interview with the author.
153 Bundesbank official, 1991, interview with the author.
154 Bundesbank official, 1991, interview with the author.
155 German Finance Ministry official, 1991, interview with the author (author's translation).
156 CBI official, 1991, interview with the author.
157 CBI official, 1991, interview with the author.
158 Although it did not advocate an immediate return of the pound in the ERM, a policy paper concluded: '[T]he CBI is urging the Government to operate policy in a way which leaves the door open for participation in any future moves towards monetary union' (CBI, 1992).
159 RPR stands for Rassemblement pour la République (the Gaullist political party).
160 CNPF official, 1991, interview with the author (author's translation). An example of such a joint statement is BDI + CNPF (1990).
161 CNPF official, 1992, interview with the author.
162 CNPF official, 1992, interview with the author.
163 CNPF official, 1992, interview with the author.
164 BDI official, 1992, interview with the author (author's translation).
165 TUC official, 1991, interview with the author (emphasis in the original).
166 TUC official, 1991, interview with the author.
167 TUC official, 1991, interview with the author.
168 TUC official, 1991, interview with the author.
169 TUC official, 1991, interview with the author.
170 TUC official, 1992, interview with the author.
171 TUC official, 1992, interview with the author. The 'cooperative growth strategy' was a follow-up to the 1986 'cooperative strategy'. It aims at employment and growth. One of the ways in which this could be obtained, according to an European Trade Union Confederation (ETUC) policy statement on this matter, was by reducing interest rates (ETUC, 1992: 3). See also TUC (1992a, 1992b).

172 TUC official, 1992, interview with the author. See also TUC (1992b).
173 CFDT official, 1992, interview with the author (author's translation).
174 CFDT official, 1992, interview with the author.
175 DGB official, 1991, interview with the author (author's translation). See also: DGB (1987, 1990a, 1990b, 1990c).
176 For an interesting critical account of an overly strong focus on market principles and its subsequent effects on wages and location of business see Welzmüller (1990a, 1990b).
177 DGB official, 1992, interview with the author (author's translation).
178 Treasury official, 1991, interview with the author.
179 Treasury official, 1991, interview with the author.
180 Treasury official, 1992, interview with the author.
181 Bank of England official, 1991, interview with the author.
182 Bank of England official, 1992, interview with the author.
183 French Finance Ministry official, 1991, interview with the author (author's translation).
184 French Finance Ministry official, 1992, interview with the author.
185 German Finance Ministry, 1991, interview with the author (author's translation).
186 Bundesbank official, 1991, interview with the author.
187 Bundesbank official, 1992, interview with the author.
188 Treasury official, 1991, interview with the author.
189 Banque de France official, 1992, interview with the author (author's translation).
190 Bundesbank official, 1991, interview with the author.
191 Bundesbank official, 1991, interview with the author.
192 French Finance Ministry official, 1992, interview with the author.
193 French Finance Ministry official, 1992, interview with the author.
194 German Ministry of Finance official, 1991, interview with the author (author's translation).
195 Banque de France official, 1992, interview with the author (author's translation).
196 CBI official, 1992, interview with the author.
197 CBI official, 1991, interview with the author.
198 CBI official, 1992, interview with the author (emphasis in the original).
199 CNPF official, 1992, interview with the author.
200 BDI official, 1991, interview with the author (author's translation).
201 TUC official, 1991, interview with the author.
202 TUC official 1991, interview with the author.
203 TUC official 1992, interview with the author.
204 CBI official, 1991, interview with the author.
205 CBI official, 1992, interview with the author.
206 CBI official, 1992, interview with the author.
207 CNPF official, 1992, interview with the author.
208 CNPF official, 1992, interview with the author.
209 BDI official, 1992, interview with the author (author's translation).
210 TUC official, 1992, interview with the author.

211 DGB official, 1991, interview with the author (author's translation).
212 The Bank of England was cautious on this point in 1991.
213 Bank of England official, 1991, interview with the author.
214 Even though Stanley Hoffmann in 1982 realized that sometimes issues change from low to high politics and vice-versa (Hoffmann, 1982).

References

Agence Europe, various issues.

'All Saints Day Manifesto for European Monetary Union' (1975), *Economist*, 1 November; reprinted in Fratianni, Michele and Peeters, Theo (eds) (1978), *One Money for Europe* (London: Macmillan).

Andrews, David (1993), 'The Global Origins of the Maastricht Treaty on EMU: Closing the Window of Opportunity', in Cafruny, A. W. and Rosenthal, G. G. (eds), *State of the European Community: The Maastricht Debates and Beyond* (Harlow, Essex, and Boulder, CO: Longman and Lynne Rienner), pp. 107–24.

—— (1994), 'Capital Mobility and State Autonomy: Toward a Structural Theory of International Monetary Relations', *International Studies Quarterly*, 38: 193–218.

Artis, Michael J. (1992), 'The Maastricht Road to Monetary Union', *Journal of Common Market Studies*, 30: 299–309.

—— (1994), 'European Monetary Union', in Artis, M. J. and Lee, N. (eds), *The Economics of the European Union: Policy and Analysis* (Oxford: Oxford University Press), pp. 346–68.

—— and Winkler, Bernhard (1997), 'The Stability Pact: Safeguarding the Credibility of the European Central Bank' (London: CEPR, Discussion Paper series 1688).

Axtmann, Roland (1996), *Liberal Democracy into the Twenty-First Century: Globalization, Integration and the Nation-State* (Manchester: Manchester University Press).

—— (ed.) (1998), *Globalization and Europe: Theoretical and Empirical Investigation* (London: Pinter).

Baer, Günther and Padoa-Schioppa, Tommaso (1989), 'The Werner Report Revisited', in *Collection of Papers Annexed to the Report on Economic and Monetary Union* (Delors Report), pp. 53–60.

Balassa, Bela (1961), *The Theory of Economic Integration* (London: Allen & Unwin).

—— (ed.) (1975), *European Economic Integration* (Amsterdam and Oxford: North-Holland and American Elsevier).

Bank of England (1990), *The Hard Ecu in Stage 2: Operational Requirements* (London: Bank of England, Mimeograph, December).

Banque de France (1990a), 'Les Banques en Europe après 1992: La Création du Marché Unique Europeén et ses Consequences sur les Strategies Bancaires', Paris, 12 October 1990, *Info Banque de France*, no. 90.28, 16 October 1990.

—— (1990b), 'L'Union Monétaire Européenne. Communication de M. de Larosière, devant l'Association Europe et Entreprises', 20 September 1990, *Info Banque de France*, no. 90.26, 27 September 1990.

—— (1990c), 'L'Union Monétaire Européenne – Intervention de M. Jacques de Larosière devant la Société Royale d'Economie Politique de Belgique', 4 December 1990, *Info Banque de France*, no. 90.34, 7 December 1990.

Barre Report (1969) *see* Commission (1969).

Basevi, Giorgio *et al.* (1975), 'The All Saints' Day Manifesto and EMU', *The Economist* (London), 1 November 1975; reprinted in Fratianni, M. and Peeters, T. (eds) (1978), *One Money for Europe* (London: Macmillan), pp. 37–43.

BDI (1990a), *Economic and Monetary Union: A Challenge for Europe* (Cologne: BDI), January.

—— (1990b), *Europäische Wirtschafts- und Währungsunion – Voraussetzungen für eine Stabilitätsgemeinschaft* (Cologne: BDI), December.

—— (1991a), 'Britische Vorschläge zur Wirtschafts- und Währungsunion – Bewertung aus Sicht des BDI – Allgemeine Wirtschaftspolitik' (Cologne, BDI), 29 January 1991.

—— (1991b), 'Vorschlag der Bundesregierung zur Änderung des EWG-Vertrags im Himblick auf die Errichtung einer Wirtschafts- und Währungsunion – Stellungnahme des BDI' (Cologne), 19 March 1991.

——+CNPF (1990), 'Gemeinsames Arbeitspapier zur Wirtschafts- und Währungsunion der Europäischen Gemeinschaft'/'Document Conjoint du BDI et du CNPF' (Cologne and Paris), 2 October 1990.

——+DGB (1990), 'Gemeinsame Erklärung BDI/DGB zur Europäischen Wirtschafts- und Währungsunion' (Düsseldorf and Cologne), 22 August 1990.

Bempt, Paul, van den (1993), 'The Impact of Economic and Monetary Union on Member States' Fiscal Policies', in Gretschmann, K. (ed.), *Economic and Monetary Union: Implications for National Policy-makers* (Maastricht: European Institute of Public Administration), pp. 245–64.

Biehl, Dieter (1990), 'Deficiencies and Reform Possibilities of the EC Fiscal Constitution', in Crouch, Colin and Marquand, David (eds), *The Politics of 1992: Beyond the Single European Market* (Oxford and Cambridge: Basil Blackwell), pp. 85–99.

—— (1994), 'The Public Finances of the Union', in Duff, Andrew, Pinder, John and Pryce, Roy (eds), *Maastricht and Beyond: Building the European Union* (London and New York: Routledge), pp. 140–53.

—— and Winter, Horst (1990), *Europa finanzieren – ein föderalistisches Modell*, with Werner Weidenfeld, Helmut Fischer and Karin Stoll (Güthersloh: Bertelsmann).

Bini-Smaghi, Lorenzo, Padoa-Schioppa, Tommaso and Papadia, Francesco (1994), 'The Transition to EMU in the Maastricht Treaty', *Essays in International Finance*, no. 194 (Princeton, NJ: International Finance Section, Department of Economics, Princeton University).

BIS *Annual Report*, various issues.

Bloomfield, Arthur I. (1973), 'The Historical Setting', in Krause, L. B. and Salant, W. S. (eds), *European Monetary Unification and its Meaning for the United States* (Washington, DC: Brookings Institution), pp. 1–37.

Bordes, Christian and Girardin, Eric (1992), 'The Achievements of the ERM and the Preconditions for Monetary Union: a French Perspective', in Barrell, R. (ed.), *Economic Convergence and Monetary Union in Europe*, National Institute of Economic and Social Research and Association for the Monetary Union of Europe (London: Sage), pp. 98–120.

Brierly William (1987), *Trade Unions and the Economic Crisis of the 1980s* (Aldershot, England: Gower).

Britton, Andrew and Mayes, David (1992), *Achieving Monetary Union in Europe*, prepared by the National Institute of Economic and Social Research for the Association for the Monetary Union of Europe (London: Sage).

Brizay, Bernard (1975), *Le Patronat: Histoire, Structure, Strategie du CNPF* (Paris: Editions du Seuil).

Brown, Brendan (1987), *The Flight of International Capital: A Contemporary History* (London and New York: Routledge).

Brown, Richard (1990), 'British Monetary Policy and European Monetary Integration', in Sherman, H., Brown, R., Jacquet, P. and Julius, D. (eds), *Monetary Implications of the 1992 Process* (London: Pinter), pp. 99–123.

Buiter, Willem (1992), 'Should We Worry about the Fiscal Numerology of Maastricht?', CEPR Discussion Paper no. 668.

—— and Kletzer, Kenneth M. (1991), 'Reflections on the Fiscal Implications of a Common Currency', in Giovaninni, A. and Mayer, C. (eds), *European Financial Integration* (Cambridge: Cambridge University Press), pp. 221–44.

——, Corsetti, Giancarlo and Roubini, Nouriel (1993), 'Excessive Deficits: Sense and Nonsense in the Treaty of Maastricht', *Economic Policy*, 16: 57–100.

Bulletin of the European Economic Community (Luxembourg: Publishing Services of the EC, various issues).

Bulletin of the European Communities (Luxembourg: Office for Official Publications of the EC, various issues).

Bulletin of the European Union (Luxembourg: Office for Official Publications of the EC, various issues).

Bulmer, Simon (1983), 'Domestic Politics and European Community Policy-Making', *Journal of Common Market Studies*, 14: 349–63.

—— (1994), 'The Governance of the European Union: a New Institutionalist Approach', *Journal of Public Policy*, 13(4): 351–80.

—— (1998), 'New Institutionalism and the Governance of the Single European Market', *Journal of European Public Policy*, 5(3): 365–86.

Burda, Michael and Wyplosz, Charles (1993), *Macroeconomics: A European Text* (Oxford: Oxford University Press).

Burgess, Michael (1989), *Federalism and European Union: Political Ideas, Influences and Strategies in the European Community, 1972–1987* (London: Routledge).

Burley, Anne-Marie and Mattli, Walter (1993), 'Europe before the Court: a Political Theory of Legal Integration', *International Organization*, 47: 41–76 (winter).

Busch, Andreas (1994a), 'Central Bank Independence and the Westminster Model', *West European Politics*, 17(1): 53–72.

—— (1994b), 'The Crisis in the EMS', *Government and Opposition*, 29(1): 80–97.

Cairncross, Alec (1981), *The Relationship between Monetary and Fiscal Policy*, Keynes Lecture in Economics (Oxford: Oxford University Press).

Cameron, David (1992), 'The 1992 Initiative: Causes and Consequences', in Sbragia, A. (ed.), *Euro-Politics: Institutions and Policymaking in the 'New' European Community* (Washington, DC: Brookings Institution), pp. 23–75.

—— (1994), 'British Exit, German Voice, French Loyalty: Defection, Domination, and Cooperation in the 1992–93 ERM Crisis', paper prepared for the Annual Meeting of the American Political Science Association (Washington, DC) September.

—— (1995) 'Transnational Relations and the Development of European Economic and Monetary Union', in Risse-Kappen, T. (ed.), *Bringing Transnational Relations Back In: Non-State Actors, Domestic Structures and International Institutions* (Cambridge: Cambridge University Press), pp. 37–78.

Campanella, Miriam (1995), 'Getting the Core: a Neo-institutionalist Approach to EMU', *Government and Opposition*, 30(3): 347–69.

Caporaso, James (1996), 'The European Union and Forms of State: Westphalian, Regulatory or Post-Modern' *Journal of Common Market Studies*, 34(1): 29–52.

—— (1998), 'Regional Integration Theory: Understanding our Past and Anticipating our Future', *Journal of European Public Policy*, 5(1): 1–16.

—— and Keeler, John T. S. (1995), 'The European Union and Regional Integration Theory', in Rhodes, Carolyn and Mazey, Sonia (eds), *The State of the European Union: Building a European Polity?* (Boulder, CO: Lynne Rienner), pp. 29–62.

CBI (1989), 'European Monetary Union: a Business Perspective', report of the CBI European Monetary Union Working Group (London: CBI Centre Point), November.

—— (1990), 'European Monetary Union: The Next Steps' (internal document) *C 48 90* to the council for meeting on 25 July 1990.

—— (1991), 'Meeting the Challenge of Europe: Economic Priorities for 1991' (London: CBI Centre Point).

—— (1992), 'CBI Update: Europe Sans Frontières. European Economic and Monetary Union', October.

CFDT (1990), 'L'Union Economique et Monétaire', Nouvelles CFDT (internal document). February.

—— (1991), 'Position syndicale sur l'UEM' (Paris), 25 January.

Christie, Herbert and Fratianni, Michele (1978), 'EMU: Rehabilitation of a Case and Some Thoughts for Strategy', in Fratianni, M. and Peeters, T. (eds), *One Money for Europe* (London: Macmillan), pp. 3–35.

Claude, Inis L. (1966), *Swords into Plowshares*, 3rd edn (New York: Random House [1956]).

CNPF (1990), 'Cartes sur table' (Paris: Cirnov) April.

CNPF–BDI (1990), 'Document Conjoint du BDI et CNPF', 2 October 1990.

Coffey, Peter (1984), *The European Monetary System – Past, Present and Future* (Dordrecht, Boston and Lancaster: Martinus Nijhoff).

Cohen, Benjamin (1993), 'Beyond EMU: the Problems of Sustainability', *Economics and Politics*, 5(2): 187–203.

Cohen, Daniel (1989), 'The Costs and Benefits of a European Currency', in De Cecco, M. and Giovannini, A. (eds), *A European Central Bank? Perspectives on Monetary Unification after Ten Years of the EMS* (Cambridge, MA: MIT Press, pp. 195–209.

Coleman, William D. (1996), *Financial Services, Globalization and Domestic Policy Change* (London and Basingstoke: Macmillan/New York: St Martin's Press).

Commission (of the European Economic Community) (1960), *Third General Report on the Activities of the Community* (Luxembourg).

—— (1962), 'Memorandum of the Commission on the Action Programme of the Community for the Second Stage', COM(62)300, *Community Topics*, no. 10, 24 October.

—— (1963a), 'Monetary and Financial Co-operation in the European Economic Community (Communication from the Commission to the Council)', II/COM(63)216 final, *Bulletin of the EEC*, Supplement 7: 33–40, 19 June.

Commission (of the European Economic Community) (1963b), 'Medium-term Economic Policy for the Community (Recommendation by the Commission to the Council)', *Bulletin of the EEC*, Supplement 8, pp. 13–22.

—— (1963c), 'Memorandum from the Commission to the Council on the Action Programme in the Sphere of Customs Legislation', *Bulletin of the EEC*, Supplement.

Commission (of the European Communities) (1969), 'Memorandum from the Commission to the Council on the Coordination of Economic Policies and Monetary Cooperation within the Community', COM(69)150, *Bulletin of the EEC*, Supplement 3.

—— (1970), 'Commission Memorandum to the Council on the Preparation of a Plan for the Phased Establishment of an Economic and Monetary Union', *Bulletin of the EEC*, Supplement 3, 4 March.

—— (1973), 'Communication of the Commission to the Council on the Progress Achieved in the First Stage of Economic and Monetary Union, on the Allocation of Powers and Responsibilities among the Community Institutions and the Member States Essential to the Proper Functioning of Economic and Monetary Union, and on the Measures to be taken in the Second Stage of Economic and Monetary Union', Com(73)570 def, *Bulletin of the EC*, Supplement 5, Brussels, 19 April.

—— (1976), 'European Union' (Tindemans Report), *Bulletin of the European Communities*, Supplement 1.

—— (1977), 'Communication on the Prospect of Economic and Monetary Union', COM(77)620 final, 17 November.

—— (1979a), 'European Monetary System', *European Economy*, 3, July.

—— (1979b), 'European Monetary System: the First Six Months', *European Economy*, 4, November, pp. 79–81.

—— (1982), 'Documents Relating to the European Monetary System', *European Economy*, 12, July.

—— (1985), *Completing the Internal Market: White Paper from the Commission to the Council* (Luxembourg: Office for Official Publications of the European Communities), June.

—— (1988a), 'The Economics of 1992', *European Economy*, 35, March.

—— (1988b), 'Creation of a European Financial Area', *European Economy*, 36, May.

—— (1989), *Het EMS: Tien Jaar Groeiende Europese Monetaire Samenwerking* (Directoraat-Generaal Economische en Financiële Zaken).

—— (1990a), *Economic and Monetary Union*, SEC(90)1659 final. Brussels, 21 August.

—— (1990b), 'One Market, One Money', *European Economy*, 44, October.

—— (1991a), 'The Economics of EMU: Background Studies for *European Economy*, 44 "One Market, One Money"', *European Economy*, Special Edition, 1.

—— (1991b), 'Annual Economic Report 1991–92', *European Economy*, 50.

—— (1991c), *Eurobarometer Public Opinion in the European Union*, Report no. 36 (Brussels: European Commission).

—— (1992), *Eurobarometer Public Opinion in the European Union*, Report no. 37 (Brussels: European Commission).

—— (1993a), (European Commission), 'The Economics of Community Public Finance', *European Economy*, 5.

—— (1993b), (European Commission), 'Stable–Sound Finances. Community Public Finance in the Perspective of EMU', *European Economy*, 53.

—— (1997), (European Commission), *Eurobarometer Public Opinion in the European Union*, Report no. 46 (Brussels: European Commission).

—— (1998a), (European Commission), *Eurobarometer Public Opinion in the European Union*, Report no. 47 (Brussels: European Commission).

—— (1998b), (European Commission), *Eurobarometer Public Opinion in the European Union*, Report no. 48 (Brussels: European Commission).

—— (1998c), *Euro 1999, 25 March 1998, Report on Progress towards Convergence and the Recommendation with a View to the Transition to the Third Stage of Economic and Monetary Union* (Luxembourg: Office for Official Publications of the European Communities).

Committee for the Study of Economic and Monetary Union (1989), see: Delors Report (1989).

Corbey, Dorette (1993), *Stilstand is Vooruitgang: De Dialectiek van het Europese Integratieproces* (Assen and Maastricht: Van Gorcum).

—— (1995), 'Dialectical Functionalism: Stagnation as a Booster of European Integration', *International Organization*, 49(2): 253–84.

Corbin, Juliet and Strauss, Anselm (1990), 'Grounded Theory Research: Procedures, Canons and Evaluative Criteria', *Zeitschrift für Soziologie*, 19(6): 418–27.

Cornett, Linda and Caporaso, James A. (1992), '"And Still it Moves!" State Interests and Social Forces in the European Community', in Rosenau, James N. and Czempiel, Ernst-Otto (eds), *Governance without Government: Order and Change in World Politics* (Cambridge: Cambridge University Press), pp. 219–49.

Crawford, Malcolm (1993), *One Money For Europe: The Economics and Politics of Maastricht* (London: Macmillan).

Criddle, Byron (1993), 'The French Referendum on the Maastricht Treaty September 1992', *Parliamentary Affairs*, 46(2): 228–38.

Crockett, Andrew (1991), 'Monetary Integration in Europe', paper prepared for the conference in honour of Jacques Polak, Washington, DC, January.

Cullingford, E. C. M. (1976), *Trade Unions in West Germany* (London: Wilton House).

De Cecco, Marcello and Giovannini, Alberto (eds) (1989), *A European Central Bank? Perspectives on Monetary Unification after Ten Years of the EMS* (Cambridge, MA: MIT Press).

Dankert, Piet (1983), 'Introduction: the European Community – Past, Present and Future', in Tsoukalis, L. (ed.), *The European Community: Past, Present and Future* (Oxford: Basil Blackwell), pp. 3–21.

Delors Report (1989), *Report on Economic and Monetary Union in the European Community*, Committee for the Study of Economic and Monetary Union (Luxembourg: Office for Official Publications of the EC), April.

De Nederlandsche Bank (1973), *Report for the Year 1972* (Amsterdam).

—— (1974), *Report for the Year 1973* (Amsterdam).

Deutsch, Karl W. (1954), *Political Community at the International Level: Problems of Definition and Measurement* (Garden City, NY: Doubleday).

——, Burrell, Sidney A., Kann, Robert A., Lee, Maurice, Lichtenman, Lindgren, Raymond E., Loewenheim, Francis, L. and Van Wagenen, Richard W. (1957), *Political Community and the North-Atlantic Area: International Organization in the Light of Historical Experience* (Princeton, NJ: Princeton University Press).

Deutsch, Karl W. *et al.* (1967), *France, Germany and the Western Alliance: A Study of Elite Attitudes on European Integration and World Politics* (New York: Charles Scribner's Sons).

Deutsche Bundesbank (1973), *Monatsberichte der Deutschen Bundesbank*, September.

—— (1974), *Geschäftsbericht der Deutschen Bundesbank für das Jahr 1973* (Frankfurt).

—— (1990a), 'General Meeting of the Mont Pelerin Society', Presse Auszüge, no. 68. Luncheon speech by Karl Otto Pöhl, President of Deutsche Bundesbank, Munich, 3 September.

—— (1990b), 'Statement by the Governor of the Fund for the Federal Republik of Germany Karl Otto Pöhl', Presse Auszüge, no. 75 (IMF and World Bank, Washington, DC) 26 September.

—— (1990c), 'Konferenz über die Wirtschafts- und Währungsunion. Auszüge aus den Schlußfolgerungen des Vorsitzes des Europäischen Rats', Presse Auszüge, no. 84 (Rome) 27/28 October.

—— (1990d), 'Little Sympathy for Britain's Alternative EMU Proposals', Presse Auszüge, no. 88; *The Independent* (London) 12 November.

—— (1990e), 'Une Banque Centrale Européenne hors des influences politiques', Presse Auszüge, no. 92; *Le Figaro* (Paris) 27 November.

—— (1990f), 'Statement by the Deutsche Bundesbank on the Establishment of an Economic and Monetary Union in Europe', 19 September, published in Monthly Report of the Deutsche Bundesbank, October, pp. 40–44.

—— (1991a), 'Wirtschafts- und Währungspolitische Herausforderungen in einem neuen offenen Europa', Presse Auszüge, no. 5; Vortrag von Karl Otto Pöhl, Präsident der Deutschen Bundesbank (The Hague) 22 January.

—— (1991b), 'Pöhl's Presciption', *The Wall Street Journal Europe* (Brussels) 6 February.

—— (1991c), 'Statement by President Pöhl on Economic and Monetary Matters and Industrial Policy' (Brussels) 18 March.

Deutsche Bundesregierung (1974), *Jahreswirtschaftsbericht 1973 der Bundesregierung.*

Dexter, Lewis Anthony (1970), *Elite and Specialized Interviewing* (Evanston, IL: Northwestern University Press).

DGB (1987), 'Für ein soziales Europa – Prioritäten der Gewerkschaften für die deutsche EG-Präsidentschaft', Beschluß des Geschäftsführenden Bundesvorstandes des DGB vom 7 Dezember 1987.

—— (1989a), 'Für ein soziales Europa' – Aufruf zur Wahl des Europäischen Parlaments am 18. Juni 1989 (Düsseldorf).

—— (1989b), 'Gemeinsame Erklärung de Bundesverbandes der Deutschen Industrie und des Deutschen Gewerkschaftsbundes: die Chancen des Europäischen Binnenmarktes nutzen', Informationen zur Wirtschafts- und Umweltpolitik (Düsseldorf, 31 July 1989, no. 7).

—— (1990a), Abteilung Strukturpolitik: 'Diskussionspapier zur Wirschafts- und Währungsunion aus der Sicht des Deutschen Gewerkschaftsbundes' (internal document), (Düsseldorf) 16 January.

—— (1990b), 'Gemeinsame Erklärung BDI/DGB zur europäischen Wirtschafts- und Währungsunion', ID 23 (Düsseldorf) 22 August.

—— (1990c), 'Europäische Währungsunion: Start in eine ungewisse Phase', *Jahres-Gutachten 1990/91*, pp. 424–37.

Dornbusch, Rudiger (1988), 'The EMS, the Dollar and the Yen', in Giavazzi, Micossi and Miller, Marcus (eds), *Limiting Exchange Rates Flexibility: The European Monetary System* (Cambridge, MA: MIT Press), pp. 23–41.

—— (1991), 'Problems of European Monetary Integration', in Giovannini, A. and Mayer, C. (eds), *European Financial Integration* (Cambridge: Cambridge University Press), pp. 305–33.

Drazen, Allan (1989), 'Monetary Policy, Capital Controls and Seigniorage in an Open Economy', in De Cecco, M. and Giovannini, A. (eds), *A European Central Bank? Perspectives on Monetary Unification after Ten Years of the EMS* (Cambridge, MA: MIT Press), pp. 13–32.

Driffill, John and Beber, Massimo (eds) (1991), *A Currency for Europe* (London: Lothian Foundation).

Duchêne, François (1994), *Jean Monnet: The First Statesman of Interdependence* (New York and London: Norton).

Dunning, John H. (1993), *The Globalization of Business: The Challenge of the 1990s* (London: Routledge).

Dyson, Kenneth (1994), *Elusive Union: The Process of Economic and Monetary Union in Europe* (London and New York: Longman).

Dyson, Kenneth and Featherstone, Kevin (1996), 'EMU and Economic Governance in Germany', *German Politics*, 5(3): 325–55.

Dyson, Kenneth and Featherstone, Kevin (1999), *The Road to Maastricht: Negotiating Economic and Monetary Union* (Oxford: Oxford University Press).

——, Featherstone, Kevin and Michalopoulos, George (1995), 'Strapped to the Mast; EC Central Bankers between Global Financial Markets and Regional Integration', *Journal of European Public Policy*, 2(3): 465–87.

Eberlie, Richard (1993), 'The Confederation of British Industry and Policy-Making in the European Community', in Jeremy Richardson and Sonia Mazey (eds), *Lobbying in the European Community* (Oxford: Oxford University Press), pp. 201–12.

EEC Treaty: Treaty Establishing the European Economic Community, Rome, 25 March 1957 (Brussels).

Economic and Social Committee (1990), *Economic and Monetary Union in the European Community* (Brussels), January.

—— (1991), *Additional Opinion on Economic and Monetary Union* (Brussels), February.

Ehrmann, Henry, W. (1957), *Organized Business in France* (Princeton, NJ: Princeton University Press).

Eichengreen, Barry (1990), 'One Money for Europe: Lessons from the US Currency Union', *Economic Policy*, 10, April, pp. 117–87.

—— (1993), 'Is Europe an Optimum Currency Area', in Borner, Silvio and Grubel, Herbert (eds), *The European Community after 1992: Perspectives from the Outside* (London: Macmillan), pp. 138–61.

—— and Frieden, J. A. (1993), 'The Political Economy of European Monetary Unification: an Analytical Introduction', *Economics and Politics*, 5(2): 85–105.

—— and —— (eds) (1994), *The Political Economy of European Monetary Unification* (Boulder, CO and San Francisco, CA and Oxford: Westview Press).

El-Agraa, Ali M. (ed.) (1990), *The Economics of the European Community*, 3rd edn (Oxford: Philip Allan [1985/1980]).

Emerson, Michael and Huhne, Christopher (1991), *The Ecu Report* (London: Pan Books).

—— Giovannini, Alberto and Thygesen, Niels (1991), 'Towards Monetary Unification of Europe', *European Economic Review*, 35(2–3): 455–483.

—— *et al.* (1992), *One Market, One Money* (Cambridge: Cambridge University Press).

Esch, J. C. P. A., van and Bont, H. W. M. de (1980), *Documenten over de Economische en Monetaire Unie (1974–1980)* (Deventer: Kluwer).

ETUC (1984), *The Trade Union Movement in the Federal Republic of Germany: The DGB*, info 9 (Brussels: European Trade Union Institute, ETUI).

—— (1986), *The Trade Union Movement in Great Britain*, 2nd edn, Info 1 (Brussels: ETUI).

—— (1987), *The Trade Union Movement in France*, Info 20 (Brussels: ETUI).

—— (1990a), *Economic and Monetary Union in the European Community*, Info 31 (Brussels: ETUI).

—— (1990b), *The European Trade Union Confederation: ETUC*, Info 29 (Brussels: ETUI).

—— (1991), 'Economic and Monetary Union: ETUC Submission to Inter-governmental Conference' (2nd draft) (Brussels: ETUC).

—— (1992), 'The Delors II Package: A Cooperative Growth and Employment Strategy Must Be Added', ETUC Statement adopted on 11–12 June (Brussels: ETUC).

Europe Bulletin, various issues.

Europe Documents, various issues.

European Commission (see Commission of the EC).

Feld, Werner, J. and Mahant, Edelgard E. (1986), 'New Efforts for European Union: Hopes, Progress, and Disappointments', *Journal of European Integration*, 10(1): 39–58.

Feldstein, Martin (1992), 'Europe's Monetary Union: the Case Against EMU', *The Economist*, 13 June, pp. 19–22.

Fitoussi, J.-P., Atkinson, A. B., Blanchard, O. E. *et al.* (1993), *Competitive Disinflation: The Mark and Budgetary Politics in Europe* (Oxford: Oxford University Press).

Franck, Christian (1987), 'New Ambitions: from The Hague to Paris Summits (1969–1972)', in Pryce, R. (ed.), *Frameworks for International Co-operation* (London: Pinter), pp. 130–48.

Franklin, Michael (1990), *Britain's Future in Europe*, Royal Institute of International Affairs (London: Pinter).

Fratianni, Michele and Peeters, Theo (eds) (1978), *One Money for Europe* (London and Basingstoke: Macmillan).

—— and Von Hagen, Jürgen (1990), 'Asymmetries and Realignments in the EMS', in de Grauwe, Paul and Papademos, Lucas (eds), *The European Monetary System in the 1990s* (London: Longman for CEPS and the Bank of Greece), pp. 86–115.

—— and —— (1992), *The European Monetary System and European Monetary Union* (Boulder, CO and San Francisco, CA and Oxford: Westview).

——, —— and Waller, C. (1992), 'The Maastricht Way to EMU', *Essays in International Finance*, 187, Princeton University.

Frieden, Jeffry A. (1991), 'Invested Interests: the Politics of National Economic Policies in a World of Global Finance', *International Organization*, 45(4): 425–52.

Friedmann, Willy (1992), 'German Monetary Union, and Some Lessons for Europe', in Barrell, R. (ed.), *Economic Convergence and Monetary Union in Europe*, National Institute of Economic and Social Research and Association for the Monetary Union of Europe (London: Sage), pp. 144–53.

Garrett, Geoffrey (1993), 'The Politics of Maastricht', *Economics and Politics*, 5(2): 105–25.

Genscher, Hans-Dietrich (1988), 'Memorandum für die Schaffung eines europäischen Währungsrames und einer europäischen Zentralbank', *Diskussionsgrundlage*, Bonn, 26 February.

George, Stephen (1985 and 1991), *Politics and Policy in the European Community*, 2nd edn (Oxford: Clarendon, 1985; Oxford: Oxford University Press, 1991).

Germain, Randall (ed.) (1999), *Globalization and its Critics: Perspectives from Political Economy* (Basingstoke and London: Macmillan/New York: St Martin's Press).

Giavazzi, Francesco and Giovannini, Alberto (1989), *Limiting Exchange Rate Flexibility: The European Monetary System* (Cambridge, MA: MIT Press).

——, Micossi, Stefano, and Miller, Marcus (eds) (1988), *The European Monetary System* (Cambridge, MA: MIT Press).

Giovannini, Alberto (1989), 'How Do Fixed Exchange-rate Regimes Work? Evidence from the Gold Standard, Bretton Woods and the EMS', in Miller, M. Eichengreen, B. and Portes, B. (eds), *Blueprints for Exchange-rate Management* (London: Academic Press), pp. 13–41.

—— and Spaventa, Luigi (1991), 'Fiscal Rules in the European Monetary Union: a No-Entry Clause', *CEPR Discussion Paper* no. 516, London, January.

Glaser, Barney G. (1978), *Theoretical Sensitivity: Advances in the Methodology of Grounded Theory* (Mill Valley: Sociology Press).

—— and Strauss, Anselm L. (1967), *The Discovery of Grounded Theory* (Chicago, IL: Aldine).

Goodhart, Charles (1990), 'Fiscal Policy and EMU', in Pöhl, K.-O. *et al.* (eds), *Britain & EMU* (London: Centre for Economic Performance), pp. 81–99.

—— and Smith, Stephen (1993), 'Stabilization', *European Economy*, 5: 417–56.

Goodman, John B. (1989), 'Monetary Policy in France, Italy, and Germany: 1973–85', in Guerrieri, P. and Padoan, P. C. (eds), *The Political Economy of European Integration: States Markets and Institutions* (New York: Harvester Wheatsheaf), pp. 171–201.

—— (1992), *Monetary Sovereignty: The Politics of Central Banking in Western Europe* (Ithaca, NY and London: Cornell University Press).

Grauwe, Paul de (1988), 'Is the European Monetary System a DM-Zone?' CEPR Discussion Paper, no. 297 (London: Centre for Economic Policy Research).

—— (1997), *The Economics of Monetary Integration*, 3rd edn (Oxford: Oxford University Press).

——, Knoester, A., Kolodziejak, A. *et al.* (1989), *De Europese Monetaire Integratie: Vier Visies*. Wetenschappelijke Raad voor het Regeringsbeleid (The Hague: SDU).

—— and Papademos, Lucas (eds) (1990), *The European Monetary System in the 1990s* (London: Longman for CEPS and the Bank of Greece).

Grieco, Joseph M. (1995), 'The Maastricht Treaty Economic and Monetary Union and Neo-Realist Research Programme', *Review of International Studies*, 21: 21–40.

Grilli, Vittorio (1989), 'Seignorage in Europe', in De Cecco, Marcello and Giovannini, Alberto (eds), *A European Central Bank? Perspectives on Monetary Unification after Ten Years of the EMS* (Cambridge, MA: MIT Press), pp. 53–79.

Groom, A. J. R. and Taylor, Paul and (eds) (1975), *Functionalism: Theory and Practice* in *International Relations* (London: University of London Press).

—— and —— (eds) (1990), *Frameworks for International Co-operation* (London: Pinter).

Gros, Daniel (1996), 'Towards Economic and Monetary Union: Problems and Prospects', CEPS Paper no. 65 (Brussels: CEPS).

—— and Thygesen, Niels (1988), 'The EMS: Achievements, Current Issues and Directions for the Future' (Brussels: Centre for European Policy Studies (CEPS), no. 35).

—— and —— (1992), *European Monetary Integration: From the European Monetary System to Economic and Monetary Union* (London: Longman).

—— and —— (1998), *European Monetary Integration: From the European Monetary System to Economic and Monetary Union*, 2nd edn (Harlow, Essex/New York: Longman).

—— and Vandille, Guy (1994), 'Seignorage and EMU: the Fiscal Implications of Price Stability and Financial Market Integration', Geld und Währungpaper Working Papers no. 36 (Frankfurt am Main: Goethe Universität).

Groux, Guy and Mouriaux, René (1992), *La C.G.T. Crises et Alternatives* (Paris: Economia).

Haas, Ernst B. (1958, 1968), *The Uniting of Europe*, 2nd edn (Stanford, CA: Stanford University Press).

—— (1964), *Beyond the Nation State. Political, Social, and Economic Forces, 1950–1957* (Stanford, CA: Stanford University Press).

—— (1971), 'The Study of Regional Integration: Reflections on the Joy and Anguish of Pre-theorising', in Lindberg, Leon and Scheingold, Stuart (eds), *Regional Integration: Theory and Research* (Cambridge, MA: Harvard University Press), pp. 3–43.

—— (1975), *The Obsolescence of Regional Integration Theory*, Research Studies 25 (Berkeley, CA: Institute of International Studies).

—— (1976) 'Turbulent Fields and the Theory of Regional Integration', *International Organization*, 30(2): 173–212.

Hall, Peter A. (1986), *Governing the Economy: The Politics of State Intervention in Britain and France* (New York: Oxford University Press).

—— (1994), 'Central Bank Interdependence and Coordinated Wage Bargaining: their Interaction in Germany and Europe', *German Politics and Society*, 31: 1–24.

Hansard Parliamentary Debates, House of Commons and House of Lords (London), various issues.

Harrison, R. J. (1974), *Europe in Question* (London: George Allen & Unwin).

—— (1990), 'Neo-functionalism', in Groom, A. J. R. and Taylor, P. (eds), *Frameworks for International Co-operation* (London: Pinter), pp. 139–50.

Hasse, Rolf H. (1990), *The European Central Bank: Perspectives for a Further Development of the European Monetary System* (Gütersloh: Bertelsmann).

Helleiner, Eric (1994), *States and the Re-emergence of Global Finance: From Bretton Woods to the 1990s* (Ithaca, NY: Cornell University Press).

Helm, Dieter and Smith, Stephen (1989), 'The Assessment: Economic Integration and the Role of the European Community', *Oxford Review of Economic Policy*, 5(2): 1–19.

Henerson, M. E., Morris, L. L. and Fitz-Gibbon, C. T. (1987), *How to Measure Attitudes* (Beverley Hills, CA, London and New Delhi: Sage).

Henning, Randall C. (1994), *Currencies and Politics in the United States, Germany, and Japan* (Washington, DC: Institute for International Economics).

Higley, John, Deacon, Desley and Smart, Don (1979), *Elites in Australia* (London: Routledge & Kegan Paul).

——, Lowell Field, G. and Groholt, K. (1976), *Elite Structure and Ideology: A Theory with Applications to Norway* (Oslo and New York: Universitetsforlaget and Columbia University Press).

Hirsch, Fred and Goldthorpe, John H. (eds) (1978), *The Political Economy of Inflation* (London: Martin Robertson).

Hirst, Paul Q. and Thompson, Grahame (1996) *Globalization in Question: The International Economy and the Possibilities of Governance* (Cambridge: Polity Press).

HM Treasury (1989), 'An Evolutionary Approach to Economic and Monetary Union' (London: HSMO Mimeograph, 2 November).

—— (1992), 'Economic and Monetary Union: the Agreement at Maastricht', *Treasury Bulletin*, Winter 1991–2, pp. 1–23.

Hoffmann, Stanley (1966), 'Obstinate or Obsolete? The Fate of the Nation-state and the Case of Western Europe', *Daedalus*, 95(3): 862–916.

—— (1982), 'Reflections on the Nation-state in Western Europe Today', *Journal of Common Market Studies*, 21: 21–37.

Hoffmann-Lange, Ursula (1987), 'Surveying National Elites in the Federal Republic of Germany', in Moyser, G. and Wagstaffe, M. (eds), *Research Methods for Elite Studies* (London: Allen & Unwin), pp. 24–48.

Holland, Martin (1993), *European Community Integration* (London: Pinter).

House of Lords (1989), *The Delors Committee Report: Select Committee on the European Communities of the House of Lords* (London: Her Majesty's Stationery Office).

—— (1990), *Economic and Monetary Union and Political Union: Select Committee on the European Communities of the House of Lords* (London: Her Majesty's Stationery Office).

Huelshoff, Michael G. (1994), 'Domestic Politics and Dynamic Issue Linkage', *International Studies Quarterly*, 38(2): 255–79.

Italianer, Alexander (1993), 'Mastering Maastricht: EMU Issues and How They Were Settled', in Gretschmann, K. (ed.), *Economic and Monetary Union: Implications for National Policy-Makers* (Maastricht: European Institute of Public Administration), pp. 51–115.

Jenkins, Roy (1977), 'Europe's Present Challenge and Future Opportunity', the First Jean Monnet Lecture, Florence, EUI, 27 October.

Johnson, Christopher (1994), 'Fiscal and Monetary Policy in Economic and Monetary Union', in Duff, A., Pinder, J. and Pryce, R. (eds), *Maastricht and Beyond: Building the European Union* (London and New York: Routledge), pp. 71–83.

Jones, Barry R. J. (1995), *Globalisation and Interdependence in the International World Economy: Rhetoric and Reality* (London: Pinter).

Jones, Erik, Frieden, Jeffrey and Torres, Francisco (eds) (1998), *Joining Europe's Monetary Club: The Challenges for Smaller Member States* (New York: St Martin's Press).

Keesing's Contemporary Archives: Record of World Events (Edinburgh: Longman), various issues.

Keesing's Record of World Events (Harlow: Longman), various issues.

Kenen, Peter B. (1969), 'The Theory of Optimum Currency Areas: an Eclectic View', in Mundell, R. and Swododa, A. (eds), *Monetary Problems of the International Economy* (Chicago, IL: University of Chicago Press), pp. 41–60.

—— (1995), *Economic and Monetary Union in Europe: Moving beyond Maastricht* (Cambridge: Cambridge University Press).

Kennedy, Ellen (1991), *The Bundesbank: Germany's Central Bank in the International Monetary System*, Royal Institute of International Affairs (London: Pinter).

Keohane, Robert O. (1983), 'The Demand for International Regimes', in Krasner, S. D. (ed.), *International Regimes* (Ithaca, NY: Cornell University Press), pp. 325–55.

—— (1984), *After Hegemony: Cooperation and Discord in the World Political Economy* (Princeton, NJ: Princeton University Press).

—— (1989), *International Institutions and State Power: Essays in International Relations Theory* (Boulder, CO: Westview).

—— and Hoffmann, Stanley (1990), 'Conclusions: Community Politics and Institutional Change', in Wallace, W. (ed.), *The Dynamics of European Integration* (London: Pinter), pp. 276–301.

—— and —— (eds) (1991), *The New European Community: Decision-making and Institutional Change* (Boulder, CO, San Francisco, CA and Oxford: Westview Press).

—— and Nye, J. (1975), 'International Interdependence and Integration', in Greenstein, F. and Polsby, N. (eds), *Handbook of Political Science*, vol. 8 (Reading, MA: Addison-Wesley), pp. 363–414.

Kitzinger, Uwe W. (1963), *The Politics and Economics of European Integration*, 2nd edn (Westport, CT: Greenwood Press), 1st edn: *The Challenge of the Common Market* (Oxford: Basil Blackwell, 1961).

Kloten, Norbert (1987), *Wege zu einer Europäischen Währungsunion* (Berlin: Duncker & Humbolt).

Kohler-Koch, Beate (1996), 'Catching up with Change: the Transformation of Governance in the European Union', *Journal of European Public Policy*, 3(3): 359–80.

Krause, Laurence B. and Salant, Walter S. (eds) (1973), *European Monetary Unification and its Meaning for the United States* (Washington, DC: Brookings Institution).

Kruse, D. C. (1980), *Monetary Integration in Western Europe: EMU, EMS and Beyond* (London and Boston, MA: Butterworth).

Lagayette, Philippe (1990), 'Vers l'Union Economique et Monétaire', text of a conference of the German federation of industrie (BDI) Bonn, 15 October.

—— (1991), 'La Dynamique de l'Union Economique et Monétaire', text of a conference spoken on 23 November 1990; *Revue d'économie politique*, 101(1) January–February.

Landes, David S. (1969), *The Unbound Prometheus* (Cambridge: Cambridge University Press).

Landier, Hubert (1981), *Demain, Quels Syndicats?* (Paris: Editions Pluriel).

Lange, Peter (1993), 'Maastricht and the Social Protocol: Why Did They Do It?', *Politics and Society*, 21: 5–36.

Laursen, Finn and Vanhoonacker, Sophie (eds) (1992), *The Intergovernmental Conference on Political Union: Institutional Reforms, New Policies and International Identity of the European Community* (Maastricht: European Institute of Public Administration).

Lebègue, Daniel and Boissieu, Christian de (eds) (1991), *Monnaie Unique Européenne Système International: Vers Quelles Ambitions?* (Paris: Presse Universitaires de France).

Leigh-Pemberton, Robin (1990a), 'Beyond Stage 1 of EMU', speech given to the European Parliamentarians and Industrialists Council, in Strasbourg on 11 July, in *Bank of England Quarterly Bulletin* (August), pp. 378–9.

—— (1990b), 'The United Kingdom's Proposals for Economic and Monetary Union', Speech given to the European Currency Inter-Group of the EP and the European Parliamentarians and Industrialists Council in Strasbourg on 11 July, in *Bank of England Quarterly Bulletin* (August), pp. 374–7.

—— (1990c), 'Approaches to Monetary Integration in Europe', speech given at the Deutsche Bank/Ecu Banking Association Conference in Berlin on 25 October, in *Bank of England Quarterly Bulletin* (November), pp. 500–2.

—— (1991a), 'Speech Given by the Governor of the Bank of England at the Le Monde "Review of the Year"' (Paris), 18 January.

—— (1991b), 'Speech Given by the Governor of the Bank of England to the Übersee Club' (Hamburg), 22 January.

—— (1991c), 'European Monetary Arrangements: Convergence and Other Issues', Paolo Baffi Lecture, Bocconi University (Milan); *Bank of England Quarterly Bulletin*, November, pp. 516–20.

—— (1992), 'Monetary Aspects of European Integration', the fourth 1992 lecture at Oxford on 13 February, *Bank of England Quarterly Bulletin*, May, pp. 199–204.

Lindberg, Leon N. (1968), *The Politics of European Economic Integration* (Stanford, CA: Stanford University Press [1963]).

—— and Scheingold, Stuart A. (1970), *Europe's Would-be Polity: Patterns of Change in the European Community* (Englewood Cliffs, NJ: Prentice Hall).

—— and —— (eds) (1971), *Regional Integration: Theory and Research* (Cambridge, MA: Harvard University Press).

Lipgens, Walter (1982), *A History of European Integration: The Formation of the European Unity Movement, 1945–1950*, vol. 1: *1945–1947* (Oxford: Clarendon Press); originally published in German: *Die Anfänge der europäischen Einigungspolitik 1945–1950* (Stuttgart: Ernst Klett [1977]).

Louis, Jean-Victor (ed.) (1989), *Vers un Système Européen de Banques Centrales: Projet de Dispostions Organiques*, Rapport du groupe présidé par Jean-Victor Louis. Institute d'Etudes européennes (Brussels: University of Brussels).

Ludlow, Peter (1982), *The Making of the European Monetary System: A Case Study of the Politics of the European Community* (London: Butterworth Scientific).

Ludlow, Peter (1989), *Beyond 1992: Europe and its Western Partners* (Brussels: Centre for European Policy Studies).

MacDougall Report (Commission of the European Communities) (1977), *Report of the Study Group on the Role of Public Finance in European Integration*, vols 1 and 2 (Brussels), Doc. II/10/77, 2 vols, April.

Machlup, Fritz (1977), *A History of Thought on Economic Integration* (London: Macmillan).

Magnifico, Giovanni (1973), *European Monetary Unification* (London: Macmillan).

Majocchi, Alberto and Rey, Mario (1993), 'A Special Financial Support Scheme in Economic and Monetary Union: Need and Nature', *European Economy*, 5: 457–80.

March, James G. and Olsen, Johan P. (1989), *Rediscovering Institutions: The Organizational Basis of Politics* (New York: Free Press).

Marcussen, Martin (1997), 'The Role of "Ideas" in Dutch, Danish and Swedish Economic Policy in the 1980s and the Beginning of the 1990s', in Minkkinen, P. and Patomäki, H. (eds), *The Politics of Economic and Monetary Union* (Boston, MA, Dordrecht and London: Kluwer), pp. 75–103.

——— (1998a), *Ideas and Elites: Danish Macro-Economic Policy-Discourse in the EMU Process*, PhD dissertation, Aalborg University, Institute for Development and Planning, ISP-Series, no. 226, April.

——— (1998b), 'Central Bankers, the Ideational Life-Cycle and the Social Construction of EMU', EUI Working Papers, RSC no. 98/33 (Florence: European University Institute).

Marjolin, Robert *et al.* (1975), *Report of the Study Group Economic and Monetary Union 1980* (The 'Marjolin Report'), Commission of the European Communities (Brussels), Doc. II/675/3/74, 8 March.

Marjolin, Robert (1986), *Le Travail d'une Vie: Memoires, 1911–1956* (Paris: Laffont).

Marks, Gary, Hooghe, Liesbet and Blank, Kermit (1996), 'European Integration from the 1980s', *Journal of Common Market Studies*, 34(3): 341–78.

Marsh, David (1992a), *The Bundesbank: The Bank that Rules Europe* (London: Mandarin).

——— (1992b), *The New Politics of British Trade Unionism: Union Power and the Thatcher Legacy* (Ithaca, NY: ILR Press).

Martin, Lisa, L. (1993), 'International and Domestic Institutions in the EMU Process', *Economics and Politics*, 5(2): 125–45.

Maso, Ilja (1989), 'The Necessity of Being Flexible', *Quality and Quantity*, 23: 161–70.

——— and Smaling, Adri (eds) (1990a), *Objectiviteit in Kwalitatief Onderzoek* (Meppel and Amsterdam: Boom).

Masson, Paul and Melitz, Jacques (1990), 'Fiscal Policy Independence in a European Monetary Union', *CEPR Discussion Paper*, no. 414, London, April.

Mayne, R. (1966), 'The Role of Jean Monnet', *Government and Opposition*, 2: 349–71.

McIlroy, John (1988), *Trade Unions in Britain Today* (Manchester and New York: Manchester University Press).

McKinnon, Ronald (1963), 'Optimum Currency Areas', *American Economic Review*, 53, 717–25.

McNamara, Kathleen R. (1994), 'Economic and Monetary Union in Europe: Do Domestic Politics Matter? Does Hegemony?', paper delivered at the 1994 APSA Meeting (New York), 1–4 September.

—— (1998), *The Currency of Ideas: Monetary Politics in the European Union* (Ithaca, NY: Cornell University Press).

—— and Jones, Erik (1996), 'The Clash of Institutions: Germany in European Monetary Affairs, *German Politics and Society*, 14(3) (autumn): 5–30.

Milner, Helen (1995), 'Regional Economic Co-operation, Global Markets and Domestic Politics: a Comparison of NAFTA and the Maastricht Treaty', *Journal of European Public Policy*, 2(3): 337–60.

Milward, Alan S. (1984), *The Reconstruction of Western Europe, 1945–51* (London: Methuen).

—— (1992), *The Rescue of the Nation-State* (Berkeley, CA: University of California Press).

Minkkinen, Petri and Patomäki, Heikki (1997) 'Introduction: the Politics of Economic and Monetary Union', in Minkkinen, P. and Patomäki, H. (eds), *The Politics of Economic and Monetary Union'* (Boston, MA, Dordrecht and London: Kluwer), pp. 7–18.

Ministère de l'Economie, des Finances et du Budget (1990), *Vers l'Union Economique et Monétaire Européenne*, Colloque du 21 juin 1990 (Paris: La documentation Française).

—— (1991), 'Intervention de M. Pierre Bérégovoy pour la Présentation du Projet Françaissur l'Union Economique et Monétaire – conference intergouvernementale du 28 janvier'.

Mishler, Elliot G. (1986), *Research Interviewing: Context and Narrative* (Cambridge, MA and London: Harvard University Press).

Mitrany, David (1933), *The Progress of International Government* (New Haven, CT: Yale University Press).

—— (1943, 1966), *A Working Peace System* (London: Royal Institute of International Affairs, and New York and Toronto: Oxford University Press, 1943 edn; Chicago, IL: Quadrangle Books, 1966 edn).

—— (1975), *The Functional Theory of Politics* (London: London School of Economics and Political Science and Martin Robertson).

Mittelmann, James H. (ed.) (1996), *Globalization: Critical Reflections* (Boulder, CO: Lynne Rienner).

Molle, Willem (1990), *The Economics of European Integration: Theory, Practice, Policy* (Aldershot: Dartmouth).

——, Sleijpen, Olaf and Vanheukelen, Marc (1993), 'The Impact of an Economic and Monetary Union on Social and Economic Cohesion: Analysis and Ensuing Policy Implications', in Gretschmann, K. (ed.), *Economic and Monetary Union: Implications for National Policy-makers* (Maastricht: European Institute of Public Administration), pp. 217–44.

Monetary Committee (1972), *Fourteenth Activity Report* (Brussels).

Monnet, Jean (1976), *Mémoires* (Paris: Fayard).

Moravcsik, Andrew (1991), 'Negotiating the Single European Act: National Interests and Conventional Statecraft in the European Community', *International Organization*, 45(1): 19–56.

—— (1993a), 'Introduction. Integration International and Domestic Theories of International Bargaining', in Evans, Peter B., Jacobson, Harold K. and Putnam, Robert D. (eds), *Double-Edged Diplomacy: International Bargaining and Domestic Politics* (Berkeley, CA: University of California Press), pp. 3–42.

Moravcsik, Andrew (1993b), 'Preferences and Power in the European Community: a Liberal Intergovernmentalist Approach', *Journal of Common Market Studies*, 31(4): 473–524.

—— (1994), 'Why the European Community Strengthens the State: Domestic Politics and International Cooperation', Harvard University, Center for European Studies, Working Paper Series, no. 52. Presented at the Annual Meeting of the American Political Science Association, New York, September.

—— (1998a), *The Choice for Europe. Social Purpose and State Power from Messina to Maastricht* (Ithaca, NY: Cornell University Press).

—— (1998b), 'Does International Cooperation Strengthen National Executives? The Case of monetary Policy in the European Union', paper presented at the third workshop on Europeanization and Domestic Political Change, European University Institute (Florence), 19–20 June.

Moyser, George and Wagstaffe, Margaret (eds) (1987), *Research Methods for Elite Studies* (London: Allen & Unwin).

Mundell, Robert A. (1961), 'A Theory of Optimum Currency Areas', *American Economic Review*, 51: 657–65.

—— (1962), 'The Appropriate Use of Monetary and Fiscal Policy for Internal and External Stability', *IMF Staff Papers*, 9: 70–9.

Mutimer, David (1989), '1992 and the Political Integration of Europe: Neo-functionalism Reconsidered', *Journal of European Integration*, 13(1): 75–101.

OECD (Organization for Economic Cooperation and Development) (various economic surveys), Paris.

Offe, Claus (1984), *Contradictions of the Welfare State* (London: Hutchinson).

Official Journal of the European Communities, various issues.

Ostrup, Finn (1992), *The Development of the European Monetary System* (Copenhagen: DJOF/Stockholm: Nerenius).

Padoa-Schioppa, Tommaso (1987), *Efficiency Stability and Equity: A Strategy for the Evolution of the Economic System of the European Community* ('Padoa-Schioppa Report') (Oxford: Oxford University Press).

—— (1994), *The Road to Monetary Union in Europe: The Emperor, the Kings, and the Genies* (Oxford: Clarendon Press).

Panic, Milivoje (1992), *European Monetary Union: Lessons from the Classical Gold Standard* (Basingstoke and London: Macmillan/New York: St Martins).

Patomäki, Heikki (1997), 'Legitimation Problems of the European Union', in Minkkinen, Petri and Patomäki, Heikki (eds) (1997), *The Politics of Economic and Monetary Union* (Boston, MA, Dordrecht and London: Kluwer), pp. 162–204.

Pauly, Louis W. (1992), 'The Politics of European Monetary Union: National Strategies, International Implications', *International Journal*, 47 (winter 1991–2): 93–111.

Pelkmans, Jacques (1991), 'Towards Economic Union', in Ludlow, Peter (ed.), *Setting EC Priorities, 1991–92* (Brussels: CEPS), October–November, pp. 39–100.

Pentland, Charles (1973), *International Theory and European Integration* (London: Faber & Faber).

Peterson, John (1995), 'Decision-making in the European Union: Towards a Framework for Analysis', *Journal of European Public Policy*, 2(1): 69–93.

Petit, Pascal (1989), 'Expansionary Policies in a Restrictive World: the Case of France', in Guerrieri, P. and Padoan, P. C. (eds), *The Political Economy of*

European Integration: States Markets and Institutions (New York: Harvester Wheatsheaf), pp. 231–63.

Pierson, Paul (1996), 'The Path to European Integration: a Historical Institutionalist Analysis', *Comparative Political Studies*, 29(2): 123–63.

Pijpers, Alfred E. (1994), 'Internationale Integratie en de Functionalistische Verleiding', in Koch, K., Soetendorp, R. B. and van Staden, A. (eds), *Internationale betrekkingen: Theorieën en benaderingen* (Utrecht: Het Spectrum), pp. 154–76.

Pirages, Dennis, C. and Sylvester, Christine (eds) (1990), *Transformations in the Global Political Economy* (London and Basingstoke: Macmillan/New York: St Martin's Press).

Pisani-Ferry, J., Italianer, A. and Lescure, R. (1993), 'Stabilization Properties of Budgetary Systems: a Simulation Analysis', *European Economy*, 5: 511–38.

Ploeg, Frederik van der (1989), 'Towards Monetary Integration in Europe', in De Grauwe, Paul, Knoestler, A., Kolodziejak, A. *et al.* (eds), *De Europese Monetaire Integratie: Vier Visies*, Wetenschappelijke Raad voor het Regeringsbeleid (The Hague: SDU), pp. 81–106.

—— (1991), 'Macroeconomic Policy Coordination during the Various Phases of Economic and Monetary Union', *European Economy*, Special Issue, 1, pp. 136–64.

Pöhl, Karl Otto *et al.* (eds) (1990), *Britain & EMU* (London: Centre for Economic Performance in association with the Financial Markets Group).

Porter, Tony (1993), *States, Markets and Regimes in Global Finance* (London and Basingstoke: Macmillan/New York: St Martin's Press).

Portes, Richard (1992), 'EMS and EMU: after the Fall', *The World Economy*, 16(1): 1–16.

Pryce, Roy and Wessels, W. (1987), 'The Search for an Ever Closer Union: a Framework for Analysis', in Pryce, R. (ed.), *Frameworks for International Co-operation* (London: Pinter), pp. 94–110.

Puchala, Donald (1972), 'Of Blind Men, Elephants and International Integration', *Journal of Common Market Studies*, 10(3): 267–84.

Putnam, Robert D. (1988), 'Diplomacy and Domestic Politics: the Logic of Two-level Games', *International Organization*, 42(3): 427–60.

Radaelli, Claudio M. (1995), 'The Role of Knowledge in the Policy Process', *Journal of European Public Policy*, 2(2): 159–83.

—— (1996), 'Fiscal Federalism as a Catalyst for Policy Development? In Search of a Framework for European Direct Tax Harmonisation', *Journal of European Public Policy*, 3(3): 402–20.

—— (1997), *The Politics of Corporate Taxation in the European Union: Knowledge and International Policy Agendas* (London: Routledge).

Risse-Kappen, Thomas (1996), 'Exploring the Nature of the Beast: International Relations Theory and Comparative Policy Analysis Meet the European Union', *Journal of Common Market Studies*, 34(1): 53–80.

Rittberger, Volker (ed.) (1993), *Regime Theory and International Relations* (with the assistance of Mayer, Peter) (Oxford: Oxford University Press and Clarendon Press).

Robson, Peter (1987), *The Economics of International Integration*, 3rd rev. edn (London: Unwin Hyman [1980]).

Rosamond, Ben (1993), 'National Labour Organizations and European Integration: British Trade Unions and "1992"', *Political Studies*, 16: 420–34.

Rosamond, Ben (1995), 'Mapping the European Condition: The Theory of Integration and the Integration of Theory', *European Journal of International Relations*, 1(3): 391–408.

Rosenthal, Glenda (1975), *The Men Behind the Decisions: Cases in European Policy-Making* (Lexington, MA: Lexington Books, D. C. Heath).

Ross, George (1995), *Jacques Delors and European Integration* (New York: Oxford University Press).

Sachs, Jeffrey D. and Sala-i-Martín, Xavier D. (1989), 'Federal Fiscal Policy and Optimum Currency Areas', Harvard University (mimeo), June; reprinted as 'Fiscal Federalism and Optimum Currency Areas: Evidence for Europe from the United States', in Canzoneri, M. B., Grilli, V. and Masson, P. R. (eds), *Establishing a Central Bank: Issues in Europe and Lessons from the US* (Cambridge: Cambridge University Press, 1992), pp. 195–219.

Sandholtz, Wayne (1993a), 'Choosing Union: Monetary Politics and Maastricht', *International Organization*, 47(1): 1–39.

—— (1993b), 'Monetary Bargains: the Treaty on EMU', in Cafruny, Alan W. and Rosenthal, Glenda G. (eds), *State of the European Community: The Maastricht Debates and Beyond* (Harlow, Essex: Longman and Lynne Reinner), pp. 125–39.

—— (1996), 'Money Troubles: Europe's Rough Road to Monetary Union', *Journal of European Public Policy*, 3(1): 84–101.

—— and Zysman, John (1989), '1992: Recasting the European Bargain', *World Politics*, 42: 95–128.

Schmitter, Philippe C. (1971), 'A Revised Theory of International Integration', in Lindberg, N. and Scheingold, Stuart A. (eds), *Regional Integration: Theory and Research* (Cambridge, MA: Harvard University Press), pp. 232–64.

—— (1992), 'Interests, Powers and Functions: Emergent Properties and Unintended Consequences in the European Polity', Stanford University and Center for Advanced Study in the Behavioral Sciences: unpublished paper, second revised and expanded version, April.

Scholte, Jan Aart (forthcoming), *Globalisation: A Critical Introduction* (London and Basingstoke: Macmillan).

Sewell, James Patrick (1966), *Functionalism and World Politics* (Princeton, NJ: Princeton University Press).

Simon, W. (1976), *Macht und Herrschaft der Unternehmerverbände. BDI, BDA und DIHT im ökonomischen und politischen System der BRD* (Köln: Pahl-Rugenstein).

Smaling, Adri and Maso, Ilja (1990a), 'Objectiviteit in Kwalitatief Onderzoek: een Overzicht', in Maso, Ilja and Smaling, Adri (eds), *Objectiviteit in Kwalitatief Onderzoek* (Meppel and Amsterdam: Boom), pp. 13–29.

Smeets, Heinz-Dieter (1990), 'Does Germany Dominate the EMS?', *Journal of Common Market Studies*, 29(1): 37–52.

Smith, Michael E. and Sandholtz, Wayne (1995), 'Institutions and Leadership: Germany, Maastricht, and the ERM Crisis', in Rhodes, Carolyn and Mazey, Sonia (eds), *The State of the European Union: Building a European Polity?* (Boulder, CO: Lynne Rienner), pp. 245–65.

Spaventa, Luigi (1989), 'Discussion', in De Cecco, M. and Giovannini, A. (eds), *A European Central Bank? Perspectives on Monetary Unification after Ten Years of the EMS* (Cambridge, MA: MIT Press), pp. 84–8.

Stone Sweet, Alec and Sandholtz, Wayne (1997), 'European Integration and Supranational Governance', *Journal of European Public Policy*, 4(3): 297–317.

Strange, Susan (1976), *International Monetary Relations*, vol. 2, in Shonfield, Andrew (ed.), *International Economic Relations of the Western World, 1959–1971* (London, New York and Toronto: OUP for RIIA).

—— (1994), *States and Markets: An Introduction to International Political Economy* (London: Pinter [1988]).

—— (1996), *The Retreat of the State: The Diffusion of Power in the World Economy* (Cambridge: Cambridge University Press).

—— (1998), *Mad Money* (Manchester: Manchester University Press).

Strasser, Daniel (1992), *The Finances of Europe: The Budgetary and Financial Law of the European Communities*, 7th edn (Luxembourg).

Strauss, Anselm L. (1987), *Qualitative Analysis for Social Scientists* (Cambridge: Cambridge University Press).

Sumner, M. T. and Zis, G. (eds) (1982), *European Monetary Union: Progress and Prospects* (London: Macmillan).

Swann, Dennis (1988), *The Economics of the Common Market*, 6th edn (Harmondsworth: Penguin Books [1970]).

Talani, Leila Simona (1998), 'Interests or Expectations? The Problem of Credibility of Exchange Rate Policy: An International Political Economy Approach. The Cases of Italy and the United Kingdom and their Departure from the Exchange Rate Mechanism of the European Monetary System', PhD dissertation, European University Institute, Florence.

Taylor, Christopher (1995), *EMU 2000? Prospects for European Monetary Union* (London: Royal Institute of International Affairs).

Taylor, Paul (1983), *The Limits of European Integration* (London and Canberra: Croom Helm).

—— (1990), 'Functionalism: the Approach of David Mitrany', in Groom, A. J. R. and Taylor, P. (eds), *Frameworks for International Co-operation* (London: Pinter), pp. 125–38.

Temperton, Paul (ed.) (1993), *The European Currency Crisis: What Chance Now for a Single Currency?* (Cambridge, UK and Chicago, IL: Probus).

Tew, B. (1982, 1988), *The Evolution of the International Monetary System, 1945–1981*, 3rd and 4th rev. edns (London: Hutchinson).

Thiel, Elke (1989), 'Macroeconomic Policy Preferences and Co-ordination: a View from Germany', in Guerrieri, P. and Padoan, P. C. (eds), *The Political Economy of European Integration: States, Markets and Institutions* (New York: Harvester Wheatsheaf), pp. 202–30.

—— (1995), 'The Shaping of the Framework of a Single Currency in the Course of the EMU Negotiations', paper presented at the 4th biennial ECSA conference (Charleston, SC) May.

Thygesen, Niels (1990), 'Benefits and Costs of an Economic and Monetary Union Relative to the EMS', in de Grauwe, Paul and Papademos, Lucas (eds), *The European Monetary System in the 1990s* (London: Longman for CEPS and the Bank of Greece), pp. 1–26.

—— (1993), 'Towards Monetary Union in Europe – Reforms of the EMS in the Perspective of Monetary Union', *Journal of Common Market Studies*, 31(4): 447–72.

Tinbergen, Jan (1965), *International Economic Integration*, 2nd rev. edn (Amsterdam, London and New York: Elsevier).

Tindemans Report (1976), 'European Union: Report to the European Council of the European Communities', *Bulletin of the EC*, Supplement 1.

Tranholm-Mikkelsen, Jeppe (1991), 'Neofunctionalism: Obstinate or Obsolete? A Reappraisal in the Light of the New Dynamism of the European Community', *Millennium*, 20: 1–22.

Treaty on European Union (1992), CONF-UP-UEM 2002/92 (Brussels: Office of the European Communities).

Triffin, Robert (1961), *Gold and the Dollar Crisis: The Future of Convertibility*, rev. edn (New Haven and London: Yale University Press).

—— (1968), *Our International Monetary System: Yesterday, Today and Tomorrow* (New York: Random House).

Tsoukalis, Loukas (1977), *The Politics and Economics of European Monetary Integration* (London: Allen & Unwin).

TUC (Trades Union Congress) (1989), *Europe and 1992* (London: TUC Publications).

—— (1991), 'TUC Budget Submission 1991' (London: TUC Publications).

—— (1992a), 'Call for Action: A Programme for National Recovery' (London: TUC Publications).

—— (1992b), 'Unions after Maastricht: The Challenge of Social Europe' (London: TUC Publications).

Ungerer, Horst (1989), 'The European Monetary System and the International Monetary System', *Journal of Common Market Studies*, 3 (March), pp. 231–48.

—— (1997) *A Concise History of European Monetary Integration: From EPU to EMU* (Westport, CT/London: Quorum).

——, Evans, Owen and Nyberg, Peter (1983), 'The European Monetary System: the Experience, 1979–82', *International Monetary Fund Occasional Papers*, no. 48 (Washington: IMF).

——, ——, Mayer, Thomas and Young, Philip (1986), 'The European Monetary System: Recent Developments', *International Monetary Fund Occasional Papers*, no. 19 (Washington: IMF).

——, Houvonen, Jouko, Lopez-Claros, Augusto and Mayer, Thomas (1990), 'The European Monetary System: Developments and Perspectives', *Occasional Paper*, no. 73 (Washington: IMF).

UNICE (1990a), 'Economic and Monetary Union in the European Community: a Business Perspective', Brussels, 27 March.

—— (1990b), 'Statement in View of the Intergovernmental Conference on Economic and Monetary Union in the European Community', Brussels, 15 November.

—— (1991), 'Intergovernmental Conference on Economic and Monetary Union', letter to Mr Wim Kok, Dutch Prime Minister, President of the IGC, 13 November.

—— (1992), 'UNICE Note on Economic Convergence in the European Community', 17 September.

Vaciago, G. (ed.) (1991), *Europe 1992 and Monetary Union* (Milan: Vita e Pensiero).

Van Rompuy, Paul, Abraham, Filip and Heremans, Dirk (1991), 'Economic Federalism and the EMU', in *European Economy*, 'The Economics of EMU: Background Studies for European Economy, no. 44: "One Money, One Market"', Special Edition no. 1, pp. 107–35.

Verdun, Amy (1990), *Naar een Economische en Monetaire Unie (1970–1990): een analyse van de politieke beleidsruimte in Nederland* (Towards an Economic and Monetary Union (1970–1990): an Analysis of the Political Room for Manoeuvre in the Netherlands), University of Amsterdam (unpublished manuscript).

—— (1995), 'Europe's Struggle with the Global Political Economy: a Study of How EMU is Perceived by Actors in the Policy-making Process in Britain, France and Germany', PhD dissertation, European University Institute, Florence.

—— (1996), 'An "Asymmetrical" Economic and Monetary Union in the EU: Perceptions of Monetary Authorities and Social Partners', *Journal of European Integration/Revue d'Integration européenne*, 20(1) autumn: 59–81.

—— (1998a), 'Creating EMU: Issues of Legitimacy, Accountability and Democracy?', *CEPS Review*, no. 7, Autumn, pp. 21–30.

—— (1998b), 'The Increased Influence of the EU Monetary Institutional Framework in Determining Monetary Policies: a Transnational Monetary Elite at Work', in Reinalda, B. and Verbeek, Bert-Jan (eds), *Autonomous Policymaking by International Organizations* (London: Routledge), pp. 178–94.

—— (1998c) 'The Institutional Design of EMU: a Democratic Deficit?', *Journal of Public Policy*, 18(2): 107–32.

—— (1998d), 'The International Aspects of the EU's Exchange Rate Policy: European Integration and Dollar Dominance', in Cafruny, Alan and Peters, Patrick (eds), *The Union and the World* (London: Kluwer), pp. 175–89.

—— (1998e), 'Understanding Economic and Monetary Union in the EU', *Journal of European Public Policy*, 5(3): 527–33.

—— (1999a), 'The Role of the Delors Committee in the Creation of EMU: an Epistemic Community?', *Journal of European Public Policy*, 6(2).

—— (1999b), 'The Logic of Giving up National Currencies: Lessons from Europe's Monetary Union', in Gilbert, Emily and Helleiner, Eric (eds), *Nation-States and Currencies* (London: Routledge).

—— (2000a), 'Governing by Committee: The Case of the Monetary Committee', in Christiansen, Thomas and Kirchner, Emil (eds), *Administering the New Europe: Inter-Institutional Relations and Comitology in the European Union* (Manchester: Manchester University Press).

—— (2000b), 'Governing EMU Democratically: Some Lessons from Neofunctionalism and Fiscal Federalism', in Macmillan, Gretchen (ed.), *Canadian Perspectives on European Integration* (Calgary: Calgary University Press).

—— and Christiansen, Thomas (2000), 'Policy-making, Institution-building and European Monetary Union: Dilemmas of Legitimacy', in Crouch, Colin (ed.), *After the Euro: Shaping Institutions for Governance in the Wake of European Monetary Union* (Oxford: Oxford University Press).

Vree, Johan K. de (1972), *Political Integration: The Formation of Theory and its Problems* (The Hague: Mouton).

Wallace, Helen (1990), 'Making Multilateral Negotiations Work', in Wallace, W. (ed.), *The Dynamics of European Integration* (London: Pinter), pp. 213–29.

—— (1996a), 'The Institutions of the EU: Experience and Experiments', in Wallace, Helen and Wallace, William (eds) (1996), *Policy-Making in the European Union* (Oxford: Oxford University Press), pp. 37–68.

—— (1996b), 'Politics and Policy in the European Union: the Challenge of Governance', in Wallace, Helen and Wallace, William (eds) (1996), *Policy-Making in the European Union* (Oxford: Oxford University Press), pp. 3–36.

Wallace, Helen and Wallace, William (eds) (1996), *Policy-Making in the European Union* (Oxford: Oxford University Press).

Wallace, William (1990), *The Transformation of Western Europe*, Royal Institute of International Affairs (London: Pinter).

Walsh, James (1994), 'Politics and Exchange Rates: Britain, France, Italy, and the Negotiation of the European Monetary System', *Journal of Public Policy*, 14(3): 345–69.

Webb, Carole (1983), 'Theoretical Perspectives and Problems', in Wallace, Wallace and Webb (eds), *Policy-making in the European Communities*, 2nd edn (New York: Wiley), pp. 1–42.

Weber, Axel A. (1991), 'European Economic and Monetary Union and Asymmetries and Adjustment Problems in the European Monetary System: Some Empirical Evidence', *European Economy*, Special edition, 1, pp. 136–64.

Weidenfeld, Werner (1989), *European Deficits, European Perspectives – Taking Stock for Tomorrow: 'Strategies and Options for the Future of Europe. Basic Findings 1'* (Gütersloh: Bertelsmann Foundation).

Weiler, Joseph H. (1981), 'Supranationalism Revisited – Retrospective and Prospective', *European University Institute Working Paper* 2 (Florence: EUI).

Welzmüller, Rudolph (1990a), 'Konjunktur- und Beschäftigungspolitik in der EG. Vorherrschaft der Geldpolitik, Lohnpolitik als Restgröße?', in WSI Mitteilungen 9/90.

—— (ed.) (1990b), *Marktaufteilung und Standortpoker in Europa. Veränderungen der Wirtschaftsstrukturen in der Weltmarktregion Europa* (Cologne: BundVerlag GmbH).

Wendon, Bryan (1994), 'British Trade Union Responses to European Integration', *Journal of European Public Policy*, 1(2): 243–58.

Werner Interim Report (1970), 'A Plan for the Phased Establishment of an Economic and Monetary Union', Commission of the EEC, *Bulletin of the EC*, Supplement 3; COM(70)300, 4 March.

Werner Report (1970), 'Report to the Council and the Commission on the Realization by Stages of Economic and Monetary Union in the Community', Council and Commission of the EC, *Bulletin of the EC*, Supplement 11, Doc. 16.956/11/70, 8 October.

Wessels, Wolfgang (1997), 'An Ever Closer Fusion? A Dynamic Macropolitical View on Integration Processes', *Journal of Common Market Studies*, 35(2): 267–99.

Williams, Neil (1992), 'Passing the EMU "Tests"', *CBI News*, September, pp. 12–13.

Winkler, Bernhard (1996), 'Towards a Strategic View on EMU: a Critical Survey', *Journal of Public Policy*, 16(1): 1–28.

Wolf, Dieter and Zangl, Bernhard (1996), 'The European Economic and Monetary Union. "Two-level Games" and the Formation of International Institutions', *European Journal of International Relations*, 2(3): 355–93.

Woolley, John T. (1992), 'Policy Credibility and European Monetary Institutions', in Sbragia, A. (ed.), *Europolitics: Institutions and Policymaking in the 'New' European Community* (Washington: Brookings Institution), pp. 157–90.

Wyplosz, Charles (1991), 'Monetary Union and Fiscal Discipline', in *European Economy*, 'The Economics of EMU: Background studies for European Economy 44 "One Money, One Market"', Special edition 1, pp. 165–84.

Subject Index

accountability, 26, 90, 212
    in interviewee responses, 132,
        141–2, 144, 146, 163
All Saints' Day Manifesto, 71
asymmetical EMU, 14(n. 8), 20,
    196, 201, 211
asymmetric shocks, *see*
    country-specific shock

Bank of England (BoE)
    in response to Question 1,
        118–19, 127–8
    in response to Question 2,
        130–2, 145
    in response to Question 4,
        147–53
    perceptions of EMU in
        comparison to other
        central banks, 161–4,
        181–3, 200
    perceptions of EMU in
        comparison to other British
        actors, 173–7, 181–3, 200
Banque de France (BdF)
    in response to Question 1, 120,
        127–8
    in response to Question 2, 130,
        133–5, 145
    in response to Question 4,
        147–53
    perceptions of EMU in
        comparison to other
        central banks, 161–4,
        181–3, 200
    perceptions of EMU in
        comparison to other
        French actors, 177–9,
        181–3, 200
Barre Report/Barre Plan, 54–6
benefits and costs of EMU, 17–18,
    23–6(n. 12), 186–7, 212
    in questionnaire, 113

in interview responses, 146,
    157, 164–6, 177–8
Black Wednesday, 142, 175;
    see also ERM crisis
Bretton Woods system, 51, 192–3
    in interviewee responses, 120,
        123, 128–9, 165
budgetary deficit, 1, 6–8, 12, 14,
    25, 89–93, 97, 196, 203, 209
    in interviewee responses, 132,
        138, 145, 147–8, 159, 162,
        166–7, 169, 175, 180
budgetary policy, 14, 60, 68, 196
    coordination of, 7,
    in questionnaire, 114, 146
    in interviewee responses,
        132–3, 137, 139, 141, 147,
        149, 158–60
budgetary policy committee,
    53(n. 35), 57
Bundesbank (BB), 38(n. 23), 81,
    85–6(n. 91), 198, 202
    in response to Question 1, 118,
        121–3, 127–8
    in response to Question 2, 130,
        136–7, 145
    in response to Question 4, 147,
        149–53
    perceptions of EMU in
        comparison to other
        central banks, 161–4,
        181–3, 200
    perceptions of EMU in
        comparison to other
        German actors, 179–83,
        200
Bundesverband der Deutschen
    Industrie (BDI),
    in response to Question 1,
        123–5, 128–9
    in response to Question 2, 137,
        140–1, 145

Author Index